RUNNING THE RED LIGHTS

RUNNING THE RED LIGHTS

Putting the Brakes on Sexual Temptation

FOREWORD BY
RAY AND ANNE ORTLUND

CHARLES MYLANDER

Regal Books

A Division of GL Publications
Ventura, California, U.S.A.

Rights for publishing this book in other languages are contracted by Gospel Literature International (GLINT) foundation. GLINT also provides technical help for the adaptation, translation, and publishing of Bible study resources and books in scores of languages worldwide. For further information, contact GLINT, Post Office Box 6688, Ventura, California 93006, U.S.A., or the publisher.

Published by Regal Books
A Division of GL Publications
Ventura, California 93006
Printed in U.S.A.

Library of Congress Cataloging in Publication Data

Mylander, Charles.
    Running the red lights.

    Bibliography: p.
    1. Sex—Religious aspects—Christianity.
2. Sexual ethics. 3. Adultery. I. Title
HQ63.M95   1986   261.8'357   86-444
ISBN 0-8307-1103-1

To
Bill and Pam MacLaren
for their friendship,
generosity and encouragement

Contents

Foreword

When our marvelous Creator-Lord gave mankind the gift of sex, and when He handled the description of it and the rules for it in His book, He did it all with strength, dignity, firmness, tenderness, beauty, and clarity—all at once.

And so Dr. Charles Mylander, our friend Chuck, has dealt with this wonderful and elevated subject. The warnings are powerfully strong; the commendings are warmly tender. This is a beautifully and thoughtfully written book; it, too, fits the quiet, strong personality style of the author.

And most of all, it is a much needed book! In today's Christian scene there is much confusion about sexual issues. The two of us pray that this writing will get a wide reading by the Body of Christ, and with all our hearts we commend it to you.

Sincerely in Christ,

Dr. Raymond and Anne Ortlund
Newport Beach, California

Preface

Running the Red Lights is about winning over sexual temptations and sins, but it is more. I am writing about winning in all of
life as a Christian and so I deal with a number of topics related to
sexual immorality. While the focus is on sex, the principles apply
to any battleground experience where temptation seems overwhelming.

Our friends ask about my motives. Why did I write a book on
sex? My wife Nancy jokes back, "You can get your copy in a
brown paper wrapper!" No, I have not had an affair. Yes, I have
struggled hard and long with lustful thoughts. One time at lunch,
author and psychologist Lawrence Crabb asked if this book
started when I was about 14! Yes, in some ways it did. This is a
life message book.

Much of my motivation comes from counseling. Like most
pastors I have talked, hurt and prayed with many people who are
victims or perpetrators of sexual sins. Our conversations over
the past 20 years impact my thinking and writing. I am grateful
for the people who allowed me to share their stories. For the
most part they are winners. They have fought the battle and
overcome. I have, of course, changed names, places and identifying information in order to protect their privacy.

The subject of sexual sin is serious and sometimes intense. The humor that pops up here and there is meant to give you a break! My dad used to quote the old folk-saying, "All work and no play makes Jack a dull boy!"

I do not believe the abuse of sex is the only kind of sin, or even the worst, but it does cause incredible pain and damage. If we as Christians will not *do something,* the sexual revolt will destroy us as a people. As radio speaker and Christian psychologist James Dobson writes,

> Anthropologist J.D. Unwin conducted an exhaustive study of the eighty-eight civilizations which have existed in the history of the world. Each culture has reflected a similar life cycle, beginning with a strict code of sexual conduct and ending with the demand for complete "freedom" to express individual passion. Unwin reports that *every* society which extended sexual permissiveness to its people was soon to perish. There have been no exceptions.[1]

This is not a textbook on ethics—what we *ought* to do. Rather, it offers practical help for real life struggles—what with Christ's resources we *can* do. My goal in writing is to communicate in a way that is biblical, sensitive and straightforward without coming across as preachy or judgmental.

I am so grateful for what the Lord Jesus has done in my life and the lives of many of my fellow Christians that I want to spread the good word. In Christ it is possible to win over sexual sins and temptations, even deviations, and come out an overcomer. If this book helps you make the journey from the losers' arena to the winners' circle, I will be delighted.

I am praying that when you finish reading this book you will pass it on to family members or friends caught in a sexual sin. The best chance of their reading it will come because someone they like and trust gives them a copy with a prayerful appeal to think about it.

Acknowledgments

What a wonderful family the Lord has given to me, and how they have supported me in writing this book. About half of the original chapter drafts were written during family vacations and most of the rest were written at home or at the library. The sacrifice of family time seems obvious, but rather than griping and complaining I have received support and encouragement from my wife Nancy, our son Kirk and our daughter Lisa. *Thank you Lord, for each of them.*

Sandi Perry Leach typed the early chapters before going to Guatemala with her husband Stan as missionaries. Cheryl Hamblin did a wonderful job typing the remaining chapters and in the word processing of all of them. She made the deadlines in spite of computer breakdowns and a heavy work and study schedule in her pre-med major. Her sister Jill helped in the last weeks before the deadline.

Many people have prayed for me and for this book. They are too numerous to mention by name, but the Lord will reward them accordingly. Any eternal impact of these writings may well be traced to these intercessors.

The staff at Gospel Light have given incredible encouragement and support. Bill Greig, Jr. first asked for the manuscript. Earl Roe and Don Pugh gave helpful guidance on the tone and slant of the book after reading the first proposal. My editor, Joan Bay Klope, did a marvelous job of making it more warm and personal. I am deeply grateful. The production and sales staffs have been so supportive and affirming. My thanks to the Gospel Light family.

My friend Brandon McGrath took an evening to do an audio promotional tape. I promised him a book. Cheap labor! Thanks, Brandon.

Our staff at the Friends Church Headquarters in Whittier, California, where I work, read parts of the manuscript and made helpful suggestions. They cheered me on, pumped me up and covered the bases. Thanks, team.

A host of people read part or all of the manuscript and gave their suggestions. They include Neil Anderson, Toni Baldwin, Doug Clark, Ken Cowl, Earl Henslin, Don Lamm, Carlos Mauritz, Ray and Anne Ortlund, C.W. Perry, Harold Slick and the Partakers young singles group of Rose Drive Friends Church in Yorba Linda, California.

Finally, my heartfelt gratitude to the people who have graciously given permission to use their stories. Their experiences give this book a ring of reality!

Battleground and Holy Ground

Ever since God created male and female, each sex has found something fascinating about the other. At its best, this powerful attraction leads to some of life's profound joys: romances catch fire, marriages mature and healthy friendships between men and women flourish. At its worst, misused sex leads to ugly wounds and lasting scars: romances decay into bitter routines, marriages end in divorce and once-healthy friendships decline into conflict or immorality. Sooner or later almost every Christian struggles with sexual temptation. Very few escape this battle without a skirmish or two. Some fight the war every day.

Sex as God planned it leads to much of the best in life. Bonding of personalities, delightful children and satisfying pleasure all come from pure sex within marriage and controlled sexuality outside of marriage. Immoral sex, on the other hand, ignites emotional explosions, burns personalities, leaves ugly scars and sometimes ends in death. This book is about how to win on the battleground of sexual temptation.

THE STRESS OF SEXUAL TEMPTATION

It is by no means the only enticement to sin, but sexual temptation plagues many. *Time* magazine reports that for millions it causes great stress.

> When psychiatrist George Serban of New York University conducted a nationwide poll of 1,008 mostly married men and women aged 18-60, he found that the greatest source of stress was the changes in society's attitudes toward sex, including sexual permissiveness and "the new social role of the sexes."[1]

Stress comes not only from seeing these changes in others but also from personal wars with sexual temptation, especially when guilt follows a moral defeat. I know, firsthand. I am not especially proud of my own inner war. For years I struggled with lustful thoughts. They plagued my mind and irritated my soul. Nothing seemed to help for long; not self-discipline, not prayer, not Bible memorization, not new experiences with God, not anything. I felt I had no one to talk to about my private battle with lust. In fact, I began to think that no answers existed.

I seldom spoke of the savage struggle going on within me. I avoided pornography like the plague, but the lustful thoughts did not stop. This was the battleground, not the rose garden, of my Christian growth. Just as I would gain one inch of ground I would lose two. Then I would regain three inches and lose two of them again. A progress check showed I was at a standstill.

Some of my wars with temptation were short, hard-fought victories. Other battles strung out an incredibly long time with more losses than wins. I prayed during these times of struggle and defeat; God knows I prayed. The Lord answered my prayer, too, at the moment. I confessed my sins often and repented (or at least I thought I did) more times than I can recall.

Nothing seemed to give lasting relief. I tasted brief periods of obedience and then grew sick from repeated times of disobedience. I experienced defeat after defeat. Guilt and discouragement dogged my steps. Yet there was no question in my mind that I belonged to Jesus Christ. He was my Lord and Saviour, my God and leader. He had touched my life and, in spite of my inner struggles, I experienced a daily fellowship with Him.

NEW HOPE

The turning point for me came when I viewed a Christian film about a different subject altogether. In the film was one short prayer that grabbed my attention: "Lord Jesus, protect me by your blood." In a flash of insight, I knew that Christ's power was as near to me as that quick prayer. The inner voice of the Holy Spirit came with convincing force, "Chuck, it's time for you to shape up your thought life. If you don't, I'm through with you. I'm simply not going to use you for my purposes anymore. You'll go through all the motions. You'll also stay busy and remain in the ministry. But when everything is said and done, nothing will remain that really counts."

I was terrified because in my way of thinking, this was the Lord's worst possible threat next to everlasting damnation. I would rather die on the spot than live a useless life. I could think of nothing more horrible than to stand before the judgment seat of Christ empty-handed, with rottenness on the inside and nothing on the outside. To me this was the final failure. Except for eternity without Christ, what could be worse?

Believe me, my thought life turned around. For six months I was rigid in my self-discipline. Like a watchdog on the prowl, I guarded against the lust of the eyes. The simple prayer, "Lord Jesus, protect me by your blood," came often to my lips or thoughts. I prayed it with authority and meant it from my innermost heart.

God honored it and a strange thing happened. The temptation did not just vaporize, but its power was broken. When I prayed, something like an invisible curtain came down between me and the lustful thought. It was not a solid curtain, but one that blocked enough of the tempting sight that I was able to resist it if I so chose. I found that I could freely turn away from the picture or mental image that stimulated lust. I had what it took to replace sexual lust with thoughts of Christ.

Obedience to God became a daily pattern and then lasting victory came—year after year. I was not perfect. I encountered some brief setbacks and at times I slipped. But the trend of my life with Christ was trust and obedience. With every inner victory came renewed joy and restored confidence. The Holy Spirit began to assure me that I need not stand before the judgment seat of Christ empty-handed. I could look forward to entering His presence with the fruit of a Christ-formed character. I could expect the legacy of Spirit-filled influence on people whose lives were touched, helped, changed.

WE'RE NOT ALONE

Is my experience unique? Am I the only one who failed miserably in combating lust while seeming to succeed in most of my Christian life? Don't others struggle, too? And if not lust, then what about other problems? Does not every Christian fight a battle on some front? Weight? Anger? Money? Resentment? Pride? Apathy? Does not every Christian spend some time in his own kind of lion's cage?

I remember the night a group of friends who are sincere followers of the Lord Jesus discussed obedience to Christ. They were routinely sharing basic insights on how to obey in the Christian life. Then one spoke up, "I agree with what is being said—with one exception. It seems to me that these ideas work in every area of life except one. The one weak point shows up as a besetting sin, an inner weakness." (See Heb. 12:1.)

The conversation turned from drab to electric.

"Is it easy to live with?"

"Oh yes, it's very attractive."

"And that is where Satan tempts you?"

"Yes, the devil always fights dirty."

"This fits what I know about conflict resolution," a psychologist in the group added. "In each person's life some central questions must be resolved. They become the keys to everything else."

A pastor who was present commented, "It'll take every resource and every ounce of spiritual energy within you, and more, to win over sin in this one area. It'll also take everything you can receive from Christ."

The group talked about the major temptation in each life that most often gets people down. In colorful terms, one man summarized the group's critical concern. "That is where your game is played. Everything else is warm-ups and practice. The real game, however, is played on this field and this field only."

Spiritual warfare on some front—temptation, suffering or service—will face every Christian. The truth is that we won't come to maturity in the Christian life until we begin obeying God at our point of greatest struggle. This is our own battleground. Only as we obey Christ here will we understand how to lead others to be overcomers. Only as we give our all, at times fighting to a standstill (see Eph. 6:13), will we feel compassion for our fellow strugglers.

HOLY-GROUND EXPERIENCES

My story does not end here. No soldier spends all his time on the battleground. In His sovereignty, our beloved King also leads us, His children, on to "holy ground." In fact, the more time I spend on holy ground the more effective I become on the battleground. The Bible reminds me that our gracious God wants to do far more in the life of each Christian than we can ask or imagine (see Eph. 3:20-21). My holy ground times come when I meet God in a life-changing way.

When Moses heard God speaking to him, it was a holy-ground experience (see Ex. 3:4-6). His life was never the same again. Joshua, just before receiving marching orders to capture

Jericho, met the angel of the Lord. Commanded to remove his sandals, Joshua soon learned he was standing on holy ground (see Josh. 5:13-15). Dramatic experiences with God occur again and again in the Bible. The place where we meet God becomes holy ground.

Like most other Christians, I recall a few times when God moved upon my life in an intense, life-changing way. My childhood was stable and happy—anything but a hotbed for offbeat psychological experiences. I grew up in a warm and loving family just outside of Boise, Idaho. Although all of my schooling and most of my life was in the city, I also grew up milking a cow by hand and doing chores.

My parents are very special people. Our home never lacked for love and laughter or for firm and fair discipline. They were the kind of parents who believed in taking their three sons with them to church on Sundays and Wednesday nights. My folks know Christ in a personal and vital way, and they have always practiced what they preach. From my perspective, at least, real Christianity was both taught and demonstrated in my childhood home.

When I was quite young a traveling evangelist came to our church. Unlike the highly emotional, hellfire and brimstone stereotype, his preaching was loving, logical and sincere. I recall going forward and kneeling at the wooden altar at the front of our sanctuary, a customary response to the message of a visiting evangelist. I did not weep or undergo any great vision of God, but in childlike faith I prayed a simple prayer. It was not a superemotional experience for me, but it was real. I never forgot it. It stands in my mind to this day as the time I first invited Christ into my life. It was a child's decision, yes, but as my understanding and experience enlarged, so did my renewals and commitments to Christ.

In the passing years other times came when hot tears of sorrow for my sins fell from my cheeks onto that same altar. I knew what I had done wrong and deeply repented. I came to grips with giving Christ the right to rule in every part of my life.

Through the years God provided a few other holy-ground experiences in a variety of times and places: a film about India, a routine prayer meeting, a Christian concert and a pastor's talk each turned into a holy-ground confrontation with Christ. The only thing these experiences held in common was the inner working of the Holy Spirit in a life-changing way.

My spiritual life surged with a sudden, even dramatic, spurt of growth following each encounter with Christ. God seemed close and personal. Life brimmed with purpose. On the inside was an inner excitement about serving the Lord and obeying Him in so many ways became a life-style. This sense of personal growth lasted for days, weeks or sometimes even months. I love holy-ground experiences, and like to hear about them in others.

As you read these words you may recall holy-ground moments, quiet or stunning, when God moved in. While enjoying summer camp, hiking in majestic mountains, walking along the beach with surf pounding, reading a moving book, or listening to good preaching or gospel music, you can suddenly meet God in a holy-ground experience. How can you forget it? You are never quite the same again.

THE SPURTS AND LONG HAUL OF IT ALL

Most committed followers of Jesus Christ understand both holy-ground and battleground kinds of growth. Sometimes God makes Himself known in striking ways, convincing us of His power and presence—holy ground. At other times He allows trials and temptations that dog our steps to the point of despair—battleground. Holy-ground growth comes in dramatic spurts. Battleground growth follows the long hard pull. Holy-ground experiences sometimes lead to exhilarating times with God. Battleground progress comes from slugging it out with temptation day after day, learning the hard way how Christ turns a loser into a winner.

No two of us are the same in every detail, nor are our patterns of progress toward Christian maturity identical. Some of us experience more of one kind of growth than the other. Hal was led to Christ in a quiet way, but for several years he did not make much change for the better. Eventually he moved to a new community where his wife spent a week praying for guidance to the right church. Within a few days they had three invitations, all from people who attended the same church. Taking every opportunity to participate, Hal soon learned of his need to identify with Christ and serve Him. His spiritual life took an upward trend as he studied, learned and began to teach. Hal had a minimum of holy-ground experience and seemed to need very little.

Lance's experience was different. He found the Lord in an emotion-charged moment and his life was immediately revolutionized. His experiences with God were vivid and colorful—just what he needed.

In different ways each man sensed God's grace and power up close. However, when it comes to battleground growth, both Hal and Lance understand the struggle. So does every sincere disciple of Christ.

What did it take to win on the battleground of my life? It took all the grace of God I could possibly grab hold of. It took an ever-deepening dependence on Christ and His power. Then it took all the self-discipline I could somehow muster. On top of all of this, it took tireless diligence and unending determination day after day after day. No one paints the picture of a battleground as a grassy green field where athletes do calisthenics. I felt like a lone soldier trying to take a mountain infested by well-armed enemy soldiers in concrete bunkers. Battleground growth came only through struggle with temptation, trial or weakness. It was hard fighting and not much fun!

For constant progress in the Christian life, winning on the battleground is more important than searching for a new holy ground. *Not one of us will come to maturity in the Christian life until we begin to win the struggle on our unique battleground.* Whatever the temptation—an unruly tongue, misused money, a shattered relationship, a bad attitude or misguided sexual attraction—only those who overcome will reach maturity in their life with Christ. Whether our temptation is in the mind or the body, the way to win is to trust God on the holy ground and obey Him on the battleground.

CHRIST'S RESPONSE TO SEXUAL SIN

The Bible teaches that the Lord has a heart for our human weaknesses.

> As a father has compassion on his children, so the Lord has compassion on those who fear him; for he knows how we are formed, he remembers that we are dust (Ps. 103:13-14, *NIV*).
> For we do not have a high priest (referring to Jesus the Son of God) who is unable to sympathize with our weaknesses, but we have one who has been tempted in every way, just as we are—yet was without sin. Let us then approach the throne of grace with confidence, so that we may receive mercy and find grace to help us in our time of need (Heb. 4:15-16, *NIV*).

What these verses teach is that Christ offers love, grace and forgiveness. The Lord is compassionate and eager to give refuge when no one else understands. In His life on earth, Christ revealed both compassion and conviction when it came to sexual sins.

One afternoon, during a counseling session, a pastor asked Edith, who was herself involved in an affair, "Do you recall the incident of Jesus and the woman caught in adultery"? (See John 8:1-11.) Edith did not remember. Their conversation went something like this.

"She was caught in the act and the condemning Pharisees brought her to Jesus as bait for their trap," the pastor began. "They quoted the law of Moses and called for a stoning, even though Roman law didn't allow the Jews to execute anyone. Jesus bent down and wrote on the ground, appearing unthreatened by their phony games. They kept probing, interrogating, questioning. It looked like they'd caught Him on the horns of a dilemma. Either He had to violate the clear teaching of Moses or allow a public execution—which the Roman authorities outlawed. But no one ever trapped Jesus. He quietly exposed the hypocrisy in their hearts."

"If any one of you is without sin, let him be the first to throw a stone at her," Jesus said. (See John 8:7.) Again He stooped down and wrote on the ground.

The pastor added, "I picture a sudden silence sweeping over this group of sneering, accusing men. No one knew what to say. One of the younger men turned around to a wise elder for an answer but his older friend was walking away in defeat. It took only a matter of moments for the self-appointed judges to disperse. The first stone had already hit its mark—the guilty consciences of the accusers."

Edith was listening intently, fascinated.

"Jesus asked, 'Woman, where are they? Has no one condemned you?'

"'No one, sir,' she said.

"'Then neither do I condemn you,' Jesus declared. 'Go now and leave your life of sin'" (see John 8:10-11).

Edith's quick mind grasped the main point. "He meant, 'I'll forgive you this time, but don't do it again,'" she said.

"You've got it," replied the pastor.[2]

What a loving balance between compassion for the person and conviction about God's truth! "Neither do I condemn you," shows compassion. Jesus loved and accepted the woman. If she had asked forgiveness, I am sure He would have granted it. "Go now and leave your life of sin," reveals conviction. The form of this command means, "Stop your sinful habit."[3] Jesus never put His stamp of approval on sin of any kind, but He did help this woman out of her lion's cage.

With God, your past is never so full of mistakes, failures and sins that your future is hopeless. Christ loves you, no matter what you have done. In fact, He delights in forgiving the worst of sex sins and rebuilding the lives of those who suffer its consequences. The Bible gives us plenty of examples:

• With David, it was adultery
• With Samson, it was compulsive lust
• With Gomer, Hosea's wife, it was a series of illicit affairs
• With some Corinthians, it was homosexual sin
• With an unnamed church member in Corinth, it was incest.

A friend of mine thought he would have to clean up his act before Christ would accept him. He had it backwards. When he came to Christ, the Lord cleaned up his act. Listen to Jesus' invitation. He never says, "Clean up and then come to me." He simply says, "Come."

> Come to me, all you who are weary and burdened, and I will give you rest (Matt. 11:28, *NIV*).
> I am the bread of life. He who comes to me will never go hungry, and he who believes in me will never be thirsty (John 6:35, *NIV*).
> "If a man is thirsty, let him come to me and drink. Whoever believes in me, as the Scripture has said, streams of living water will flow from within him." By this he meant the Spirit, whom those who believed in him were later to receive (John 7:37-39, *NIV*).

God looks at the intent of your heart. As you come to Jesus, this prayer may guide you.

> Lord Jesus,
> I turn from my own selfish ways and come to you. Please forgive my sins and make me fresh and new on the inside. I invite you into my innermost being as my Lord, Saviour and Ruler. Make me the kind of person you want me to be. I will go wherever

you want me to go. I will say whatever you want me to say. I will give up whatever you want me to give up. I will give away whatever you want me to give away. I will do whatever you want me to do. Thank you for taking charge of my heart, my spirit and my will. In your powerful name I pray. Amen.

If you have prayed this prayer and have committed yourself wholeheartedly to Christ, you are on holy ground.

MORE THAN WILLPOWER

Once we trust Christ on the holy ground we become ready to obey Him on the battleground. It will never be a piece of cake; Christ promised an abundant life, not an easy one. It will also take willpower, but willpower alone will never win the battle. In his fun book, *Frog and Toad Together,* Arnold Lobel wrote the following delightful conversation about willpower.

> Toad baked some cookies. "These cookies smell very good," said Toad. He ate one. "And they taste even better," he said. Toad ran to Frog's house.
> "Frog, Frog," cried Toad, "taste these cookies that I have made."
> Frog ate one of the cookies. "These are the best cookies I have ever eaten!" said Frog.
> Frog and Toad ate many cookies, one after another. "You know, Toad," said Frog, with his mouth full, "I think we should stop eating. We will soon be sick."
> "You are right," said Toad. "Let us eat one last cookie, and then we will stop." Frog and Toad ate one last cookie. There were many cookies left in the bowl.
> "Frog," said Toad, "let us eat one very last

cookie, and then we will stop." Frog and Toad ate one very last cookie.

"We must stop eating!" cried Toad as he ate another.

"Yes," said Frog, reaching for a cookie, "we need willpower."

"What is willpower?" asked Toad.

"Willpower is trying hard not to do something that you really want to do," said Frog.

"You mean like trying hard not to eat all these cookies?" asked Toad.

"Right," said Frog.

"Frog, put the cookies in a box. There," he said. "Now we will not eat any more cookies."

"But we can open the box," said Toad.

"That is true," said Frog.

Frog tied some string around the box. "There," he said. "Now we will not eat any more cookies."

"But we can cut the string and open the box," said Toad.

"That is true," said Frog.

Frog got a ladder. He put the box up on a high shelf. "There," said Frog. "Now we will not eat any more cookies."

"But we can climb the ladder and take the box down from the shelf and cut the string and open the box," said Toad.

"That is true," said Frog.

Frog climbed the ladder and took the box down from the shelf. He cut the string and opened the box.

Frog took the box outside. He shouted in a loud voice, "Hey, birds, here are cookies!" Birds came from everywhere. They picked up all the cookies in their beaks and flew away.

"Now we have no more cookies to eat," said Toad sadly, "not even one."

> "Yes," said Frog, "but we have lots and lots of willpower."
>
> "You may keep it all, Frog," said Toad. "I am going home now to bake a cake."[4]

Willpower alone is never enough. Only Christ can open the door to the cage of sexual bondage. You might be able to identify with some of the following situations. Perhaps you struggle with memories of sexual exploits in the past or mental images of pornography. Do you live in a work or social environment full of suggestive sex? You may have a history of fornication, adultery, homosexual activity or a variety of other sexual sins. You may find it difficult to relate in any deep way with *my* struggles, for sexual temptation does not bother you as much as some other battle. But whatever the battle may be, what gives us *all* hope is this: Jesus meets us at our point of greatest need. This holds true even if our lack of willpower involves adultery and running the red lights.

Running the Red Lights

Anyone looking for an affair can always find one. In the climate of today's society, adultery is easy to come by. What comes as a surprise to many is that Christians may fall into extramarital affairs even when they are not looking for them. Too often well-meaning believers make unwise moves and suddenly realize they are in love with someone other than their spouse. The "If I had only known what was happening . . . " revelation dawns too late.

NEGLECTFUL BEGINNINGS

A married Christian can cause pure sex to catch fire and build a wall of protection around his/her spouse. This involves building attention and love into the marriage every day. Compliments, tender talk, resolving conflict, meeting needs, coping with stress, forgiving and starting over are all a part of a good marriage. The most common cause of an affair is neglect. What is tricky about neglect is that a little goes a long way. For example, a husband may provide well for his family's financial needs yet neglect his wife's heartfelt need to be cherished. Any major area of continued neglect gives the devil a foothold to tempt the other spouse toward infidelity.

Ella Wheeler Wilcox wrote the following insightful poem almost a century ago and yet it speaks to us today. Keep in mind that neglect never excuses adultery; it simply increases the downward pull of temptation.

An Unfaithful Wife to Her Husband

Branded and blackened by my own misdeeds
I stand before you; not as one who pleads
For mercy or forgiveness, but as one,
After a wrong is done,
Who seeks the why and wherefore.
                                   Go with me,
Back to those early years of love, and see
Just where our paths diverged. You must recall
Competitors and rivals, till at last
You bound me sure and fast
With vow and ring.
I was the central thing
In all the Universe for you just then.
Just then for me, there were no other men.
I cared
Only for tasks and pleasures that you shared.
Such happy, happy days. You wearied first.
I will not say you wearied, but a thirst
For conquest and achievement in man's realm
Left love's barque with no pilot at the helm.
The money madness, and the keen desire
To outstrip others, set your heart on fire.
Into the growing conflagration went
romance and sentiment.
Abroad you were a man of parts and power—
Your double dower
Of brawn and brains gave you a leader's place;

At home you were dull, tired, and commonplace.
You housed me, fed, clothed me; you were kind;
But oh, so blind, so blind.
You could not, would not, see my woman's need
Of small attentions and you gave no heed
When I complained of loneliness; you said,
"A man must think about his daily bread
And not waste time in empty social life—
He leaves that sort of duty to his wife
And pays her bills, and lets her have her way,
And feels she should be satisfied."

                                        Each day,
Our lives that had been one life at the start,
Farther and farther seemed to drift apart.
Dead was the old romance of man and maid.
Your talk was all of politics and trade.
Your work, your club, the mad pursuit of gold
Absorbed your thoughts. Your duty kiss fell cold
Upon my lips. Life lost its zest, its thrill,

                                        Until
One fateful day when earth seemed very dull
It suddenly grew bright and beautiful.
I spoke a little, and he listened much;
There was attention in his eyes, and such
A note of comradeship in his low tone,
I felt no more alone.
There was a kindly interest in his air;
He spoke about the way I dressed my hair.
And praised the gown I wore.
It seemed a thousand, thousand years and more
Since I had been so noticed. Had mine ear
Been used to compliments year after year,
If I had heard you speak
As this man spoke, I had not been so weak.
The innocent beginning
Of all my sinning

Was just the woman's craving to be brought
Into the inner shrine of some man's thought.
You held me there, as sweetheart and as bride;
And then as wife, you left me far outside.
So far, so far, you could not hear me call;
You might, you should, have saved me from my fall.
I was not bad, just lonely, that was all.

A man should offer something to replace
The sweet adventure of the lover's chase
Which ends with marriage. Love's neglected laws
Pave pathways for the "Statutory Cause."[1]

A DANGEROUS DETOUR

Unwary Christians often become vulnerable because the tender talk with their own spouses is missing. Surface subjects like "Pass the toast" and "The weather is nice today, isn't it?" become all too typical. It may start with a sexual problem they no longer talk about. Then the finances pose trouble and the only communication is a fight. If a discipline problem with one of the kids continues and each blames the other, they touch the limit. Soon almost no tender talk takes place between them. Neither is there genuine sharing of real feelings about each other, about their goals or their hurts in life.

Then, with another employee or a neighbor, one of them begins confiding in someone of the opposite sex. This person, often divorced or hurting in his or her own marriage, listens intently and seems to care. Nothing in the conversation seems to hint of any immoral activity. Each feels it is innocent, harmless and even helpful to the other. Tender talk about real feelings, and often about marriage problems, is going on outside of marriage and not within it. The married spouse begins to lose respect in the inner chambers of the thought life. Yet the outsider who listens and cares moves up the ladder of likability.

The Light Turns Amber

Before long "innocent" touching begins taking place. If she is his secretary, he puts a hand on her shoulder while giving instructions. If he is a friend, there's a social embrace, a warm pat, a friendly nudge. Both would insist nothing is wrong with the limited physical contact between them because it is not related to sex. They are good friends and no more—or so they tell themselves. In fact, sometimes they are not even aware of how much innocent touching is going on. Yet in the new friendship each is aware of the other's genuine admiration and acceptance.

A man came to his pastor to share about a compelling attraction to a woman at work. All of his feelings were electric toward her and he no longer felt anything toward his wife. His pastor asked a pointed question.

"How much are you touching your secretary?"

"Why, I'm *not* touching her!" he responded.

"This week," the pastor suggested, "keep track of how often you touch her and let me know when we get together again."

The next time they met the man told his pastor what he discovered. "I'm touching her all the time—and liking it, too." The pastor pinpointed the danger of finding emotional delight outside the marriage. People only need so much emotional delight and if it all happens outside the marriage, then there is nothing left for the spouse.

Barbara tells how attractive emotional delight was for her even though her life was happy and her marriage was satisfying.

> When I heard the rumors about an apparent affair between two people I knew, I was horrified. I had no patience with people who found themselves in immoral situations. I felt there was no way wrong could happen if you were where you should be, doing what you should be doing. Somehow I felt I was "above that sort of thing." *My* life centered—happily—around my hus-

band, children, home and job.

And then a new family moved into our neighborhood. They were our kind of people, fit right into our community and church. But over the months it became clear that the husband and I shared more of the same interests than the other family members did. Still, we were merely good neighbors, good friends.

Then something changed. It was nothing tangible, but a light in his eyes seemed to reflect the growing interest and excitement I too felt. I knew that our mutual attraction could easily go one step further . . . then another. And the terrible truth was that I was tempted to go along with it. I plunged from the heights of romantic imaginings to the depths of self-condemnation. What was happening? I was a Sunday School teacher, church leader, devoted wife and mother. Why couldn't I simply banish these thoughts from my mind?

But in actual practice it was not so easy. Temptation worked like an undertow, and the harder I fought it, the more fiercely it pulled: What was so wrong about what was happening? I rationalized. Who would be hurt? Could this man and I help it if we were "meant for each other"? And didn't other people flirt and fib and cheat all the time—on television, in the news, even in our neighborhood?[2]

Barbara was a winner. She recalled God's love, confessed her wrong desires and asked for His supernatural power. She faced up to her lustful longings and released them. In His faithfulness the Lord channeled her desires where they belonged, toward her own husband. She overcame the temptation, avoided the adultery and became a more humble and compassionate Christian. She now understands how easy it is for others to run the red lights.

THE LIGHT TURNS RED

Mark the principle well. When emotional delight and "innocent" touching come from outside the marriage, the light is changing from amber to red. Every driver knows this signal means put on the brakes. We cannot change our feelings in an instant, but we can change our actions. We can decide whom we will see and under what conditions. We can decide whether or not to send a card or note. We can control whom we talk to on the telephone. By taking the right actions and making no provision for wrong desires, we can slow down and stop before the light turns red (see Romans 13:14).

If neither the man nor the woman puts on the brakes, the wrong relationship enters the next stage. The couple begins spending time together. At first, they just happen to work on the same projects or they end up at the same events. It feels good to be together. But before long, the two are making excuses to spend extra hours with each other. Lunch or dinner, special gifts and hidden times for just the two of them soon become the norm.

By now both know they have much more than a casual friendship. They rationalize that it is not adultery because, after all, they are not sleeping together. A solid red light is glowing. Once an emotional affair is underway, the danger becomes intense.

The man wakes up to his erotic and emotional feelings of "love" for this other woman, although he tells himself he also loves his wife. The woman knows she is "madly in love" with this other man and often feels she made a mistake about the man she did marry. By this time, the two who are bound emotionally become one in the flesh. No more warning lights—the "accident" has occurred (see Ex. 20:14).

POWER TO TURN AROUND

Watching for the lights can warn us about the impending danger of temptation. To overcome, a Christian must want God's best at any cost. Unfortunately, too many believers are not single-minded at this point. If secret desires from the old sin nature are not crucified, the emotional appeal of a wrong relationship will intensify. Worse yet, when sinful longings take charge, our living relationship with the Lord Jesus Christ becomes mere talk or theological theory. The up and down struggle for victory often ends in defeat. The bottom line in winning over sexual temptations is death to sin, death to selfish desires and life in Christ (see Rom. 6; Eph. 2:1-10; Col. 2:13—3:14).

The apostle Paul presents three concepts to highlight this truth—fact, faith and force.

Fact

The fact is "that our old self was crucified with him so that the body of sin might be rendered powerless, that we should no longer be slaves to sin" (Rom. 6:6, *NIV*). Every genuine Christian is to know, not feel, this fact. A Christian has been crucified with Christ and Christ lives in him (see Gal. 2:20). When tempted, he must tell himself this truth from God's point of view: the sinful and selfish nature within was crucified with Christ.

Faith

Faith grabs hold of redemptive history, makes a personal union with Christ's death and resurrection, and applies it to life now. "In the same way, count yourselves dead to sin but alive to God in Christ Jesus" (Rom. 6:11, *NIV*). By faith, figure out the effects of your own death to sin. See yourself as unresponsive to misguided sexual appeal or to emotional warmth from the wrong person. Then consider yourself alive to God in Christ Jesus, appropriating His resurrection power to win over temptation. This step of faith is the turning point between victory and defeat.

We are into some pretty heavy stuff. Before going further let me tell you a silly story. It just might help you to take this step of faith with greater confidence. It seems that a photographer learned about a haunted house where, he was told, a ghost became visible at midnight. Wanting a picture badly enough to lay aside his fears, the camera buff waited in the dark house until the magic hour. Sure enough, the spook appeared and visited with him. In fact, he even consented to pose for a picture. The photographer snapped a bulb into his camera, took the picture and rushed back to his studio. With great care and eager anticipation, he developed the film. However, to his disappointment, the picture was too dark and the ghost was not visible at all. The moral of the story is this: the spirit was willing, but the flash was weak![3]

A serious application can follow for you and me. We must remember that the flesh is weak and so we must humble ourselves before God (Jas. 5:5-6). Even as we take the crucial step of picturing ourselves as dead to sin but alive to God, we can call on Christ for help. Since the Lord has commanded every Christian to exercise his faith in this way, He will always answer prayer and provide the needed grace.

Faith means that we believe God's truth and trust Him to bring it into reality. Faith can often take root by talking to yourself. *It is sheer nonsense to think that in Christ I cannot control my physical passions. All my unhealthy urges and longings died with Christ. I'm raised up to a new life of righteousness. Every wholesome desire is under His rule and designed for His purpose. With Christ's supernatural power, I can set my mind on the Spirit rather than on the flesh (see Rom. 8:5-7). I once again give Him every part of my body for His use—my eyes, my brain, my tongue, even my glands. I now see all my feelings and emotional needs as a call to prayer rather than a summons to self-indulgence.*

Force
With the facts of God's Word in mind and with faith claiming Christ's life and power, the Christian must put his resources into

force. This is a call for obedience. "Therefore do not let sin reign in your mortal body so that you obey its evil desires. Do not offer the parts of your body to sin, as instruments of wickedness, but rather offer yourselves to God, as those who have been brought from death to life; and offer the parts of your body to him as instruments of righteousness" (Rom. 6:12-13, *NIV*). With each action the Christian chooses to make the parts of his body a force for God or a force for Satan. The thoughts of one's brain, the gaze of one's eyes, the words of one's tongue, the touch of one's caress must all be yielded to God. What a Christian does with the physical parts of his or her body shows whether or not faith is put into force.

It is at this point of putting faith into action that many Christians falter, hesitate and take a nosedive. A touch of humor may make the point here. Did you hear about the Indian called Chief Running Water? His daughters were named Hot and Cold and his son was called Luke. Does that remind you of what Jesus said about lukewarm Christians in Revelation 3:16? Warm fellowship with Christ Himself is what turns a lukewarm believer into one who is hot! (See Rev. 3:20.)

The halfhearted, double-minded, lukewarm Christian remains a sitting duck for the enemy's shotgun of sensual temptation. By neglect or compromise he has left himself vulnerable to a sneak attack. *A genuine believer does not slip into sexual sin (or any other kind) because he cannot avoid it. Rather, he does so because he inwardly cherishes a hidden love for it. The truth is, he loves this sin more than he loves Jesus Christ.* In contrast our Lord Jesus says, "If you love me, you will obey what I command" (John 14:15, *NIV*).

A Christian can never conquer the one sin that gets him down until he loves the Lord Jesus more than that sin. Then he will repudiate his sin and turn to Jesus, his greater love. Even then, the alert Christian will build practices into his life-style that keep him or her out of an extramarital or premarital trap. We should note that the guidelines apply to both heterosexual and homosexual temptations.

TAKING CHARGE OF YOUR DIRECTION

Thought Control

The best place to win over sexual temptation, or any lack of self-control, is in the mind. Paul's command to "be transformed by the renewing of your mind" is the key in Romans 12:2. He also directs us to let our minds dwell on "whatever is noble, whatever is right, whatever is pure" (see Phil. 4:8, *NIV*). I have often found that a good defense against lust is to turn my thoughts at once to Christ. Quoting Scripture, mental prayers and meditating on the best things in life all help. This subject is so important that the next chapter will deal with it in detail. At this point, however, it is vital to note that adultery gets its first foothold in one's thoughts.

At what point in one's thoughts does sexual attraction become mental adultery? In the Sermon on the Mount, the Lord Jesus taught: "Anyone who looks at a woman lustfully has already committed adultery with her in his heart" (Matt. 5:28, *NIV*). The context shows he is exposing the *intent of the heart.* Whenever a man looks at a woman with the intent of sinning sexually, he is into lust. When a woman thinks *I would do anything with him* (and means an affair), the intent of her heart is adultery. Sinful lust is mental adultery springing from the heart's desire. Even before the point of actual sin, we can follow the Holy Spirit's prompting to keep our thoughts in the right place.

In most cases, a person plays with the idea of love, romance and sex with someone other than his spouse long before he takes any action. Mental adultery always precedes physical adultery. It seems popular today to think that sexual fantasies are harmless and normal. But wait a minute! The direction of these fantasies, if not toward one's spouse, may destroy healthy relationships. They may inflame feeling for the wrong person. Little by little they can break down the Christian's defenses. Subtle lies such as "God wants me to be happy" and "God will forgive me" begin to excuse wrong actions. They erode the resistance to sin.

THOUGHTS (FANTASIES) ARE NOT HARMLESS!

J. Allan Petersen summarizes what happens next. "So our minds feed the fantasy, the fantasy creates the emotions, and the emotions scream for the actual experience. This is why when one is emotionally committed to an affair, all the truth and logic in the world don't seem to faze him. In a contest between emotion and truth, emotion usually wins."[4] An emotional affair lacks substance and depth. It is a fantasy and a dreamworld that crowds out reality. What goes on in the mind makes all the difference in what happens later.

A friend of mine gives some down-to-earth advice to other men who feel trapped and unhappy. In frank honesty he counsels them to think straight. "Sexual release can only be so good; everything else is in your mind. I believed the lie that it could be better and better. It was a pleasurable game, but it left only misery behind. If the Christian man can get it in his head," he continues, "that sexual release can only be so good, and God's intended release is his wife, then it doesn't matter how big-chested she is or isn't. The release will feel the same. It's what is in his mind that gives him satisfaction or a feeling of discontent."

Our minds stand wide open to attack during a time of emotional turmoil. Or it may come following a peak experience when our guard is down. Satan always fights dirty. He hits below the belt at the worst possible moment. When our emotions are far from feeling satisfied, we can expect the power of temptation to multiply.

Have you ever had the persistent problem of wrong thoughts coming back even after crucifying them with Christ? I have. Even after claiming the *fact* of my sinful nature's death with Christ and by *faith* considering myself dead to this sin and alive to God, the sensual thoughts came back again. I had even put my faith into *force* by avoiding the obvious sources of temptation and concentrating on God's Word. Yet the lustful fantasies kept popping into my mind unbeckoned and unwelcomed. Of course I know that temptation often lasts a lifetime and that every Christian has times when he is vulnerable. But for years defeat, more often than victory, was my mental life-style. In time, I learned that both grace and discipline are essential in keeping my thoughts focused on Christ.

Based squarely on the Scripture, John R.W. Stott gives a powerful solution to this problem.

> If besetting sins persistently plague us, it is either because we have never truly repented, or because, having repented, we have not maintained our repentance. It is as if, having nailed our old nature to the cross, we keep wistfully returning to the scene of its execution. We begin to fondle it, to caress it, to long for its release, even to try to take it down again from the cross. We need to learn to leave it there. When some jealous, or proud, or malicious, or impure thought invades our mind we must kick it out at once. It is fatal to begin to examine it and consider whether we are going to give in to it or not. We have declared war on it; we are not going to resume negotiations. We have settled the issue for good; we are not going to re-open it. We have crucified the flesh; we are never going to draw the nails.[5]

What a Christian does with his thought life will determine what he says and does in other parts of his behavior. Through the apostle Paul the Holy Spirit commands, "Set your minds on things above, not on earthly things" (Col. 3:2, *NIV*). "Things above" relate to Christ and all that pleases Him. "Earthly things" refer to the attitudes and actions that the Christian is to put aside and consider dead. Included in the Bible's list of earthly things that a Christian must not spend his time thinking or doing anything about are "immorality, impurity, lust, evil desires" (Col. 3:5, *NIV*).

The Christian mind-set is our most important discipline. Prayer, Bible study, Christian fellowship and obedience to the Holy Spirit all help us to keep our minds in the right place.

For those who are according to the flesh *set their minds* on the things of the flesh, but those who are according to the Spirit, the things of the Spirit. For the *mind set* on the flesh is death, but the *mind set* on the Spirit is life and peace (Rom. 8:5-6, *NASB*, italics added).

Little decisions make a big difference and casual thoughts can determine a destiny. As Joyce Mayhew once wrote, "The mind may be compared to a garden, which is as necessary to cultivate as any plot of earth, if order and beauty are to be manifested through it . . . . Ideas, as well as flowers, in order to attain their full beauty, must be kept free from encumbering influences, whatever tends to weaken or degrade or detract from planned perfection . . . . The riotous bramble is not to be compared to the perfect rose. The bramble may manifest a certain freedom and vigor, but it is the rose which, petal by petal, shows forth the Great Artist's shaping hand."[6] Now ask yourself an obvious question: What kind of a thought life am I cultivating, a briar patch or a rose garden?

Word Control

In winning bouts with sexual temptation, thought control is only the first line of defense. Word control comes next. For a young woman, the problem of lust takes a different focus than it does with a man. He desires her body while she desires him—all of him. The body is only one part of her total man. She responds to his personality, his attention, his caring. So her greatest temptations come from the one she currently considers Mr. Wonderful. What most often leads her astray is love language. If he promises more than he intends to deliver, he is seducing her. Christian men must beware; women, too.

A wise Christian husband will make a personal pact never to share love language or tender talk with someone other than his mate. This includes a note or card in the mail and even a phone call just to talk.

The real test is not the question, "Shall I have an affair?" because by the time you're at that point, it's probably already too late. The crucial decisions are the little ones you've made earlier, such as "Shall I pick up the phone and call?" or "Would it hurt if I sent just this one postcard?" These are the little but crucial intersections at which your destiny is determined. The way to win the battle against infidelity is to win the little skirmishes one at a time.[7]

Word control may also involve whom you speak with when discussing a relationship. A good guideline is: "Never take counsel from losers." In matters of morals and sex, a person picks up the values of those he or she listens to. If a person listens to those who have been losing the moral battle for a long time, he will likely follow their example. But if he takes his counsel from winners, he will probably learn how to overcome. If you had $10,000 to invest, would you follow the advice of someone who became bankrupt three times or would you listen to the one whose $10,000 increased to $10 million? With advice, as with money, it's time to heed winners.

A young mother found that the counsel of committed Christians worked for her. "Often, after talking the temptation over with a trusted Christian friend, I find the Lord seems to remove it from me." One young man made a pact with a fellow Christian to talk and pray together whenever temptation's appeal began to look too good. A college girl commented that it helped to phone a Christian friend, even if they did not talk about the specific temptation. Her friend's godly values somehow came through to her. Everyone who struggles with self-control needs a friend who will hold him/her accountable.

Contrast the help that comes from Christian friends with the crazy ideas that pervade the world system today. A spirit of prostitution is loose in the land, but it tries to disguise itself with nice-sounding words. (See Hos. 5:4.) It is amazing how the vocabulary changes when one wants to dismiss the fact of sin.

"Sexually active" sounds more inviting than "adultery" or "forni-cation." "Amoral" often glosses over an activity that is "immoral." Somehow "pro-choice" has a better ring to it than "killing the unborn." "Motherhood before marriage" has a finer sound than "illegitimate." The Bible warns against these empty words that deceive and confuse the differences between good and evil (see Eph. 5:6).

Touch Control

Thought control and word control are next to impossible without touch control. Within families healthy touching has its benefits. Children who grow up with lots of hugs and kisses from parents build a greater resistance to promiscuity. The tingle from touching a boyfriend or girlfriend seems less demanding for those who have no inner need to be stroked. However, without careful controls, touching can lead to disaster outside of the fam-ily circle. Without becoming prudish or standoffish, it is time to take a fresh look at where our culture is leading us. Touching the opposite sex in casual relationships is now so common that many people are blind to its dangers.

What are a Christian's guidelines about touch? A single disci-pline will keep the married from falling into an extramarital affair. It's a simple matter of not touching someone of the opposite sex *when it brings comfort or inner delight*. Sexual attraction some-times gives an electric excitement. The more this electricity is present, the more one must back off from physical contact. When the voltage runs high, even touch given as a mere social gesture will lead to sensual pleasure for one or both. As my pas-tor, C.W. Perry, once said, "If you are looking forward to the next hug, you are in big trouble."

When it comes to touching, another key word is discretion. Proverbs tells us, "A beautiful woman lacking discretion and modesty is like a fine gold ring in a pig's snout" (Prov. 11:22, *TLB*). The discreet use of touching can radiate the love of Christ, but without discretion the dangers are greater than most people imagine. It is high time to say no to hugging as a social game of sex appeal and suggestiveness. If it suggests the desire for sexual immorality or sends signals of sexual interest it is out of bounds for the Christian. We depend on the Spirit, not on the flesh (see Rom. 8:9,12-13).

Are there occasions for hugs between Christians of the opposite sex? Of course! It will happen naturally enough within the bounds of the Christian family. Respect is the key word. Paul instructs Timothy to treat "older women as mothers, and younger women as sisters, with absolute purity" (1 Tim. 5:2, *NIV*). A man may hug his Christian mother or sister with a clean mind and a pure heart. Most of the time it will be no problem. If it becomes a problem touch control is essential. And if a Christian ignores the electricity of sensuality when it does occur, he is either naïve or in trouble.

GETTING OFF THE DETOUR

What if all this talk about avoiding an affair comes too late? What if the adulterous relationship is already in full swing? How does someone break it off and get out? The amazing thing is that often a husband feels greater loyalty to the mistress than to his wife and kids who love him most. In his guilt and warped thinking, he often feels more responsible for the adulterous woman than for his own family. Gross insensitivity is one of the sad by-products of adultery.

The truth is that affairs blow up faster than marriages. Much of the appeal of an affair is fun and games without the burden of responsibility. As the relationship progresses, the expectations of one or both of the participants begin to rise. The grass may look greener on the other side of the fence, but it still has to be mowed. Tensions begin to build within the affair. The wrong relationship is built on a shifty foundation of deceit and adultery. It is not unusual for an affair to collapse.

Sometimes the spouse who is trying to hold the marriage together can give the shaky affair a big shove. Almost everyone in Kent and Cherie's family learned about the adultery, except Kent. No one wanted to hurt him, so they gave only gentle hints. Kent suspected an affair, even accused Cherie of being an adulteress wife, but she denied it over and over again. He wanted to believe her, and so he did. He backed off and asked her forgiveness for accusing her.

Not too long afterward, Kent's sister took him to lunch and told him about the whole sordid mess between Cherie and Warren. Kent felt shock, hurt and pain. He also felt like a fool since he was the proverbial last one to know. Without wasting time he went to Cherie's work. She was surprised to see him and even more astounded at what he did next. Taking her hand, he slipped off her wedding ring and put it in his pocket. "When you get home, we've got something to talk about," he said, and left.

Kent was tough at times. He had a way of acting by surprise, taking a drastic step with no warning. And it scared Cherie. He told her that if she kept going the way she was, divorce was inevitable.

"I won't tell you when. I'll just do it. One day you'll come home and find that I've filed for divorce and for custody of the kids."

Cherie knew he meant it. She broke off the affair with Warren—or did *he* break it up? Anyway, it was over for now.

In spite of Kent's best efforts, Cherie was on again, off again with the affair for some time. Eventually the wrong relationship did blow up for good and both Cherie and Kent renewed their commitments to Christ and to each other. Through supportive relatives, a Bible study group and Christian marriage counseling, they turned around a seemingly impossible situation.

Most often an affair shatters because of its own internal pressures. This means the faithful spouse needs extraordinary patience. When the time is right, however, one of those in the affair will want to break it up. What counsel can help them?

Amputation

The best way to break off an affair is to amputate. Because sex makes two people "one flesh" (see 1 Cor. 6:16), an amputation will cause intense pain. It is impossible to break up an affair without someone getting hurt. God never wants more pain directed toward our marriages. He always wants the adultery amputated rather than the marriage bond severed. It all boils down to somehow saying, "We must part forever. I cannot go on with this relationship."

Marci, a divorcee, was gradually led into a promiscuous lifestyle. She said, "I found myself in the role of mistress, lover, plaything of married men. I was locked into a behavior and lifestyle without the keys to get out. To walk away meant the certain collapse of my world." One day her brother pointed out what the Bible said about her behavior. Soon after his loving confrontation she heard a strong inner voice. "Thou shalt not commit adultery" (Ex. 20:14, *KJV*). She knew it was God speaking.

Marci began to obey by amputating her promiscuous lifestyle. Then one by one she severed adulterous relationships with various men. She called on God for help in what to say. "Lord, show me how I can tell him how I feel in a manner that he'll understand." She felt God's answer impressed on her thoughts, "Tell him it is inconsistent with your beliefs!" For Marci, this approach worked. She was able to state her position without feeling like she was passing judgment or injuring dignity. With stark realism she commented, "However, the man who bases a relationship on sexual intimacy usually doesn't call again unless he wants to see if I've changed my mind."

The deeper problem came in not wanting to break off the emotional ties. Marci prayed, "Lord Jesus, raise your double-edged sword high over your head and sever the cords that connect me to wrong relationships with (she named the men)." Twenty-four hours later God's strength came to say no firmly. "When the conversation was terminated I felt the roots of the umbilical cord yanked from my stomach. Anguish and sobbing followed. In time, however, the void was replaced through the Holy Spirit's filling my life with new opportunities for growth."

Grief

The next stage, grieving, seems to come as a shock to many

who leave an affair and two surprises follow. The first is that the marriage seems less satisfying than the affair. The problems that built up for years and were intensified by adultery do not vanish overnight. It will take months to rebuild the marriage until it fully satisfies. Both partners must remind themselves often that their marriage is worth all the time and effort invested until it pays rich dividends.

The second surprise is that strong feelings of attraction, affection and desire for the one involved in the affair persist for a long time. Because adultery means a person has become one flesh with two partners, he or she will often feel torn in two, trapped, caught in the middle, confused and not sure whom he/she loves most. All these are common feelings. Wrong appetites do not subside all at once. Misplaced affections must be reset like a fractured bone. Instead of bouncing back and forth between spouse and lover, the wise step is to set the splintered bone with a cast of grief.

As Marci's experience aptly illustrates, not all kinds of grief are of the same sort. "By the time the relationship with Mr. *A* ended, I was so devastated that I was in a murderous rage. I went on a shopping spree, whipped the dead horse and cut off contacts. In therapy I acted out my frustration by clawing him and wringing his neck. I grieved, hated and pitied him. I asked countless whys and did not speak to him for months. I was deeply resentful."

Following other adulterous relationships Marci's grief was far less hostile but the pain lasted much longer. "Five years have elapsed since Mr. *C* and I have spoken on the phone. This has been the most difficult to sever. This man eventually dropped me. That hurt but I wouldn't admit that it was over. I wouldn't let go of the hope that we'd be together again some time when he was free. I also held tightly to the hope that maybe today he'd call. Just today the Holy Spirit revealed to me that I'm in emotional bondage to the fantasy of this relationship. It is over! I'm excited because I'm aware of the open wounds that still need our Lord's help. I'm free, truly free!"

To grieve well is to face up to recurring emotional cycles of distress, pain and loneliness. In fact, it is a rare exception when a person does not go through this grieving process. Since this is a normal part of God's healing, it is always right to turn to Him for comfort and relief. The Lord never wants the grieving person to return to the adulterous affair.

Healing

The final stage, healing, will certainly come. Consider Marci's progress on her journey to recovery. "I've lived a celibate life for four years. This is definitely a time of cleansing and renewal. The old is passing away and the whole new person of me is emerging. I have an identity again. I see who I am. My past is dead; that person who lived this story is dead. She has been reborn. She's a new person in Jesus Christ. The joy of knowing that God has worked life-changing miracles in my life gives me a sense of awe. I know that my Redeemer lives. My greatest personal victory is winning over sexual temptation."

For those who return to a marriage, an interesting surprise often waits. Maybe it is God's reward to the faithful spouse. The renewed marriage often develops into a deeply satisfying relationship, far better than before. Please do not misunderstand. The adultery did not make the marriage better. Never. The determination to save the marriage, the spiritual growth that came to both spouses through crisis and the all-out efforts to rebuild God's intended relationship are what made it better. People in good marriages can invest this kind of effort without the devastation of adultery. The dividends for them are even higher.

No wonder Solomon penned these words in Proverbs 5:15-19 *(NIV)*:

> Drink water from your own cistern,
>   running water from your own well.
> Should your springs overflow in the streets,
>   your streams of water in the public squares?
> Let them be yours alone,

never to be shared with strangers.
May your fountain be blessed,
and may you rejoice in the wife of your youth.
A loving doe, a graceful deer—
may her breasts satisfy you always,
may you ever be captivated by her love.

Prayer

Thank you, heavenly Father, that you loved me before the foundation of the world. I praise you for sending the Lord Jesus Christ, who was pre-existent with you in the Trinity, as the Creator of the heavens and earth and all that are in them. I praise you for revealing yourself in the written Word of God. Thank you for your mighty acts, your commands and your promises. I especially praise you for the life, ministry and work of the Lord Jesus Christ.

I claim the fact that I was crucified with Christ so that the sinful self might be rendered powerless, that I should no longer be a slave to sin. By faith I count myself dead to sin but alive to God in Christ Jesus. By your grace and in obedience to your command, I refuse to let sin reign in my mortal body so that I obey its evil desires. I put this commitment into force by offering the parts of my body—eyes, brain, glands, hands, feet, mouth and all of me—to God as instruments of righteousness. I believe your Word that I have been set free from sin and have become a slave to righteousness.

Build within my life the fruit of the Spirit, including love and self-control. Express it in thought-control, word-control and touch-control. I love you more than any sin, even the one sin that most often gets me down. Pick me up and set me free. In Jesus' holy name I pray. Amen.

A Clean Mind 3
in a
Dirty World

"I understand you're going to tell them how to never have another lustful thought," my friend remarked with a sly smile. I was on my way to speak to our church's college group on the assigned topic, "Dealing with Lust." Tough assignment. Hard enough to teach and even more difficult to live.

"Hopefully, I'm going to share with them how to win the battle."

"When you figure out the first one, let me know," he said.

"You mean no more lustful thoughts at all? I'm sure I don't have the answer to that one!"

Everyone wants an instant solution. "What I want is a quick fix that requires no self-discipline!" one Christian friend exclaimed. When it comes to lust, only a few find the quick fix. In His wisdom, the Lord allows no shortcuts to Christian maturity. If not resisted lust turns into a stubborn habit. And habits, especially mental habits, are tough to break. This chapter will offer an arsenal of spiritual weapons for attacking these entrenched thoughts.

GOD-CREATED SEXUALITY

The Bible speaks of living "in the power of God; with weapons of righteousness in the right hand and in the left" (2 Cor. 6:7, *NIV*). To ignore the firepower that God provides leaves a person open to Satan's sabotage. One of the enemy's first points of attack lies in the emotions and the mind. Unlike some spiritual losers, Jesus never wants His disciples to turn a blind eye to the strategies of the adversary. Smart servants of God will arm themselves with both offensive and defensive weapons—the right hand and the left. The Word of God and the mind of Christ give a strong *offense*. Righteousness in our thoughts presents a powerful *defense*.

Win the battle with lust in the mind, and you will never fight it on the more lethal fronts of sinful actions or ingrained habits. Lust is always a strong desire gone astray. The heart of healthy desires stem from God-created sexuality. They emerge from deep longings within the personality. Intimacy, companionship, understanding, pleasure, security, communication, relationships—all these and more underlie the expression of God's intended sexuality. God never condemns a person's basic sexual desires. In his excellent volume entitled *The Myth of the Greener Grass*, J. Allan Petersen explains the difference between healthy desires and selfish ways of satisfying them.

> Desires for friends, love, praise, success, acceptance, intimacy—these are all good. To satisfy these by dishonesty, manipulation, selfishness, and violation of God's truth leads us to sin.
>
> Exactly so with sex. Every person is a sexual being, with sexual desires, sexual attractions, and sexual feelings. All of this is God's idea. Nothing is or ever could be wrong with sex. Because sexuality is God's gift, there can be no fault, flaw, or evil in it. But man has a history of prostituting God's gifts and using them to his selfish advantage and detriment.[1]

God-given urges are never wrong, but rejecting His source of satisfaction and pursuing a substitute is always sinful and self-destructive. "Lust produces bad sex, because it denies relationship," writes Richard J. Foster in *Money, Sex and Power.*[2]

> My people have committed two sins: They have forsaken me, the spring of living water, and have dug their own cisterns, broken cisterns that cannot hold water (Jer. 2:13, *NIV*).

God Himself intends to satisfy the inner thirst from all of the created longings of the human personality. He is our spring of living water. Looking to sex outside of marriage as the source of inner satisfaction amounts to seeking a false god, a broken cistern. Like trying to satisfy thirst with saltwater, lust only aggravates unsatisfied longings and perverts them. It causes one's system to scream for more, but fails to quench the thirst. Sexual lust intensifies the inner ache.

MALE AND FEMALE LUST

Often men and women experience different kinds of lust. Most men battle with *impulsive lust* based on physical attractiveness. Most women battle *selective lust,* desiring men whom they consider special. Men are led into sexual sin by lusting after women's bodies, most often beginning with the eye gates. Women are led into sexual sin by lusting after men's attentiveness, most often beginning with the ear gates.

Men fall into lust because of the enticement of physical pleasure. Lustful male fantasies prompt a physical stimulation that raises his voltage. Women fall into lust because of the enticement of emotional pleasure. Female lust most often takes the form of mental fantasy about romance with drama, a love affair with excitement or a triangle with intrigue. Lustful female fantasies cause emotional stimulation that likewise raises her voltage.

Much of the attraction of lust is this voltage-raising stimulation.

Selective lust sets its focus on one person. It feels quite different than impulsive lust stimulated by physical beauty or surface sex appeal. It often accompanies a good relationship, which makes it all the more dangerous. Selective lust plagues women more often than men. A woman may think, *For this one guy I'd do almost anything. I'm in love with him and he's in love with me. I want him, no matter what it takes.* By "no matter what" she even means an adulterous affair or breaking up his marriage.

Some people believe that lust is only a male problem. Not true. A woman who spends her time fantasizing about old boyfriends or viewing TV or films with strong sexual content is programming her emotions for potential adultery—physical or mental. Emotional magnetism can be more powerful than physical attraction. When the emotional and the physical mix, it has a catalytic effect. The woman now finds herself drawn to this man in body and soul. But no matter how each of us is wired, lust leads to the same place—trouble. Men and women are equally vulnerable.

Most men are first tempted by physical attraction while most women seem more vulnerable to emotional appeal. However, it is also true that some men find emotional attraction a powerful pull upon them and some women feel strong sexual urges from the visual sight of a well-built male. The Christian who finds both kinds of urges, physical and emotional, stimulated by the opposite sex must be doubly careful. When channeled in the right direction, this man or woman is often warm, attractive and caring—wonderful qualities in a Christian. Outside of Christ's control, however, this same person can fall easily into sexual immorality.

WINNERS AND HOW THEY DID IT

I asked some adults in a class to write me notes about how they won over temptation. The funniest one went like this:

Dear Chuck,
   I believe in learning by experience. Therefore, when temptation knocks, I open the door wide, submit to it, then repent. After all, isn't that the American way?
   Love, Jake

He was a friend of mine and teasing (I hope!). A shocking number of professing Christians live by what Jake calls, "the American way." It's time we memorize 1 John 1:6 *(NIV)*: "If we claim to have fellowship with him yet walk in the darkness, we lie and do not live by the truth."

In these next few pages we will consider some specific techniques used by winners.

Get Squeaky Clean on the Inside

A man in Montana told me how much guilt he felt because of his lust. And the more guilty he felt, the more lust tightened its grip on his mind. He wondered if he were really a Christian. He did not know how God could love him. Then one day he really saw for the first time the inner meaning of the cross of Jesus Christ for himself. He understood that what Jesus did in offering Himself as "the atoning sacrifice for our sins" (see 1 John 2:2) was for his own lust. As he meditated on the cross his guilt left and power replaced it. He saw with new eyes that the cross was for his sin problem. With this truth snug in his soul, other specific techniques proved helpful.

He would have liked what Heini Arnold wrote in *Freedom from Sinful Thoughts*. "Jesus came to bring healing to man's innermost life through His blood. Every heart, however tormented, can find comfort in the thought of the Cross and the healing that issues from it."[3]

One afternoon a Christian who was riding a bus found his mind going the wrong direction and felt overpowered by lustful thoughts. He confessed his mental sins often in silent prayer, sometimes every few seconds. Yet his passions surged as strong as ever. Confessing his mental adultery did not remove his burning desires. A million other Christians can identify with his experience. Then he found what worked for him. He asked the Lord not only to forgive his sin, but to cleanse him on the inside. "If we confess our sins, he is faithful and just and will forgive us our sins *and purify us from all unrighteousness*" (1 John 1:9, *NIV,* italics added). By faith he received into his mind and heart the cleansing that the Bible promises. He reported that at times he could feel the lust flowing out of his system as he set his will to accept the inner purifying.[4]

Accountability

A man who won over hard-core lust said, "I found it necessary to keep open and honest communication with God and my wife on every little temptation toward lust."[5] As a wise Christian you will find a friend or a group of church elders who will hold you accountable. This step may not come easy. My friend Earl Henslin, a competent Christian psychologist, points out that men who struggle with lust often have trouble sharing at a deep level with a male friend. He affirms that a close male friendship can make a powerful difference in finding relief from lust's compulsive grip.

The Bible speaks of the therapy of confessing sins to each other, especially to church elders, in relation to physical healing (see Jas. 5:14-15). I believe the same practice brings mental and moral healing as well. "Therefore confess your sins to each other and pray for each other so that you may be healed. The prayer of a righteous man is powerful and effective" (Jas. 5:16, *NIV*).

Try Sexual Fasting

Jesus calls for drastic action to deal with lust.

> You have heard that it was said, "Do not commit adultery." But I tell you that anyone who looks at a

woman lustfully has already committed adultery with
her in his heart. If your right eye causes you to sin,
gouge it out and throw it away. It is better for you to
lose one part of your body than for your whole body
to be thrown into hell. And if your right hand causes
you to sin, cut it off and throw it away. It is better for
you to lose one part of your body than for your whole
body to go into hell (Matt. 5:27-30, *NIV*).

Is Jesus teaching that we must gouge out our physical eye if
it wanders into lust? Stuart Briscoe has a stimulating answer in
his book on the Sermon on the Mount.

What is Jesus saying here? That we should follow
his command literally? No, I don't believe so, for
where would we stop with this self-mutilation? After
the right eye, would the left eye have to go? What
about the man who can be turned on by the smell of
perfume? Does he cut off his nose? Or the seductive
sound of a woman's voice? Does he cut off his ear?
Sexual arousal can come from any one of our senses,
and Jesus is calling for us to control our senses and
deny ourselves in all these areas—not to destroy
our senses.[6]

Our Lord, like the Hebrew prophets before Him, was using
picture language to drive His message home to our hearts. The
graphic picture illustrates a great spiritual truth. Jesus is teaching sexual fasting, namely, *act as if* an eye were gouged out. The
winner over lust will discipline his eyes so radically that he acts
as if he were blind. In fact, he blinds himself to any sight that
arouses lust. He simply acts as if he cannot see lust-provoking
images. He fasts from sexual stimuli.

Some people will respond that strict self-discipline of the
eyes will make a person out of step with his friends, a misfit.
Jesus teaches that it is better to be maimed socially or culturally

than to go to hell. What if a woman's flirtatious eyes lead her into sexual sin? What if her feet take her to places where temptation becomes irresistible? What if a man's hands fondle, caress and stimulate lust in his mind? (See Matt. 18:8-9.) To paraphrase Jesus' statement, if it cripples your style to discipline your eyes, then live as a cripple. It is far better to see only half the beauty in life than to go to hell forever. If your hands touch where they should not, then have no mercy on your hands. It is far better to keep your hands to yourself than to end up in hell for eternity. Stomp on your toe when your foot takes that first step in the wrong direction. It only takes a few weeks to recover from a sore toe; but how long does hell last? No measures are too radical to deal with an ingrained habit of lust.

Sexual fasting has an important and powerful effect. Psychiatrist John White first brought this term to my attention in his insightful book, *Eros Defiled.*

> Starving people can be in one of two states. Some experience hunger as torture. They fight, steal, even kill to get food. Others experience no hunger at all.
>
> It depends upon the attitude (or mindset) of the starving person. If, for instance, I decide voluntarily to fast I will experience hunger for a couple of days and then suddenly a strange absence of hunger. If, on the other hand, I have no wish to fast and you deprive me of food, I will spend my days drooling over visions of it and my nights dreaming about it. My hunger will grow intolerable.
>
> In many ways sex urges differ little from hunger urges.
>
> But what of single men and women and of all those for whom the hungers of sex cannot be satisfied? What of those who twist and turn in restless half sleep haunted by fantasies that mock and inflame them?

There *is* such a thing as sexual fasting. Many people, I am well aware, are not able to find it, but it exists.

Just as the fasting person finds he no longer wishes for food while the starving person is tortured by mental visions of it, so some are able to experience the peace of sexual abstinence when they need to. Others are tormented. Everything depends upon their mindset or attitude. The slightest degree of ambivalence or double-mindedness spells ruin.[7]

Fasting from food often has a by-product of building self-control in other areas of a person's life, including sex. A missionary I know began fasting from three consecutive meals each week. With a touch of realism, he committed himself to continue the practice until his next furlough. While in progress he reported it as "a positive spiritual experience." A nice surprise came in the form of increasing control over his thought life. In a letter he wrote he explained, "Not to be controlled by superficial hunger pains has helped me to better know myself and my urges. To be able to yield to or reject such hunger pains has had an overflow effect of being able to yield to or reject other thoughts, urges or desires, especially in the sexual realm, much better than before."

If both agree in advance, the Bible recommends brief periods of sexual fasting for married couples (see 1 Cor. 7:3-5). The purpose is to devote yourselves to prayer. Fasting from sex can deepen your prayer life just as fasting from food can. The two kinds of fasting often go together. Abstaining from food for 24 hours or more produces a side effect of diminished sexual desire. When the physical cravings for food and sex subside, the human spirit seems more responsive to the inner nudgings of the Holy Spirit. Sexual desire returns in full force when a person eats again.

The apostle Paul makes it clear that sex within marriage is the normal pattern for serving the needs of one's spouse. He even calls it a marital duty. Although the ideal may be mutual pleasure, the apostle's sound counsel states that neither partner should withhold sex except by mutual consent. Even sexual fasting for prayer must be temporary. As Richard J. Foster once preached, "There is a time to fast and a time to feast. The disciplined person can fast when it's time to fast and feast when it's time to feast." In his book, *Money, Sex and Power,* he adds:

> Discipline is the language of self-control. The disciplined person is the person who can do what needs to be done when it needs to be done. The disciplined person is the person who can live appropriately in life . . . . We experience self-control over self-indulgence by the power of God.[8]

Sexual fasting means the utmost discipline for the eyes, hands, feet and especially the brain. When linked to Christ's power, it works. In the inner core of the Christian's personality lies a desire to please a holy God and discover the joy of the beatitude, "Blessed are the pure in heart, for they will see God" (Matt. 5:8, *NIV*). Sexual fasting is good for us. After the initial shock and necessary adjustments, it is quite possible to feel no pain—or at least very little. The benefits far outweigh the price we pay to become winners.

Shout "No!"

At the entrance of any military base stand soldiers on guard. Their one task is to prevent unauthorized people from entering the restricted area. As Christians we also need an early warning system to alert us as moral danger comes near. When temptation approaches, the moral guards within us can send it away with a firm "no admittance." The Bible gives sound counsel, "For the grace of God . . . teaches us to say 'No' to ungodliness and worldly passions" (Titus 2:11-12, *NIV*). A man I know took this advice seriously. When wrong thoughts popped into his mind, he mentally shouted, "No!" For him it worked and the thoughts were rejected.

Christian psychologist Earl D. Wilson teaches a similar technique to his patients who are battling sexual obsessions. When their minds start drifting into wrong thinking he instructs them to slap themselves on the leg and say, "Stop!" The louder, the better, he suggests. Wearing a rubber band loosely around the wrist can also provide help. When destructive thought patterns begin, a sharp flip of the rubber band will interrupt the thought with a slight punishment. It brings the person back to reality and for the moment, at least, sidetracks the undesired thinking.[9]

The best place to win over sexual temptations is in the mind. The winner will guard with diligence what he or she thinks, reads and watches. Soap operas and romantic novels lead many women to think of adultery as a dramatic and exciting part of life. When it comes to leading Christians astray, women seem more vulnerable to the influence of soap operas than the pornographic flicks often shown on cable TV. Saying "No!" may translate into turning off the TV or buying clean novels at the Christian bookstore.

Chase off the Gorillas

After teaching on mental temptation one evening, a man came to me with a common problem—and an interesting solution. He pondered why evil thoughts come with strange force to a good person, one who desires God's best. Startled at the compelling power of evil he asked, "Where are these thoughts coming from? How can this be? This is not like me." Then he began to play a mental game that made all the difference.

"When these thoughts come into my mind," he reported, "I say to myself, 'That is not me.' So I assign the thought to an imaginary gorilla. Then I say to the Lord, 'Take that gorilla back into the woods. Get him out of here!' and He runs it off. Once in awhile the gorilla pokes his head out of the woods again. I just ask the Lord to take him away again and He does." A mental exercise like this gets results because it assigns alien thoughts to an alien power to be dealt with by a supernatural Lord. At the same time a touch of humor will help you keep your mental balance.

Whatever the method, as Christians we can be assured that it is God's grace that ultimately wins our battle. "For the grace of God . . . teaches us . . . to live self-controlled, upright and godly lives in this present age" (Titus 2:11-12, *NIV*). The amazing truth is that self-control leads to a more satisfying sex life within marriage. It is never God's goal to turn a virile Christian into a passive male or female. He wants all of life, including sex, to be at its best. This happens as all of our thoughts, including sexual ones, are in line with His Word and controlled by His Spirit.

Find the Escape Hatch

My favorite Bible verse about temptation (and well worth memorizing!) is 1 Corinthians 10:13 *(NIV)*. It promises, "When you are tempted, he [God] will also provide a way out." Since God always provides an escape hatch, the task is to find one and use it. But a word of warning: some Christians wait too long and bypass this exit. When it comes to lust, there is a point of no return. It seems easy then to accuse the Lord of being faithless, of providing no way out. How much better to take the escape hatch on time.

John Blattner writes of a married Christian man who struggled with masturbation and the lustful fantasies that preceded it. Although the Bible is silent about masturbation, this man felt guilty, ashamed and defeated. After a period of remorse and "being good," he would fall into the same old rut again. Blattner helped him find the escape hatch by dissecting the pattern of his behavior before the masturbation occurred. A couple of times a week the man stopped at a convenience store for a few groceries. The rack of erotic magazines on aisle three always caught his attention. Before he knew it, he was glancing through the pages which set off raging fantasies in his head. Not long afterward he was masturbating again.

Blattner recommended that he use an escape hatch. He could send his wife to the store or select a market that kept sex magazines out of view. When he did go to that store, he could refuse to walk down aisle three. The man did change his routine, short-circuited the old habit pattern and won over masturbation. The excellent counsel he received also included more frequent intercourse with his wife, accountability to a Christian friend and calling upon the Lord for supernatural energy for the struggle.[10]

Taking the escape hatch may mean moving to the other side of the car seat or getting out of the apartment or going to visit some strong Christian friends. It may mean more time in Bible studies or church activities and bypassing bars. David invited Bathsheba over for a quiet evening in the presidential suite and ignored the warning from his attendants that she was Uriah's wife (see 2 Sam. 11:2-3). He missed the escape hatch and suffered devastating consequences. Joseph, on the other hand, ran out of the house when Potiphar's wife tried to seduce him, leaving his cloak in her hand (see Gen. 39:11-12). The Bible commands, "Flee the evil desires of youth, and pursue righteousness, faith, love and peace, along with those who call on the Lord out of a pure heart" (2 Tim. 2:22, *NIV*).

Use the Son Screen

John noticed something compulsive about his lustful thoughts. Even after asking God's forgiveness, he found himself flipping through magazines looking for sexy pictures. He repented and then visually checked out every pretty girl in sight. His thoughts went far beyond a healthy appreciation of beauty and he couldn't seem to stop—at least not for long. Something was driving him.

Two things made a difference. First, John learned to resist Satan and his demonic spirits. The next chapter will investigate this subject in more detail. At this point simply observe John's story. He followed Jesus' example when He was tempted. "Away from me, Satan! For it is written: 'Worship the Lord your God, and serve him only'" (Matt. 4:10, NIV). John put Jesus' rebuke of the devil into his own words and when he used the Son screen, the power of the name of the Lord Jesus Christ made a noticeable difference. Like Jesus, "the devil . . . left him until an opportune time" (Luke 4:13, *NIV*).

Second, John admitted the fact that he had set up an idol in his heart. He was like the elders of Israel who came to Ezekiel to hear a word from the Lord. But God exposed their hypocrisy. "These men have set up idols in their hearts and put wicked stumbling blocks before their faces" (Ezek. 14:3, *NIV*). John came to see that at times his source of ultimate satisfaction was not Jesus. He looked to lust to satiate his desires and appease his longings. This wicked idol blocked his view of Christ to satisfy him fully. The idol in John's heart gave the evil spirits a compulsive power over him.

Once John clearly saw the idol within, it was an open choice between Jesus Christ and Satan. He pulverized the idol in every way he knew how. (Remember, the Holy Spirit is faithful to give each of us specific ways to smash the idols in our hearts.) Every temptation to lust became a reminder that Jesus was John's source of satisfaction, not sensuality. John stopped putting wicked stumbling blocks before his face.

John also forced himself to look women in the eye instead of everywhere else. In social settings he began talking more to men and only to their wives or girlfriends in passing. He stared straight ahead after a glimpse of a sexy billboard and flipped past the suggestive pictures in magazines. He cleaned out of his house everything that aroused him wrongly. He rejected paid TV channels that featured sex films from coming into his home and controlled the knob as often as possible the rest of the time. He was careful about how he hugged friends of the opposite sex and refused to touch a woman when others were not present.

The results were dramatic. Far from burning up with sexual desire, going mentally crazy or having wild fantasies, John's longings and thoughts came under control. His worship of Jesus became more meaningful than ever and he heard the Lord's inner voice often. With discipline and an idol-free heart came a sense of release from bondage. While he still had to be careful not to let his eyes wander or grant the little self-indulgences of his former bad habits, the compulsive drive of his lust was gone. Using the Son screen to win over lust became a life-style.

Go for the Positive Addiction

Before a specific temptation ever starts is the time for you to build healthy habits. Learn to enjoy the right kind of films. Frequent Christian book stores. Try slow-pitch softball or maybe rent a jet ski. Family camping or even jogging can lead to a positive addiction. I love the T-shirt for a pregnant woman that says across the front, "I should have been jogging." Positive addictions do not get at the heart of the problem, but they can make life a lot more fun.

Fire Bullet Prayers

Bullet prayers are a fine response to impulsive temptations. Already I have mentioned, "Lord Jesus, protect me by your blood." How about, "Help!" (Not bad.) Or, "Ring my bell just before I fall, instead of just after." In Psalms the Lord says, "Call upon me in the day of trouble; I will deliver you, and you will honor me" (Ps. 50:15, *NIV*). Try a bullet prayer such as, "Get my mind in the right place" or "Lead [me] not into temptation but deliver [me] from evil" (see Matt. 6:13). Satan has a way of attacking when you are witnessing, praying, teaching or even preaching. An arsenal of bullet prayers can make all the difference at a moment of unexpected temptation.

Think 777

Try a simple experiment. Think about the number 666 for a moment. You may know its association with the beast in Revelation 13:18. Next, tell yourself to stop thinking 666. Concentrate on not thinking 666. If you find it tough to turn off your mind about this infamous number, you are normal. The problem with directly resisting a powerful, negative thought like 666 is one of focus. Like lust, the more you think, "I won't fantasize about 666 anymore" the more you bring it to mind.

For a moment think about 777. Divide it by 7. Multiply by 3. Can you divide the answer by 2? Are you still thinking 666? Probably not. Why? After thinking 777 and dividing by 7, you come up with 111. Multiply by 3 and you're now at 333. Can you divide 333 by 2? No, it's an odd number. Now your mind is onto something helpful.

A time-proven, powerful method of resisting lust is to memorize Scripture. When the lustful thought strikes, begin quoting the Scripture and thinking about its application to life today. When you finish, turn your thought life to something positive and helpful. Creativity emerges from a mind that knows how to concentrate on a problem and then relax and wait for the right idea to emerge at an unexpected moment. "Finally, brothers, whatever is true, whatever is noble, whatever is right, whatever is pure, whatever is lovely, whatever is admirable—if anything is excellent or praiseworthy—think about such things" (Phil. 4:8, *NIV*).

A friend of mine summed up for me how he wins over temptation. "I do it by filling my mind with Scripture, praise and spiritual songs; repeating them often so that the thoughts and temptations are soon crowded out. It's not easy, nor is it a 'get spiritual quick' scheme. But a moment-by-moment pattern of praising God for His blessings leaves less time for the temptations."

In *Living with Your Passions,* Erwin W. Lutzer recalls the adage: "The smaller your God, the bigger your problem; the bigger your God, the smaller your problem."[11] Daryl started the practice of spending at least five minutes a day in nothing but worship of God. He meditated on Psalms of praise, read the great doxologies of the New Testament, sang worshipful hymns and choruses addressed to God and worshipped with the songs of adoration in the book of Revelation. The better his worship, the less pull that sensual temptations had on him. Better yet, he found himself growing in his prayer life and overall relationship with Jesus Christ. The mind that values worship and practices it often leaves little room for sexual lust.

ASK THE RIGHT QUESTIONS

In *The Other Side of Love*, Mel White lists some excellent questions for self-examination. Give yourself honest answers and watch as you are steered in the right direction.

1. Do I really believe there is a war being waged this moment between God and Satan for my soul?

2. Do I really believe that God has won that war for me in the life and death and resurrection of Jesus?

3. Where will evil attack me next, and what should I do about it?

4. Will I control my body today, or will I let my body control me?

5. Does the Bible give me a clear warning against this specific sexual thought or act?

6. If there are no specific warnings, what general biblical guidelines are there to help me make my own responsible decision?

7. What have I done today to know God better?

8. Before I decide, I ask:
   "Is this good for me?"
   "Is this good for others?"
   "Does this honor God?"

9. Will my proximity to this person at this time lead us both to health and wholeness—or to sexual lust?

10. Who is there in the body of Christ who could hear my confession, understand my problem, pray with me, and share my burden?

11. Am I still looking for an easy miracle, or am I willing to trust God in my lifelong struggle with temptation?[12]

What if you try all these weapons and still fail? What then? I do not pretend to have all the answers, but I do have three suggestions that might help. (1) Talk with a pastor or professional Christian counselor. The insights that emerge may help you get at the heart of the problem. (2) Ask the Holy Spirit to teach you what will work in your own heart and mind. Commit yourself in advance to obey God's Word and His leading. Begin now to trust and obey in every part of your life, sexual and otherwise. Progress on battleground comes inch by inch, so be patient. (3) Keep reading this book. Something in another chapter may help you find freedom in Christ.

Trample the hungry lion of lust in the thought life and come out a winner. Try to make a friend of the angry beast and you will come out bloody and wounded. Worse yet, lustful thoughts will inevitably lead you toward impure actions and immoral habits. With Christ's grace you can win over lust. Your thought life can become a spring of purity, power and creativity. Begin telling yourself, "Through Christ I will overcome."

Prayer
I surrender my deepest desires and inner longings to you, heavenly Father. I ask you to satisfy them with living water and the bread of life that comes from our Lord Jesus Christ. Keep me from substitute satisfactions and broken cisterns that provide only sand instead of pure, refreshing water. I rebuke sinful lust and sensuality within me and replace it with the Spirit of God. Here is my mind to worship God and to enjoy fellowship with my Lord Jesus Christ. Amen.

I Can't Help It

Teresa felt terrible about "how many lives I'm messing up." A thoughtful woman, she regretted the damage caused by her adulterous affair. She was married to Pete and they were the parents of two small children. In secret she was committing adultery with Cliff who was also married with youngsters at home. While she felt miserable about hurting both families, the sinful affair with Cliff brought her enough pleasure that she did not want to break it off. She said it was like taking a bite of delicious lobster for the first time and knowing that she *had* to eat the rest of it. "I can't help it. I'm in love. What am I supposed to do?" she asked her pastor.

"Wait a minute," he responded with a kind voice. "You're lying to yourself when you say, 'I can't help it.' Let's suppose you're in bed with Cliff, just about to make love. All at once your husband breaks into the room with a gun in his hand. Would you go ahead as if he weren't there?"

"Of course not," Teresa snapped.

"So much for being helpless!" quipped the pastor.

"Well OK. I guess it's not that I can't help it. It's just that I don't *want* to help it," she admitted.

"Now you're being more honest," her pastor replied.

*   *   *

Karen was talking with her Christian friend, Janet, when somehow the subject of her illicit lover came up. She knew Janet was aware of what was going on, but neither of them had ever spoken about it before now. "You know, my . . . my . . . " Karen stumbled for words to make her illicit relationship not sound so bad.

"Your sin," Janet said with a knowing look.

"Yes, my sin," Karen spat it back with a touch of humor.

As they talked, Janet urged Karen to turn away from her sin and break off the relationship with Brett, a married man.

"I don't think Brett can stay away from me and I don't think that I can stay away from him," was her reply. It was another way of saying, "I can't help it."

*   *   *

NO GOOD EXCUSES

The "I can't help it" excuse has dozens of forms and I'm sure you have heard some of the following:

"I'm sorry, but that's just the way I am."

"It's not my fault that I'm made this way."

"I know this relationship doesn't exactly have God's blessing, but I can't get out of it. It's impossible."

"I do things that I'm sorry about later, but I just can't help it."

In His timing, the Lord has a way of getting the attention of people who, like Teresa and Karen, do not *want* to "help it." But emotional highs do not last forever and conflict, disease, pain, stress, emptiness and isolation all follow sexual sin. Before sin pays its final wage of death, it extracts a full share of torture.

Sooner or later, a person wants relief.

Evelyn's Story

It may take drastic action to break the grip of secret sin. Evelyn had wanted out of her marriage for a long time, believing it was a mistake in the first place. Her husband Robert seemed insensitive to her needs, inconsiderate and bitter with his tongue. All her hopes and prayers that he would change came to nothing. Her feelings for him were all but dead. She felt like committing suicide.

A mutual friend of Robert and Evelyn's held a job with flexible hours during the day. He often came over to chat with Evelyn like good friends should and often do. His warmth and attention moved beyond friendship but Evelyn ignored the red lights. Their relationship soon turned into outright adultery. Then the shock came when Evelyn discovered she was pregnant by him. For the sake of both of their marriages he insisted on an immediate abortion. Evelyn hesitated. She had always believed abortion was wrong. Yet the pressure was on and if she waited much longer Robert would find out. A few days later she and her lover made the trip to the abortion clinic.

In a remarkably short time, his apparent love for Evelyn cooled and she felt used. Because of her Christian background and training, guilt also swamped her emotions. She hated herself, broke off the adulterous affair and even confessed to Robert what she had done. When he guessed the culprit, she lied, telling herself that she wanted to protect the friendship between the two men. She rationalized that since the wrong relationship was over, refusing to tell her husband would not make any difference.

It was not all over, however. There were more marriage problems, a vulnerable moment, a seductive line from the family friend and she was in bed with him again.

A pastor helped Evelyn to realize that there was no way to rebuild her marriage on a foundation of dishonesty. She would only find freedom when she told Robert the identity of the other man. Evelyn agreed at the moment, but when the time came to talk about it she felt that she was not strong enough. The depths of depression followed as she looked for every possible way out. But neither the Lord nor her own conscience would let her off the hook.

The pastor made an appointment for Robert and Evelyn to meet together with him to soften the blow of the brutal truth. Healing of their relationship began in that meeting as Evelyn made a full and brokenhearted confession. To her surprise, Robert responded in a sensitive and thoughtful way even though he was deeply hurt. The power of her adultery was broken.

The next time you catch yourself saying, "I can't help it," change the *can't* to *won't*. "I won't stop lust," is more honest, and more painful, than "I can't." The reality of telling Christ Jesus, "I won't" often shocks the honest Christian enough to change it to, "By your grace, I will." As you renew your mind in Christ you will find it repulsive to say, "I can't help it." To utter such words amounts to saying, "Christ in me can't help it." Instead, say, "Step by step, day by day, I'm becoming more like Christ." Even more vital is getting to the crux of the matter and using the power of our crucified and risen Lord. When you are alive in Jesus Christ, you can "help it"! This is not arrogance. It is nothing less than the promise of God (see Ps. 145:13-14, *NIV*).

What's Your Excuse?

"I can't help it" is not the only excuse people think up. The human mind turns up the creative juices when it needs to rationalize. A humorous example comes from a track coach who posed a list of excuses for his team. All they had to do was check the right alibi.

ate too much	I didn't think
weak from lack of	I thought too much
nourishment	poor judges
not enough time to warm up	poor starter

warmed up too much
over-trained
not enough training
not enough sleep
too much sleep
need wheat germ oil
need yogurt
not enough weight lifting
too much weight lifting
snowblindness
got lost
thought there was another
   lap to go
thought the race ended a lap
   sooner than it did

poor track
footing too hard
footing too soft
too warm
too cold
shinsplints
blisters
spikes too short
spikes too long
I didn't have red shoes
forgot to bring shoes
can't run when I'm behind
can't run when I'm ahead
I don't want to improve
too rapidly[1]

Because sin causes us to build strong defense mechanisms, it helps to think through our answers to common excuses. Please recall that prayer and love prepare the heart to receive good answers to objections. And strong answers for weak excuses serve as excellent preventive medicine. My grandmother used to quote the folk saying, "An ounce of prevention is worth a pound of cure."

Excuse: We're in love . . . .

Answer 1: Genital sex outside of marriage is always wrong, always sinful. Why? Because God said so.

Answer 2: "It might come as a shock to your system to learn that when 'falling in love' includes sexual immorality, it is not real love at all. It is only a dream image of real love. As long as the other person reflects this false dream, the magic will last. When one or the other no longer lives up to the dream image, disillusionment and pain will follow."[2]

Excuse: It feels so right.

Answer 1: Feelings are powerful, but not stable. They

cycle up and down and will not last. No lasting relationship can be built on feelings alone.

Answer 2: Suppose you learn that someone you love is embezzling money from his company. You go and talk with him and he says, "It's not the money, it's the feeling of power I get from getting away with it." Do you think his feelings make it okay?

Excuse: "I'll lose him/her if I don't . . . .

Answer 1: If this is true, then he/she doesn't really love you, only your body. Real love is willing to wait.

Answer 2: A relationship built on immorality is vulnerable to unfaithfulness with someone else later on.

Excuse: It's a natural part of any meaningful relationship.

Answer 1: What do you mean by natural? Are you referring to the blood chemistry that causes sexual attraction or romantic feelings without God's direction? Do sex urges and romantic feelings make an action right? Any appetite is natural but hunger does not excuse gluttony. Neither does thirst justify drunkenness. Every appetite must have a limit or it enslaves us. God sets the limit. "It is God's will that you should be holy; that you should avoid sexual immorality" (1 Thess. 4:3, *NIV*).

Answer 2: A meaningful relationship never excuses sexual sin. God never made an exception to the seventh commandment by saying, "Thou shalt not commit adultery unless thou hast a meaningful relationship."

Excuse: We know it's wrong but we can't seem to stop.

Answer: How much do you want to stop? Are you willing to be accountable to someone you both trust? How about changing your dating patterns? Will you consider taking drastic action? If you really *can't* stop there may be a deeper problem. Have you thought about talking with a pastor or seeking Christian counseling?

Excuse: We don't go all the way, so it's not sinful.

Answer to the married reader: Are you having an emotional affair? Your marriage vows include your affections, your emotional delight and your body. If it's so wonderful, why do you hide it? Why don't you tell your husband/wife about it? Why not discuss it in your Bible study group or Sunday School class? Stop kidding yourself. You know it's wrong, don't you?

Answer to the single reader: God looks at your heart. Is your heart really free from sexual lust? Are you treating your body as a temple of the Holy Spirit? The more physical intimacy you save for marriage the happier your sexual adjustment will become within marriage.

Excuse: I've already committed adultery in my mind by lusting. I might as well do it in the body since I'm guilty anyway.

Answer: This is like saying, "I've already committed murder in my mind by hating. I might as well kill him since I'm guilty anyway." This reasoning can excuse rape, murder or the worst crime you can imagine. It amounts to greed and anyone accepting this line of reasoning will think, *What I desire I take.* Remember, two wrongs do not make a right and help is needed.

Excuse: I'm the only one who is still a virgin . . . .

Answer 1: God never determines right and wrong by a majority vote. The Ten Commandments are not up for negotiation.

Answer 2: God rewards the Christian who stands alone against peer pressure (see Matt. 5:11-12).

Answer 3: Begin praying for a few close friends who share biblical convictions to strengthen and encourage you. "Blessed are the pure in heart, for they will see God" (Matt. 5:8, *NIV*).

Excuse: I already blew it. I'm not a virgin and it's too late.

Answer to the woman caught in adultery: "'Neither do

I condemn you,' Jesus declared. 'Go now and leave your life of sin'" (John 8:11, *NIV*).

Answer to the woman who had five husbands not counting her present common-law husband: "If you knew the gift of God and who it is that asks you for a drink, you would have asked him and he would have given you living water" (John 4:10, *NIV*). "I who speak to you am he" (John 4:26, *NIV*).

Answer from the apostle Paul to the Corinthians: "Do you not know that the wicked will not inherit the kingdom of God? Do not be deceived: Neither the sexually immoral nor idolaters nor adulterers nor male prostitutes nor homosexual offenders nor thieves nor the greedy nor drunkards nor slanderers nor swindlers will inherit the kingdom of God. *And that is what some of you were. But you were washed, you were sanctified, you were justified in the name of the Lord Jesus Christ and by the Spirit of our God*" (1 Cor. 6:9-11, *NIV,* italics added).

Answer to you: It is never too late for anyone who desires to come to Jesus. God will give you a new heart and a fresh start.

Excuse: It's a decision I've made and I'll live with the consequences.

Answer: Do you know what you are saying? The consequences are far more devastating than you might imagine! Let me share a short list of possibilities. You can count on some of these happening to you:

- Real guilt before God
- God's eternal judgment
- Confusion
- Permanent damage to your children, grandchildren and great grandchildren
- Influence on friends that may lead them into similar sins and consequences
- An unhappy marriage
- Venereal disease, possibly even AIDS
- Death

• Nagging guilt feelings in your conscience.

Excuses Never End
When I list so many excuses together it seems pretty heavy.
Why not relax a minute and enjoy Frank L. Smith's rendition of
Noah's excuses to the Lord.

And the Lord said unto Noah, "Where is the ark
which I commanded thee to build?" And Noah said
unto the Lord, "Verily I have had three carpenters
off ill. The gopherwood supplier hath let me down—
yea, even though the wood hath been on order for
nigh unto 12 months. What can I do, O Lord?" And
God said unto Noah, "I want that ark finished even
after seven days and seven nights." And Noah said,
"It will be so."

And it was not so. And the Lord said unto
Noah, "What seemeth to be the trouble this time?"
And Noah said unto the Lord, "Mine subcontractors
hath gone bankrupt. The pitch which Thou comman-
dest me to put on the outside of the ark hath not
arrived. The plumber hath gone on strike. Shem, my
son who helpeth me, hath formed a pop group with
his brothers Ham and Japheth. Lord, I am undone.
Bring on the rains."

And the Lord grew angry and said, "And what
about the animals, the male and female of every sort
that I ordered to come unto thee to keep their seed
alive upon the face of the earth?" And Noah said,
"They have been delivered unto the wrong address
but should arrive Friday." And the Lord said, "How
about the unicorns and the fowls of the air by sev-
ens?"

And Noah wrung his hands and wept, saying,
"Lord, unicorns are a discontinued line; Thou canst
not get them for love or money. And fowls of the air

are sold only in half-dozen lots. Lord, thou knowest how it is."

And the Lord in his wisdom spoke, "Noah, my son, what about insurance in case thou shouldest run this ark aground atop Mt. Ararat?"

And Noah was downcast, saying, "My independent insurance agent telleth me there doth exist a market crunch. Companies liketh not writing insurance for an ark. They fear it will be used for water skiing. They doubt my wisdom as captain. Only one company hath said they would insure this vessel, and they would charge 70 times seven pieces of silver with a 250-pound sacrificial lamb deductible. Verily, the tribute is higher than Heaven and yet we cannot get delivery of the policy for three months for the company hath changed to an abacus and the beads are stuck fast.

Having spoken thus, Noah wept and the Lord went forth and did likewise. [3]

Out of Control?

Poor Noah, some things were just simply beyond his control. But behind the "I can't help it" excuse and other rationalizations all of us use at one time or another lies a terrifying truth. Outside of the grace and power of the Lord Jesus Christ, we really *cannot* help it. Oh, Jane may change her behavior in one part of her life. John may lose weight, stop drinking and even break off an affair. But sin will pop up its ugly head somewhere else unless Jane and John utilize Christ's power. The Bible tells of the inner turmoil this dilemma creates.

I know perfectly well that what I am doing is wrong, and my bad conscience proves that I agree with these laws I am breaking. *But I can't help myself,* because I'm no longer doing it. It is sin inside me that is stronger than I am that makes me do these evil things (Rom. 7:16-17, *TLB*, italics added).

The Bible never leaves us with no hope and no way out. "Who will rescue me . . . ? Thanks be to God—through Jesus Christ our Lord! . . . Therefore, there is now no condemnation for those who are in Christ Jesus, because through Christ Jesus the law of the Spirit of life set me free from the law of sin and death" (Rom. 7:24—8:2, *NIV*).

"AM I GOING CRAZY OR IS THE DEVIL AFTER ME?"

When you read about Jesus Christ's promise to rescue, do you think, *This all sounds too easy. It's fine for people who don't have a deep problem, but I'm different. No matter how hard I try or how much I pray, I can't stop. Am I going crazy or is the devil after me?*

Long before she became a Christian, Marci divorced her husband and was seduced into a promiscuous life-style. Later she wrote about her devastating experiences before coming to Christ.

I was looking for love, appreciation, acceptance, admiration, a friend, glamour, excitement, riches. I trusted persons who were not worthy of my trust and made decisions based upon emotions. I know now that I was not equipped to begin to recognize the subtle whisperings in my ear that were suggestions to try something totally foreign to my experience and moral code.

Adventure beckoned and I left my children in their father's care and traveled the highways of our nation intoxicated with the joys of discovering new people, places and activities. Quickly I discovered the dark side of the rose-colored glasses, but I was stubborn. I had made a commitment, burned bridges, and was determined to make this job and relationship work. I had never done anything like this before I met Mr. *A*. He was very crafty in drawing me into his life-style. I must have been ripe for adventure because I bought the whole program one bite at a time. It still amazes me that I was so gullible but I did want the relationship and I did want to please him.

Acceptance had everything to do with getting into both the life-style and relationships. Little did I know that my so-called freedom was really white slavery. I was involved in all of these specific sins: lust, fornication, adultery, pornography, wife swapping, prostitution, homosexuality, bisexuality, group sex. I am repulsed to the point of nausea as I recall the years of my life in which I walked the streets of Sodom and Gomorrah.

As a child I remember seeing pictures of a devil whispering in one ear and an angel whispering in the other ear. When I put my foot on the path of a promiscuous life-style I did not know the evil forces really existed. I thought demons and evil spirits were figments of people's imaginations. At first I did not have any awareness of evil spirits in control of me. I do recall not realizing that I could say no, nor that I could set limits if I had the courage. I did not really understand manipulation. In time I had the feeling of being controlled by powers other than the Lord—namely demons. It became a life and death battle both in the earthly, physical world and in the spiritual world that most of us don't believe exists.

Eventually my finely tuned system of spirit, body and mind began to short-circuit. Prior to a massive blowout, I returned to my home city to begin to rebuild my life. I sought help through therapy, family, friends, business and finally church. The contributions from all areas were valuable within limitations.

The church, Bible study and fellowship played the most prominent role in my return to God's family.

Where is the freedom from compulsive habits that stem from Satanic attacks? Is self-control possible or is our lack of control an absolute fact of life? As in every part of the Christian life, power and freedom come only in Jesus Christ. He won the decisive battle in the war with Satan and his evil spirits on the cross and through His resurrection. The war goes on, but those believers who fight with Christ's weapons consistently win over the devil and his legions. All others consistently lose.

Demons and Sexual Sin

The Bible teaches that the Christian's body is the temple of the Holy Spirit (see 1 Cor. 6:18-20). Deliberate sins against our bodies, such as sexual immorality and drug abuse, pollute His temple. A grave warning must be made at this point. Those who work in a deliverance ministry of spiritual confrontation against demons (something of a Christian specialty) often refer to sexual sins as gateways for unclean spirits to enter a person. Neil Anderson, professor of Practical Theology at Talbot Theological Seminary in La Mirada, California has considerable experience in helping people find release from the spiritual bondage of demons. He believes that those who indulge in illicit sex make room for major demonic attacks. "Almost every person that I have dealt with that had demonic problems was carrying on some type of sexual perversion," says Anderson.[4]

What lies behind sexual child abuse, rape, incest and violent sex crimes? Could it be that further investigation will sometimes reveal demonic influence? When a person suspects demonic involvement it seems wise to seek out a pastor or Christian counselor who has experience in a deliverance ministry. Christian bookstores also have books on the Christian versus demon activity. A helpful, balanced introduction is *The Adversary* by Mark I. Bubeck.[5]

While no one should dismiss the devil and his demons as a

serious threat, neither is any undue fear warranted. Many sexual problems, even sins, reflect other underlying causes rather than demonic problems. An obsession with sex is most often a *learned* pattern of thinking that must be unlearned. Compulsive sexual behavior sometimes stems from emotional causes related to childhood sexual abuse, incest, rape or molestation. No matter what the cause of the problem, ask for the guidance of the Holy Spirit and only accept counsel from those who are in harmony with the Scripture. A skilled pastor, Christian counselor or deliverance ministry specialist can help.

Claim Christ's Victory

It is of the utmost importance that every Christian know about Christ's victory over Satan, then and now. Colossians 2:15 *(NIV)* tells how our Lord Jesus humiliated the evil spirits. "And having disarmed the powers and authorities [evil spirits], he made a public spectacle of them, triumphing over them by the cross." This verse illustrates a dramatic picture that the original readers of the New Testament recognized at once. When Rome ruled the world, any general who won on the battlefield was a great hero. When he came home throngs of people turned out for the victory parade.

Behind a general's chariot would walk his prisoners of war. Once-proud combat troops who opposed him were reduced to spoils of war. Their final defeat was the disgrace of stumbling along behind the general's chariot as chained slaves.

When Jesus went to the cross, He was our spiritual general who won the greatest battle of all for us. He publicly defeated the evil spirits, including every demon of lust and sensual sin. Stripped of their weapons they are disgraced forever. As victor over them, Christ keeps those evil spirits, those rulers and authorities, on a spiritual chain. They can go only as far as He allows them.

Although Christ has triumphed over the devil and his demons, spiritual warfare for us as believers goes on. Satan and his cohorts tempt every Christian. They constantly search for hidden sin within a believer to exploit. They use guerrilla tactics to sabotage the children of God and their goal is to capture and consume every follower of Christ. For this reason the Bible warns, "Be self-controlled and alert. Your enemy the devil prowls around like a roaring lion looking for someone to devour. Resist him, standing firm in the faith . . . " (1 Pet. 5:8-9, *NIV*).

The good news is this: every disciple who lives in Christ can share the victory of the Lord Jesus over the evil spirits. He can resist them and chase them away. His spiritual weapons are prayer and the Word of God spoken in faith. Claiming Christ's victory by His shed blood on the cross defeats Satan and the evil spirits in each personal battle. This power is yours in Christ and not limited to mature Christians only. The smallest child, the moot simple disciple and the newest believer all possess this authority in Christ. This is a wonderful truth and an enormous power.

Marie listened to the pastor tell why he saw hope for her marriage. Then an old fear of hers surfaced. She felt it was impossible for her to break off her illicit affair. "I'm not strong enough to stop," she stated firmly.

"What would it take for you to get out of this adulterous relationship?" the pastor asked.

"For Tim to break up with me," she insisted.

"There is one more possibility," the pastor added. "Christ can give you the strength to break it off."

What some believers do not know is that in Christ they have everything they need to conquer Satan and his wicked forces of evil. Look again at Colossians 2:9-10 *(NIV)*:

> For in Christ all the *fullness* of the Deity lives in bodily form, and you have been given *fullness* in Christ" (italics added).

Every true believer shares the same Spirit and strength of God that dwells in Jesus Christ. Do not miss the power of these statements. The awesome truth is that the same presence and power of God that fills Jesus Christ also fills every believer. Grab hold of this fact and never let it go. Further, the Bible teaches that the true Christian shares the position of authority with Christ (see Eph. 1:19-21), seated at the right hand of the heavenly Father and far above Satan and all his evil spirits. "God raised us up with Christ and seated us with him in the heavenly realms in Christ Jesus" (Eph. 2:6, *NIV*). These basic doctrines involving the fullness of Christ within and His position of authority over Satan both serve as powerful weapons against the adversary.

Need a break? Did you hear about the two little boys who were walking home from Sunday School? One asked, "What do you think about all that devil stuff?"

The other replied, "You know how Santa Claus turned out. I bet it's your dad."

We laugh but in the real world the "devil stuff" is a formidable foe. Recall the excellent theology in Martin Luther's famous hymn, "A Mighty Fortress Is Our God."

> And though this world with devils filled,
> Should threaten to undo us,
> We will not fear, for God hath willed,
> His truth to triumph through us.
> The prince of darkness grim,
> We tremble not for him—
> His rage we can endure,
> For lo, his doom is sure:
> One little word shall fell him.

The next stanza of this great hymn explains that the "one little word" is the "word above all earthly powers." We can use it because "the Spirit and the gifts are ours through Him who with us sideth."[6]

SPIRITUAL WARFARE

Every Christian engages in spiritual warfare, "For our struggle is not against flesh and blood, but against the rulers, against the authorities, against the powers of this dark world and against the spiritual forces of evil in the heavenly realms" (Eph. 6:12, *NIV*). The Bible commands us to put on the full armor of God which includes the belt of truth, breastplate of righteousness, feet fitted and ready with the gospel of peace, shield of faith, helmet of salvation and sword of the Spirit which is the Word of God. Once armed and prepared with God's armor, every Christian is commanded to pray and keep on praying. (See Eph. 6:10-20.) How comforting it is to remember that "The prayer of a righteous man is powerful and effective" (Jas. 5:16, *NIV*).

Spiritual warfare prayers apply the truths and doctrines of the Word of God against the wicked forces of darkness. When prayed in faith, they bring a fresh sense of freedom in Christ and increased resistance to temptation. "Doctrinal praying" as Pastor Mark Bubeck calls it, fills us or our situation with the light of Christ.[7] Bill Gothard suggests the following brief warfare prayer for resisting the devil.

> Heavenly Father,
> I ask You, in the name and through the blood of the Lord Jesus Christ to rebuke Satan for tempting me to (be rebellious, lie, etc.). For it is written: "Obey them that have the rule over you." "Lie not one to another," etc.[8]

This format can apply to any sin, including a sexual one.

> Heavenly Father,
> I ask you, in the name and through the blood of the Lord Jesus Christ, to rebuke Satan for tempting me with lustful thoughts. For it is written, "Set your minds on things above, not on earthly things" (Col.

3:2, *NIV*) and "whatever is pure . . . think about such things" (Phil. 4:8, *NIV*). Amen.

A longer warfare prayer, like the one that follows, can make a tremendous difference in overcoming sex sins. At first it may seem difficult, too long or even foreign. The devil may resist it by giving you a sense of uneasiness or even physical symptoms such as dizziness, a choking sensation or a repulsive feeling. I encourage you to turn every hindrance into a fresh determination to win. For maximum power, pray this prayer daily for at least 30 days in a row—90 days is better.

Daily Warfare Prayer

Heavenly Father, I humble myself in worship before you. To your holy name be glory, honor and praise forever! You are worthy of my adoration, devotion and thanksgiving. I commit myself to love you with all of my heart, mind, soul and strength—including my energy output and all of my best efforts. I submit myself to you and to all whom you have put in authority over me. I yield my money, sex and power to you. Here is my body as a living sacrifice, consecrated to you and made holy as a temple of the Holy Spirit. I give myself to you completely and without holding anything back.

By faith I claim the protection of the blood of the Lord Jesus Christ around and within me. I give myself to abide and remain in Christ during this day. In union with Christ, I take my stand against all efforts of Satan and his demons to hinder me in this time of prayer. I address myself only to the God and Father of our Lord Jesus Christ and reject any involvement of Satan in this prayer.

Satan, I command you in the all-powerful name of the Lord Jesus Christ to leave my presence with all your demons and to go to the place where Jesus

Christ sends you. I bring His blood between us and around me as a shield. In the name of the Lord Jesus Christ I order you not to approach me in any way except by the heavenly Father's permission.

Righteous Father, by faith and in obedience to your command, I put off the old self which is being corrupted by its deceitful desires and put on the new self, created to be like God in true righteousness and holiness. I resist all the forces of darkness that stimulate the desires of my sinful nature and claim the appearing of the Son of God to destroy the devil's work in my life. By the power and authority of our Lord Jesus Christ, I retake any ground given to the devil and release its full control to the Holy Spirit.

By faith I come into union with the incarnation, crucifixion, burial, resurrection, glorification, ascension, exaltation, session (seating), outpouring of the Holy Spirit and intercession accomplished by our Lord Jesus Christ. I submit to His authority as the head of the Church and rejoice in His rule and reign in the universe. I live in the confidence of His Second Coming in power and great glory.

I claim the power of the incarnation of our Lord Jesus Christ including His virgin birth and sinless life. I confess that Jesus Christ has come in the flesh and is fully God and fully man.

I claim the power of His crucifixion on my behalf as an atoning sacrifice for my sins, and not for mine only but also for the sins of the whole world. I claim the victory over death and hell accomplished by our Lord Jesus in His burial and by His resurrection from the dead.

I claim the power of His resurrection for my justification so that I may walk in newness of life. I claim the victory of His glorification in His resurrected body and look forward to my resurrected and glorified body when Jesus comes again to earth.

I claim the power of Jesus Christ's ascension to the right hand of the Father, exalted above all authorities, principalities and powers and every name that is named. I claim the authority of His being seated at the right hand of the Father in the heavenly realms with all evil powers and authorities under His feet and under mine. I share His triumph.

I claim the power of His intercession for me and for all His people. I receive the power of the outpouring of the Holy Spirit accomplished by the Lord Jesus Christ at Pentecost. For this day I also appropriate the fullness of the Holy Spirit in my life. I claim all the power of His sanctifying work within me.

I claim the loving direction of His headship over the Church which is His Body and bride—and of which I am a part. I claim the power of His victorious reign which will be open for all to see when He appears the second time on the clouds of heaven.

I bring all this power to bear against Satan, his forces of evil and his strategies against me. Heavenly Father, with the divine power of weapons of righteousness that you give in Christ, I tear down Satan's strongholds in my life and in the lives of those I love. I destroy every argument and excuse for not knowing the triune God better and better. I reject the ideas and phrases that make sin attractive and plausible. By faith I claim the mind of Christ. I take captive every thought to make it obedient to Christ. With sound judgment I refuse to take up an offense for those who disobey your will as revealed in your written Word or to defend them in any way. I ask for your insight to restore gently someone caught in a sin.

I demolish the plans of Satan formed against me today. I smash the plans of Satan against my heart

and carefully guard my affections. I break the strongholds of Satan against my emotions. I release anxiety, bitterness, anger, loneliness and lust, replacing
them with the peace of God that transcends all
understanding. I smash the strongholds of Satan
against my mind and meditate on your Word day and
night. I obliterate the strongholds of Satan formed
against my will and choose now to trust and obey the
Lord Jesus Christ. I crush the strongholds of Satan
formed against my spirit and set my path to live constantly and continually in the fullness of the Holy
Spirit. I choose to sing psalms, hymns and spiritual
songs, always giving thanks to God the Father for
everything, in the name of our Lord Jesus Christ.
Holy Spirit, I ask you to bring these songs to my
mind throughout this day. I shatter the strongholds
of Satan formed against my body and invite the Holy
Spirit to fill my body and use its parts today for the
glory of Christ Jesus. I splinter the strongholds of
the devil against my soul and yield the depths of my
personality into your care. I burst the strongholds of
the enemy against any and every part of myself and
bring my deepest desires to you for satisfaction.

In obedience to the command in your Word, I
commit myself to be strong in the Lord and His
mighty power. Thank you for the full armor of God
that you provide. Right now I put on the belt of
truth, the breastplate of righteousness and the boots
of readiness that come from the gospel of peace. I
hold up the shield of faith that extinguishes all the
flaming arrows of the evil one. I put on the helmet of
salvation. I grasp the sword of the Spirit, the Word of
God. Train me to use it with supernatural ability.
Stimulate me to pray on all occasions with all kinds of
prayers and requests.

Thank you, Lord Jesus, for loving me and laying

down your life for me. Open my eyes today for the opportunity to love others and to lay down my life for them. Grant me opportunities to use the spiritual gifts you have given to me in a spirit of humility, joy and service. Help me to take my focus off myself and to fix my eyes on Jesus Christ and on those whom you want me to love and serve. I enter this day with thanksgiving and praise. Open my eyes to what you are doing, Holy Father, and allow me to be used of the Holy Spirit as a part of it.

I pray in the confidence of the wonderful name of our Lord Jesus Christ who is able to keep me from falling and to present me before your glorious presence without fault and with great joy. Amen.

Help, My Spouse Is Having an Affair! ⑤

The discovery by a faithful husband that his wife is committing adultery hits his emotions with a greater shock than death! Again and again I have seen grown men sob in tears and agony while learning of the news. When the tables are turned, faithful wives feel the same way. Women in pain pour out feelings of shock and deep anguish. The phrase "It hurts so bad," comes out over and over. Betraying trust in this most intimate of all human relationships rips open the emotions like slashing someone with a knife.

What's surprising is that the spouse involved in the adulterous affair seems to feel no pain, at least not at first. He appears totally insensitive to the ones who love him most—his own wife and children. All his feelings of tenderness and understanding seem centered on the other woman. (It works the same way when she has another man.) Fortified by lies and deceptions, sexual sins build emotional barriers as high as a fortress. When an affair first comes to light, these self-justifying defenses look formidable. In reality adultery builds a relationship on a foundation of sand. It can seldom stand the test of time.

Did you hear about Vera Czermak of Prague, Czechoslovakia who discovered her husband was committing adultery? In her shock and despair she decided to commit suicide and flung herself out of the third story window of their home. It did not work. As fate would have it, she landed on her unfaithful husband and killed him. Sometimes justice does indeed triumph! Anyone who goes through the painful emotions I am writing about will love this story![1]

While the adultery remains a secret, in a few strange cases the marriage actually seems better. The faithful spouse has no idea that anything is wrong and describes his/her marriage as good or improving. The unfaithful spouse acts out the part of a good husband or good wife yet lives in hidden immorality. Motives for a double life vary. Guilt drives some to try to compensate for the wrong in hopes of making themselves feel better. Others are testing the marriage to see if it really might work. For some, the marriage itself was good and not the cause of the adultery at all. Their own evil desire met a tempting person and enticed him/her into sin.

MATT AND SUSAN'S STORY

What can the faithful spouse do? Is there any hope? Is there any help? Yes indeed! The starting point comes from the *faithful* partner. The first and most important question is, *Am I willing to work on my marriage?*[2] If the answer is yes, some time-tested counsel will offer help and encouragement. Even when the marriage is not put back together, the faithful partner who takes this approach becomes stronger in character and Christian vitality.

The story that follows is a composite picture of many marriages. While it represents a common pattern, it results from a myriad of incidents, not just one. The couple I write about does not exist, but their story has parts that fit a thousand and more marriages.

Matt and Susan started dating in college. Both enjoyed sports and social activities. Susan made better grades than Matt, partly because she studied harder but also because good verbal skills come more naturally to her. Matt was lots of fun.

They found an electricity, an excitement about being together. The sparks of romance led to wonderful dreams of their future together.

Susan always said she did not believe in premarital sex, and before dating Matt she always stuck to her convictions. She was not quite sure why—was it because she had gone to Sunday School as a child? Did her morality come from church or from her parents? She did not know. What she *did* know was that Matt did not feel the same way about it. And she knew that she loved him intensely.

One thing led to another. It all seemed so natural, so exciting. Matt expected Susan to make love with him if their relationship became serious. So she did. For awhile it occurred only on "special" occasions. After their engagement, however, it became a regular part of their relationship. Susan was genuinely surprised that she felt no guilt.

For a couple of years their married life seemed romantic and fun. Without children they had enough time for each other and kept up a steady diet of sports and social events. What surprised both of them was that the opposite sex still looked good, often vibrant and attractive. Somehow they had believed that marriage would close their eyes to everyone but each other. It did not. At least they were faithful. Neither had any intention of cheating on the other.

With both working, it was easy to go into debt for a condo, furniture, a sporty pickup and much more. Without thinking much about it, they lived just above their income. With mounting debt came financial pressure and bitter arguments. In fact, they fought about finances more than anything else. Susan accused Matt of wasting money on his selfish whims. Matt countered by calling Susan stingy and tightfisted, until *she* wanted something. She took over the checkbook, but he kept his credit cards.

After Ryan was born, fatigue set in. Susan was up often during the night with their new baby. Sometimes Matt took a turn, sometimes not. In so many ways little Ryan was the joy of their lives, yet the tension in their marriage kept increasing. They both wanted Susan to quit work and stay home with the baby, but financial pressure made it impossible. Baby-sitters. Diapers. Dishes. Doctor bills. Susan was dying on the inside and becoming more and more irritable on the outside. Matt was retreating, spending more time in front of the TV watching sports with his six-pack or out with his friends.

Susan asked for help around the house and with the baby and Matt gave a little, but his heart was not in it. As the more verbal one, Susan's tongue lashings evened up the score. Why didn't he turn off the football game so they could talk? Why couldn't he pick up his own clothes? When was he going to get a decent job that made some more money? Why did he keep spending all their money on himself while she was going without? She burned with resentment.

Matt had his share of questions, too, although he kept them to himself most of the time. Why was she so easily upset, so irrational? Why did Susan lay guilt on him if he relaxed? Didn't she know he was tired when he got home from a hard day's work? Most of the jobs around the house were women's work anyway. By the way, when was the last time they made love? Matt knew the answer and did not like it. She was always too tired or in a bad mood. Like a delayed time bomb, guilt over their premarital sex was fouling up her desires and performance *now*.

Susan went to church first and liked it. The people seemed friendly, warmhearted. The nursery looked first-rate and the attendants seemed competent and caring. She enjoyed the music and found the pastor's messages practical, helpful and even inspiring at times. The women's Bible study gave some much-needed support at a crucial time. For awhile she and Matt fought about religion, but then he began coming to church, too. He liked the slow-pitch softball team and the other men accepted him with a sense of genuine friendship. Before long both Matt and Susan accepted Christ into their lives as Lord and Saviour.

The next couple of years were some of their best. After attending a Marriage Encounter seminar they began communicating better and making love more often. Matt became more helpful without complaining. They both adored Kelli, their new baby girl who was recently added to the family nest. At church their friendships were genuine and satisfying. They learned more about the Bible than they ever knew before. Life took on new meaning and purpose—for awhile.

Matt kept climbing the corporate ladder and his responsibilities included more travel, sometimes on weekends. Then the company transferred the family to a new city. Somehow they never found a church that satisfied them quite like their former one so they eventually dropped out. The stress of Matt's job was increasing. Both liked the added income, although they were still far in debt. To compensate for his increased busyness Susan kept taking on more responsibility including the things Matt used to take care of. Matt's pattern was an aggressive style at work and a passive one at home. Susan focused on his faults and griped about his laziness around the house but Matt did not want to talk about it.

One day it happened. Matt simply announced, "I don't want to be married anymore. The responsibility of a wife and family is just too much. I need some time away alone. I need some space to get my head on straight."

"There's someone else! You're seeing another woman," Susan accused. "You are having an affair, aren't you?"

"Absolutely not!" Matt insisted. "You're so paranoid. What's the matter with you, anyway? You're the one with the problem!"

Susan cried most of the night, heartbroken. True to his word, Matt packed his suitcase the next day and left. Three days later he was back home, grouchy and uptight. He still claimed that there was no one else. Susan wanted to believe him, so she tried to convince herself that he was telling the truth. On the inside she felt desperate. Her world was crumbling and Matt did not seem to care.

Open Heart, Open Door
Susan recalled something from the Marriage Encounter

weekend that she and Matt had attended. One of the couples had spoken of the value of keeping the door to the heart and door to the bedroom open to each other, especially when things were not going well. With all the tension and insecurity these days, Susan did not feel like making love. But as a survival instinct she renewed her efforts. She even tried to think of sex with Matt as loving obedience to Christ. What hurt most was that Matt seemed very interested in sex, but not in her as a person. She felt used, unclean. Only a focus on Christ Himself gave her joy and with it came a new sense of freedom in bed.

In some ways their sex life became better than ever. In other ways it felt far worse. It was better because Susan was giving herself away like never before. It was worse because Matt never seemed satisfied. His me-first, I'm-number-one attitude was hard to take. He also seemed distant most of the time, except when he wanted something from her. The emotional coolness between them was driving Susan crazy.

The Discovery

One Friday evening Susan was on the way to fill her car with gas. Ryan and Kelli were staying overnight at Grandma's. Matt was working late, a frequent pattern that she hated. Suddenly she spotted Matt in his car with a female sitting close to him. Susan followed at a distance until they stopped at an apartment building. She watched with horror as they walked in together. Susan waited and waited. Three hours later Matt came out alone. She tailed his car back to his office and then went home.

When Matt showed up long after midnight, Susan confronted him. He admitted everything but showed no guilt or regret. Susan was boiling mad and verbally ripped Matt up one side and down the other. Then she burst into tears and ran to the bedroom sobbing. Matt followed but offered no sympathy. His response to her rage was seething anger of his own. "I've had it," he snapped and started packing his suitcase. Then and there he moved out.

Since Matt did not take all of his clothes, Susan secretly

hoped he intended to come back. In spite of her heartbreak she still loved him. But her hopes were dashed when Matt moved into an apartment with some single guys from work, all of whom were either divorced or separated. Every time Matt came home, he moved more of his belongings to the apartment. The few times they did talk turned into a fight. It looked like they were headed for a long separation, maybe a permanent one.

Tough Questions

Susan felt betrayed and crushed, almost to the point of despair. A friend suggested that she see the pastor at a nearby church. Matt refused to have anything to do with marriage counseling so she went alone. In the quiet atmosphere of the pastor's office Susan found herself pouring out her story with many tears. The pastor listened intently and then asked some tough questions.

"Are you willing to work hard on your marriage?"

"Oh, yes, otherwise I wouldn't be here," responded Susan in earnest.

"Are you willing to pay any price to have God's best in your life—whether or not your marriage is saved?"

"What do you mean?" Susan asked.

"God is always for marriage and He hates divorce. So as you trust and obey Him, the Lord will do His part to heal your marriage. But as you know, the heavenly Father doesn't force His will on those who refuse to turn to Him. At this point in time no one can guarantee that Matt will change. You can expect God to change you for the better, however."

"Yes, I see that."

The pastor paused. "What I'm about to recommend will seem like the hardest thing anyone has ever suggested. And if you follow this counsel only to manipulate Matt or to bribe God, it'll never work. If, on the other hand, you give yourself afresh to Jesus Christ with all of your heart, you'll become a better person. I can't guarantee a rescue for your marriage. The Bible makes no promises about couples being reconciled when adultery is involved. Yet sometimes God puts marriages back together again even when one spouse is involved in an affair. I know several restored couples in this church."

"Really?" Susan looked surprised. "I'm impressed."

The pastor returned to the main subject. "The key question for you is, 'Are you willing to pay any price to have God's best?'"

Susan thought for a minute and then said with quiet determination, "Yes, I am."

THE FREEDOM TRAIN

"Think of a train with four cars," the pastor began. "Let's name the locomotive *Relationship,* the second car *Behavior,* the third car *Mind-set* and the caboose *Results.*" He sketched it out. "We will call it the freedom train. It'll set your spirit free to become all God intends."

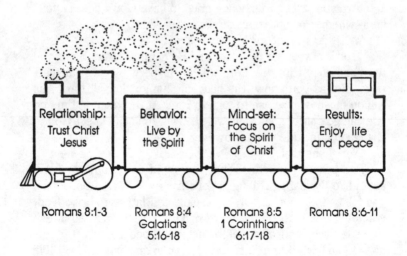

Relationship: Behavior: Mind-set: Results:
Trust Christ   Live by   Focus on   Enjoy life
Jesus   the Spirit   the Spirit   and peace
                                      of Christ

Romans 8:1-3   Romans 8:4   Romans 8:5   Romans 8:6-11
                   Galatians   1 Corinthians
                   5:16-18   6:17-18

"A right *relationship* with Christ Jesus, using the power of the Holy Spirit, leads to constructive *behavior.* This enables a healthy *mind-set* which produces good *results.* Our task is to fill each train car with the right cargo. We want God's power fueling the engine and the right freight filling the cars. Then the caboose of peace will follow."

"What about Matt?" Susan interrupted. *"He's* the one who left and he's not even here to listen to this."

"Marriage is like a teeter-totter," the pastor responded. "When one person changes position, it affects the other. If you make a definite change for the better, Matt will also change. He may change for better or for worse, but most often the change is for the better."

"It looks to me like he's out running around and I'm supposed to do the changing," Susan mused sadly.

"You're right. You're the only one here today," the pastor responded with understanding. "And if Matt will talk with me, I've got some ideas for him, too. But at this point, the only one you can change is Susan. So let's apply these principles to her."

"Okay," Susan agreed.

The Powerful Locomotive

"A right relationship with God through Jesus Christ pulls the Freedom Train," the pastor said with a sparkle in his eye.

"If ever I've needed God's help it's now," Susan blurted out. "That's why I came to see you."

"In the time of greatest need, our Lord Jesus Christ meets His wounded children with compassion and power," the pastor responded with warmth. "He alone is the Great Physician, the one who changes habit patterns and attitudes for the better."

Together Susan and the pastor turned to several verses in the Bible for comfort and help.

> Cast all your anxiety on him because he cares for you (1 Pet. 5:7, *NIV*).

When I said, "My foot is slipping," your love, O
Lord, supported me. When anxiety was great within
me, your consolation brought joy to my soul (Ps.
94:18-19, *NIV*).

Do not be anxious about anything, but in everything,
by prayer and petition, with thanksgiving, present
your requests to God. And the peace of God, which
transcends all understanding, will guard your hearts
and your minds in Christ Jesus (Phil. 4:6-7, *NIV*).

I have told you these things, so that in me you may
have peace. In this world you will have trouble. But
take heart! I have overcome the world (John 16:33,
NIV).

Humble yourselves, therefore, under God's mighty
hand, that he may lift you up in due time. Cast all
your anxiety on him because he cares for you" (1
Pet. 5:6-7, *NIV*).

"As you claim the Bible's promises, you'll find yourself drawing closer and closer to your heavenly Father. Consciously come
into His presence, pouring out all your feelings and emotions,"
the pastor suggested.

"You make it sound so easy," Susan said, "but to be honest,
well, sometimes I'm so confused. Some days I'm so mixed up. I
don't know what I feel."

"I understand," the pastor responded. "Let me suggest an
exercise that may help you get honest with God about what
you're really feeling. Try finishing this sentence. 'If I were *not* a
Christian, I would . . . . ' Then tell the Lord exactly what you'd
feel like saying or doing."

Susan looked surprised, but she agreed to try it when she
was alone.

"After all your 'non-Christian' feelings come out, commit yourself to Christ anew. Tell Him, 'Since I'm a Christian, I choose *not* to act in any way that displeases you.' Then consciously reject the unchristian actions that you described to the Lord in this exercise.

"Simply give the Lord all your anger, fear, anxiety and hurt," the pastor continued. "Ask for His peace and presence to replace them. Your emotions will cycle, so you'll find it essential to repeat this process again and again. Marital turmoil always puts our feelings on a roller coaster so when you feel near the peak, praise the Lord for His grace. When you plunge to the depths, cry out to Him for help. Make His presence your minute-by-minute refuge from the raging storm you feel inside."

"This sounds like it'll be good for me, but what do I do about Matt?" Susan asked.

"Good question. Let's move to the car called Behavior," said the pastor.

Exhibit Tough and Tender Behavior

"In his fine book, *Love Must Be Tough*, Dr. James Dobson shares a 'two-hands illustration' for separated spouses.[3] Let one of your hands represent you and the other stand for Matt. Hold them up, facing each other but separated. Every time your hand moves toward Matt's, he backs off. Right?"

"Yes. That's the way it's been going." Susan looked discouraged.

"If you verbally back off and set Matt free, then he'll stop to think about what he's losing. Watch! As you move your hand away from his, it seems to move slowly toward yours."

Susan was listening intently now, watching the pastor's two hands. She sensed in her spirit that he was right. The more she had tried to straighten Matt out, the more he resisted. If she backed off and quit telling him what to do, would he change at all?

"If Matt takes a step toward you," the pastor interrupted her thoughts, "then you take a step toward him. If he backs off further, then you move back, too."

"It doesn't seem fair," Susan was thinking out loud. "Matt's in control even though he's the one who's messing around. I'm the one who's trying to save our marriage."

"No, it's *not* fair, Susan," the pastor agreed. "Neither was it fair for Jesus to go to the cross. The way of suffering love leads to an understanding of the hidden power of our Lord Jesus Christ in your life. After the Crucifixion on Friday comes the Resurrection on Sunday. Between Friday and Sunday there are some other steps you can take. Do you want to hear them?"

"Yes, I do," said Susan without hesitation.

Remove the excuses. "Every unfaithful husband has a list of excuses to rationalize his behavior. The only way he can live with his conscience is by blaming you, using your faults to justify his selfish actions. His excuses often show up in statements such as, 'You always . . . ' or 'You never . . . ' or 'If you'd just . . . ' or 'It's your fault because . . . ' or 'You're not so perfect either!' or 'You do so and so . . . . '"

Susan was able to come up with a mental list of Matt's excuses in a few seconds. "Are you saying this whole affair was really *my* fault?" she asked.

"Not at all! Nothing you have done gives him the right to commit adultery! When he tries to sling arrows of guilt at you, simply let them fly past. Only if you reach out to catch one does it pierce your soul. Remember that he looks for excuses so he'll not have to face his guilt."

"Then why should I work on changing *my* actions just to remove *his* excuses?" Susan probed.

"For two good reasons. First, it'll help you grow as a person. Next, it'll allow God to convict Matt's conscience."

"How does that work?" Susan was fascinated.

"You'll grow in self-respect and be able to remove Matt's excuses if you 'fix your thoughts on Jesus' (see Heb. 3:1). With your focus on Christ, each change will improve your self-image. You'll look to Him for approval and He will assure you that by His grace you're becoming a better person. This will cause you to feel better about yourself and you'll like it as your self-esteem grows."

"It sure won't be easy," Susan predicted. "Ever since I found out about the other woman, Matt is so touchy. When he does come around I feel like I'm walking on eggshells all the time."

"Quite typical of an adulterous husband," the pastor commented. "More demands. More blame. More excuses. More anger. More defensiveness. Matt's living in a fantasy world where his adulterous partner seems dreamy and wonderful. At the same time he projects everything ugly and terrible on to you. Let me warn you in advance of an interesting twist in most adulterous husbands. As you remove his excuses, he'll not be pleased. He'll simply come up with a new list. However, with Christ's help, you can work on removing anything truthful about those excuses, too. And all the time you're changing for the better and liking yourself more. Here's the bonus: God will go to work on Matt's conscience."

"What do you mean?" Susan looked puzzled.

"You can't see it and Matt will try to hide it, but something powerful will go on within him. As you remove Matt's excuses, God will stab his conscience. I don't know Matt's family background since he hasn't yet come in to talk with me. But if he grew up in a home where his family taught him strong moral convictions against adultery, he'll begin to feel some intense guilt. He'll sense that he should come back into a right relationship with God. And some *do* come back to the Lord. Not all, but some do.

"If he wasn't fortunate enough to have this childhood training, the outcome may become a little more grisly. He'll probably begin to feel confused and empty. He'll struggle to understand himself and may develop a number of psychological problems. All of this is the built-in consequence of his sin. 'A man reaps what he sows' (Gal. 6:7). This principle keeps operating even if Matt doesn't acknowledge adultery as a sin. Inner pain is God's way of getting his attention.

"If he shows any willingness to change, encourage him to come with you to see me or see a Christian marriage counselor on his own. He may not change; he may continue to reject you and refuse counseling. No matter what his response, the next step for you is filling the Mind-set train car.

Mind-Set on the Spirit

"Susan, have you ever watched sailboats going different directions in the same wind? The set of the sails makes the difference. So also can your mind-set on the Holy Spirit cause you to go God's way even when it feels like you're sailing against the wind. Your mind-set includes how you think about Matt. If you put your mental energy into how unfaithful Matt is acting, you're setting your sails wrong. If you allow the Holy Spirit to fill you afresh and anew and to concentrate on Christ, He'll teach you to smile through your tears. Would you like an insight into prayer that will increase your faith and set your mind on the Holy Spirit?"

"Sure," Susan answered.

"There's a right and wrong way to pray. The wrong way is to whine and plead and bargain with God. It's wrong to cry out to God to save your marriage while you try to manipulate, fight back, cling too tight, run away, give up or put all the blame on Matt. It's also wrong to picture Matt as a dirty, rotten, immoral, no-good, two-timing rat."

"But that is what he *is!*" Susan protested.

"Wait a minute! The Lord can never bless that kind of mental image," the pastor frowned. "It locks your faith into a no-change-barring-a-miracle attitude."

"Okay," she mused.

"The right way to pray is to bring Matt to the foot of the cross in your mind's eye. Pretend that you can only see him as you look through Jesus hanging on that blood-spattered cross. Then think and meditate about what Christ wants Matt to become. You can be confident that this is the right mind-set because it's the reason Christ died. Picture Matt trusting Christ and being forgiven, cleansed, restored, renewed and filled with the Holy Spirit, faithful in marriage and serving others with joy. Hold this mental image as clearly as possible in your mind every time you pray for him—or even think about him.

"With this picture vivid in your thoughts, give yourself and your future to the Holy Spirit. Commit yourself to obey His Word no matter what happens. I'm quite aware that when your emotions are in turmoil, painful feelings and thoughts will often come. During such a time, follow the wise counsel of Brother Lawrence in his great devotional classic, *The Practice of the Presence of God:* 'Lift up your heart to Him, sometimes even at your meals, and when you are in company; the least little remembrance will always be acceptable to Him. You need not cry very loud; He is nearer to us than we are aware of.'[4]

"The more you turn your thoughts to Christ, the better you set your sails for the wind of the Spirit. It doesn't all happen automatically, of course. You'll need to keep one hand on the rudder of self-control as you sail. The power resides in the wind, not the sailboat. Likewise, the power of the Holy Spirit can move you in the best direction as you turn your thoughts to Him."

"The picture praying idea sounds like something I can try—and I'll turn my mind over to the Holy Spirit. Will He change Matt and bring him back home?" Susan asked.

"I wish I could point out an absolute promise in the Bible that guarantees every unfaithful husband will turn around and live right if his wife obeys Christ," the pastor said. "The Bible gives hope but no absolute guarantees (see 1 Pet. 3:1-2). Would you like one more idea that will affect Matt and increase your mind-set on the Holy Spirit?"

"I'm open to *anything* that will help," Susan replied.

The hedge of thorns. "Have you heard about praying what Bill Gothard calls 'a hedge of thorns' around an unfaithful partner?" the pastor asked.

"No, I don't think so," answered Susan.

"Based on the Bible's account of Hosea and Gomer (see

Hos. chapters 1-3, especially 2:5-7), hedge-of-thorns praying has dramatic results. Unfaithful marriage partners find themselves rejected by their lovers or in constant conflict. The adulterous affair breaks up, leaving them bewildered and confused. What this prayer does is call on God to get Matt's attention so he can have a reasonable opportunity to return home."

"How?" asked Susan. "Give me an example. How do I pray a 'hedge of thorns' around Matt?"

"The rebuke of Satan is best done when you're with an understanding prayer partner. Pray it out loud with authority."

> Heavenly Father, I ask You to rebuke and bind Satan in the name and through the blood of the Lord Jesus Christ.
>
> I ask You to build a 'hedge of thorns' around my partner, so that anyone with wrong influence will lose interest in him (or her) and leave.
>
> I base this prayer on the command of Your Word which states, "What therefore God hath joined together, let not man put asunder."
>
> Thank You for hearing and answering my prayer.[5]

"Do not be surprised," continued the pastor, "when you find this kind of prayer hard to say out loud. You'll find yourself feeling like you don't want to do it. You may think, *I've never heard of such a thing; it sounds silly. I've never done anything like this before.* Satan will provide plenty of excuses to keep you from engaging in spiritual battle. By my warning you ahead of time of these thoughts and feelings, you'll recognize them as from our enemy the devil. Then claim Christ's power and forge ahead."

Susan took her renewed commitment to Christ seriously and started praying a hedge of thorns around Matt. In her emotions she felt no hope, but by sheer faith and grit she kept praying. It looked to her like it made no difference, that everything between them was over.

Sex after separation? As it turned out, Matt and Susan's relationship was not over. Matt kept coming over to spend time with Ryan and Kelli and ended up talking with Susan for longer and longer periods of time. Sometimes they talked on the phone. Susan thought she could sense how things were going between Matt and the other woman by how often Matt showed up and by what he had on his mind. Sometimes it was obvious that Matt wanted to have sex. Once again Susan made an appointment with her pastor.

"Should I make love with Matt while we're still separated, or not?"

"There's no easy answer," the pastor insisted. "It depends on you. If you desire a physical relationship with Matt, please remember that he's still your husband. You're not committing adultery and you don't need to feel dirty. Until a divorce is final, sex is permissible—but it's not always a good idea. You may run the risk of pregnancy. An unfaithful husband can also transmit venereal disease. So please talk with your doctor before resuming a sexual relationship with Matt.

"If you don't want to have sex with Matt, it's not required under these conditions. You're free either to have it or not."

"Most of the time I don't think I want to," replied Susan, "but then he tells me he still loves me and maybe we can put things back together again. My hopes rise and making love seems like the thing to do."

"Why don't you ask the Holy Spirit for wisdom in making a firm decision?" the pastor suggested. "Either way can be a powerful tool for reconciliation if you're consistent."

"What do you mean?" Susan looked puzzled.

"If you decide to resume making love with Matt, it can serve as a powerful attraction for him to come home. It removes the excuse, 'Susan cut me off. What was I supposed to do?' If you feel the Lord wants to love Matt through your physical body, then take the proper medical precautions and enjoy sex with your husband. Tell him it will be even better when he gives you the security of being your husband, and your husband alone, all the time."

Susan nodded. "What if it just doesn't seem right?"

"It's amazing how our wonderful Lord can use two such different approaches for the same end," the pastor mused. "You can gain much self-esteem, and a good deal of respect in Matt's eyes, by exercising loving strength. You may find it helpful to write him a letter. Tell him that you're setting him free from your expectations. In the letter let him know clearly that you'll not be available sexually until he ends his relationship with the other woman and comes home to stay. Write the letter with as much loving toughness as you know how. Then stick to your convictions until he makes a real change and gives up the other woman." The pastor encouraged Susan to buy Dr. James Dobson's book, *Love Must Be Tough* and follow his example letters.[6]

Since Susan had been quite possessive in their marriage and Matt certainly felt trapped, the "no sex" approach seemed best to her. Following Dr. Dobson's suggestion, she wrote her letter.

Dear Matt,

I never thought this day would come. When we pledged our wedding vows to each other, I meant it with all my heart. It has come as a great shock to me that you have violated these vows and become unfaithful. For some time now, I have done everything I know how to demonstrate my continuing love for you. Nothing has worked. It appears that you still "feel trapped."

This letter is to let you know that I am opening the door of your cage for good. You are free to leave. Just as I did not force you to marry me in the first place, so now I cannot force you to remain married to me. Of course I will not be available to you sexually, nor should you expect any other wifely duties from me.

If you choose to marry the other woman, I hope you two will be happy. If you decide that you want to be my husband, we will talk about it. But I

am making no promises. The Lord is helping me
more than I ever dreamed possible. With Him I
will make it in the future.

   We had some great times together, Matt, and I
am grateful for these special memories. I will pray
for you and ask the Lord to guide your future.

Susan

The letter seemed to shake Matt up. He initiated a couple of
long talks about the possibility of a fresh start. Susan did not cry
or beg or yell. In fact, she maintained her self-respect so well
that even Matt was impressed. He thought about ending his
affair with the other woman but he kept telling himself, *I can't
hurt her. Since I got her into this, I must do something to take care
of her.* At times he felt torn in two.

Susan did not see any immediate changes in Matt, but a new
joy bubbled to the surface of her life. She was simply more fun to
be around. Others noticed and that caused a new problem. A
Christian man became extra helpful and friendly. He started
showing up at her place more and more often. It did not take a
genius to figure out that he was interested in more than friendship. It flattered Susan and bothered her, both at the same time.
She felt attractive and yet disgusted that this man would pursue
a married woman who was separated. In her next appointment
with the pastor she brought up the subject.

Are you vulnerable? "At this stage, Susan, you're more
vulnerable than you realize," the pastor cautioned. "If the 'right
guy' showed up, you might find yourself easy prey."

"Right now I'm not interested in any other man," Susan
replied. "The last thing on earth I want is another man in my life.
Some days I don't even want Matt back."

The pastor smiled. "The time will come when some man's
attention will seem strongly attractive to you. But watch out! A
strange thing happens in our society today. Once you're separated, your non-Christian friends (and sometimes even misguided Christians) will try to set you up with someone else.

"'I wouldn't put up with the way Matt's treating you,' they'll say. 'Don't let him walk all over you. Stick up for your rights, Susan. Go out and have some fun. In fact, I know this single guy who seems like your type.'"

Susan grinned. "They already have. My friends at work keep telling me to get on with my life. 'Why sit at home alone and rot?' they ask."

Why wait? "Why *should* I wait around all this time?" Susan spoke with a look of hurt in her eye. "He's out partying and I'm stuck at home. It doesn't seem fair."

"It's not easy," the pastor corrected her gently. "Remember that it took a long time to develop these problems and it'll take awhile to resolve them. Persevere. Make it your aim to please the Lord each step of the way. Dating during a time of separation brings disgrace on your reputation and on the Lord's. If you reject the shortcuts you'll look back and see this as a time of remarkable spiritual and personal growth. You certainly want God's blessing on your future, don't you?"

"I see what you mean," said Susan quietly. In her spirit, she sensed that the pastor's words made sense.

A Caboose Called Results

One Saturday Matt came over to play with Ryan and Kelli. He seemed in a good mood so Susan appealed to him to come home and give their marriage his full effort. "So much can happen to make things better if we both try," she suggested. Matt said he would think about it. But days dragged into weeks and Matt did not return home. He became more outspoken about his adultery, calling it "my new relationship." Susan was feeling so discouraged she began talking with friends about divorce attorneys.

Because she never believed in divorce, Susan talked with the pastor again before seeing an attorney. He assured her that separation, even with adultery involved, did not mean their marriage was over. "Affairs blow up faster than marriages," he repeated. "There's no promise that Matt will be back, but many husbands (or wives) do come home again. It's amazing what an effect it has on a spouse when you open the door of the cage, turn him loose and refuse to pursue him. This is especially true when you show a sense of self-respect and personal dignity in the Lord. Eventually Matt will ask himself, 'Is this really worth it? Am I losing something important?'"

"I've *done* all that and he shows no signs of coming home!" Susan protested.

Matt wanted Susan to do something about a divorce. She kept telling him, "If you decide to divorce me, I can't stop you. But don't ask me to sign any papers or take any part in it."

Matt thought she was crazy but he did not like the idea of a one-sided divorce either. He swallowed his guilt, however, and had his attorney file the necessary papers. At first he talked about a fair settlement. But when it came to specifics, his idea of fair was just as selfish as always. To Susan it looked like he was going for all the bucks he could get.

Susan was fortunate to find a Christian attorney who opposed divorce. In fact, the position of his firm was that they would not represent a client in a divorce case unless the other spouse sued first. Susan phoned her pastor to let him know what she had done. She was surprised that he approved. "It's right for you to protect Ryan and Kelli and your own financial interests since Matt started the divorce," the pastor said. "Remember, time is on your side. Have your attorney do all he can to extend the time line in these legal matters. Even if the divorce goes through, you can face everyone with your head held high and a light in your eye."

GOD DELIGHTS IN THE IMPOSSIBLE

The months of the divorce proceedings were almost over. In her mind and heart Susan had all but accepted the inevitable. One evening Matt invited her out to dinner, something he had not done before. Susan told herself, *He probably has some change in the settlement in mind.* In any case, she accepted his invitation. The evening came and they enjoyed a lovely dinner in a quiet restaurant. The conversation seemed pleasant as long as they avoided the old, painful subjects.

Then Matt dropped the bomb. "I've been thinking it over. I guess . . . I guess I want to come home—if you'll have me." That was all. No excuses for his behavior. No outright repentance for his sin. Just a simple request to come home. Something in Matt's tone of voice and mannerisms was different than before. Susan felt wary. She struggled with not wanting to forgive him and not wanting him back. And what about "his new relationship"?

"What about the other woman?"

"We broke it off," Matt replied flatly.

"Forever?"

"I think so."

"What do you mean, you *think* so?" Susan's voice began to rise, just like the old days. Then she caught herself.

"I mean, it's over with *her.* I just don't know if I can live with *you,*" Matt shot back.

His words cut to the bone, but for once Susan sensed sincerity in his voice. "If I can bring myself to forgive you, I'll think about it," she said softly. "After all, I've been waiting a long time for this. But how do I know you won't go back to her like before?"

"I won't. I won't." Matt's expressionless face looked empty, almost confused.

"All right," Susan consented, "but only if you promise never to see her again and come with me to see the pastor."

"I promise," said Matt.

Susan's hopes soared, but not for long. Matt moved home all right, but he acted like a porcupine with his quills out. He seemed on edge all the time. Everything bothered him and nothing seemed to please him. Susan felt dead on the inside, like she had no feelings for him. But what was different this time was that Matt stayed home. He did not leave for the other woman.

Little by little Matt began to relax. Some days he almost

seemed like his old self again—lots of fun. Gradually those days became more frequent. As the weeks went by, Susan noticed a new tenderness in him. He began going to church again—even to an adult Sunday School class. She learned to forgive both Matt and herself and to let go of the past.

Years have gone by. The whole adulterous affair seems like a bad dream to both Matt and Susan. The painful memories remain a closed book that they talk about only on rare occasions. Their marriage is happy, better than before. Both of them love the Lord Jesus and they keep active and faithful in their church. Some of the consequences of their separation lasted a long time, but today both feel so glad they did not divorce. "God is so good," they say. "We give Him the glory for saving our marriage. It was worth all the pain."

What Do I Say to My "Sinning" Friend?

6

One of the surprising changes in the last quarter of the twentieth century is the increasing number of Christian leaders who are running the red lights and falling into adultery. Traveling speakers, authors, pastors, college professors, missionaries, elders and Sunday School teachers find themselves among those who have fallen into sexual sin. A shocking number proceed to divorce their spouses and remarry the adulterous partners. Knowing full well what the Bible says, they ignore God's warning signals and deliberately disobey the explicit Word of God.

If the leaders fall, what are the followers to do? Some turn bitter and become disenchanted. Many find themselves trapped by sensuality. To change the analogy, a little lust grows into a smoldering fire. Add the gasoline of emotional pain and an explosion occurs. Marriages blow apart, children are burned and churches are charred. Without a spiritual awakening, future generations will follow in the footsteps of their forefathers.

Before it is over the sexual revolution may scar every family in America. Disease, guilt, broken relationships, shattered emotions and fractured families all result from the sexual revolt. The sad truth is that innocent victims, most often children, suffer most of all, for the lasting damage of divorce causes lifelong injury. With the spread of sensuality, sexual abuse of children also seems to be on the rise. But adults suffer, too. When a family member or close friend begins living in open immorality the stress and strain become intense.

WHAT CAN I DO?

Caring Christians feel distressed and helpless when marriages break apart. They cannot believe it when one of their good friends files for divorce. When the truth of secret adultery comes to light, it seems even harder to take. The questions arise, *What can I, as only one person, do about it? Can I offer any help to my friend who is living in immorality? Since he/she is caught in a sin, how can I have a part in restoring him gently?* (See Gal. 6:1.)

Yes, you can do something. Loving confrontation may turn a friend around. Intervention in Christ's name often brings new hope, especially when family, close friends and church unite in their actions. A personal appeal to return to Christ and biblical living makes a powerful impact. Some will respond well to a personal appeal; others will not. Some will return to Christ and their marriages will be restored; others will not. Whatever the outcome, the Christian who is spiritual will want to try to be a part of the restoration process (see Jas. 5:19-20). This may be you.

The First Step Is the Hardest

The all-important step is to talk with the right person in the right spirit. Who is the right person? The one involved in the sexual sin. Remember to talk *with* the person, not *about* him or her. God's way is loving confrontation, not gossip. The right spirit is a combination of being tender and tough. The concerned Christian will always be tender with the person and tough on the sin. Show love and acceptance of the person's feelings, but refuse to put up with the sinful life-style.

The world system all around us resists loving confrontation. From childhood most of us in Western culture find it difficult to confront an offender without anger or threats. When in conflict our society teaches us to run, fight, quit or blame. None of these methods work, however. Running away solves nothing. Fighting leads to getting even. Quitting means giving up. Blaming solves nothing and avoids any possibility of personal help.

The Christian solution involves obeying Jesus' teaching about a sinning brother. Some call this the "Matthew 18 Principle." What is amazing is how well it works.

> If your brother sins against you, go and show him his fault, just between the two of you. If he listens to you, you have won your brother over. But if he will not listen, take one or two others along, so that 'every matter may be established by the testimony of two or three witnesses.' If he refuses to listen to them, tell it to the church; and if he refuses to listen even to the church, treat him as you would a pagan or a tax collector (Matt. 18:15-17, *NIV*).

When a good friend or family member is living in immorality, at first no one wants to talk with him or her about it. "How will my friend respond?" is a common question. In fact, how the person involved in sexual sin reacts to a loving confrontation is not the Christian's first responsibility. When we obey the Holy Spirit we can also trust the Lord to use our appeal for His good purposes. Nowhere does the Bible criticize us for poorly stating our witness or for fumbling for words when confronting a sinning brother. However, when Christians accept a sinful life-style within their fellowship, it brings down God's wrath according to the inspired writers of the Bible. (For further study read Rom. 6:1-2; 1 Cor. 5:1-2; 2 Tim. 3:1-9; 2 Pet. 2:1-22; 1 John 3:7-10; the book of Jude and Rev. 2:14-16, 20-23.)

If God puts it in your heart to talk with someone caught in a sex sin, you should obey, no matter what it takes. No one ever said it would be easy. Effective—quite possibly! Easy— probably not. You are not alone. When acting in obedience to God's Word, the resources of heaven are at your fingertips— including the penetrating presence of the Holy Spirit. As you prepare your heart and spirit, you can count on Him to work through you.

Prepare with Prayer

Before taking the essential step of confronting a friend in love, wait on the Lord and humble yourself in prayer. Talking to the right person *without* the right spirit will devastate him or her. A time of fasting and prayer prepares your heart and mind with Christ's compassion and power. Searching your own heart for wrong motives or secret sins prepares the spirit for *loving* confrontation. The inner confidence in knowing that this is what Christ wants you to do makes all the difference.

Meet Face to Face

Note Jesus' words, "just between the two of you," in Matthew 18:15. This means alone, one-on-one, eyeball-to-eyeball, in private. If at all possible make this first meeting face-to-face. When two people meet together they read each other's spirits. They pick up attitudes, gestures, facial expressions and a dozen signals of non-verbal communication. The face-to-face appeal always surpasses a less personal approach such as a telephone call or a letter. In person your chances for making a difference in your friend's thinking and actions multiply.

Listen and Question

It helps to remember that the Holy Spirit works energetically to win this person back into a right relationship with God. He will sometimes open your mind to clues that will lead to naming a sin or other times reveal a problem that you did not know about. These insights may come either on a natural or a supernatural level. On the natural plane, the one caught in sin may say things that hint of another problem. On a supernatural plane, the Holy Spirit may reveal a certain sin that the person is struggling with. The Lord seldom does this unless He wants you to use the information at once for a redemptive purpose. Under the guidance of the Holy Spirit, you may ask some penetrating questions or make some revealing statements:

> "Tell me, are you having an emotional or physical affair with someone?"
> "Your problem is homosexuality, isn't it?"
> "How long have you struggled with lust?"
> "Were you molested as a child?"
> "You feel guilty because of a past abortion, don't you?"

If your discernment is accurate, the person will often look shocked and say something like, "How did you know?" The answer may range from a strong, "God told me" to a quiet, "It seemed obvious," "It showed" or simply, "I thought so." Once a person's sin or problem is exposed by surprise, his/her receptivity to God's solution increases by a quantum leap. He/she will often show a whole new openness to counsel from God and from the Bible. It may be appropriate to ask, "May I pray with you about this?" It may seem right to say, "You need a competent Christian counselor. I'm sure my pastor has one to suggest." It may well be that the Holy Spirit will give you a plan of action or a clear directive on the spot: "It's time for you to break off this adulterous affair and go home to your family—today."

These things may seem surprising or unusual. The truth is that they happen more often than most Christians think. If your motive is to win a person to Christ or restore a professing Christian back into a right relationship with God, then stay on the alert. God is at work. As you ask to be filled and directed by His Holy Spirit, He may work through you in surprising ways. On the other hand, do not be discouraged if the conversation seems quite ordinary. The most important thing is "speaking the truth in love" (Eph. 4:15, *NIV*). When a person walking away from God is cared about enough to be confronted, the Lord can use it for good.

The Second-best Approach

Because of distance or a refusal by the other person to talk about the problem, a carefully written letter must sometimes replace a face-to-face talk. When communicating on a ticklish subject, a well-composed letter succeeds better than the telephone. A Christian can write and rewrite a letter until it says exactly what he/she desires. Everyone reads his personal mail and next to being there in person, a letter remains the best way to confront in love.

What follows are letters written by two different people. Neither writer would ever pretend that they are perfect models for others to follow. They kept copies only to verify what they had written. Yet I believe they serve well in communicating what a personal appeal or a letter to a sinning friend might contain. I have changed names, dates and places and have done some editing to make it impossible to identify the people involved. The content, however, comes from the original writers.

This first letter was mailed from a pastor to a parishioner. At the time the letter was sent, Jeff, formerly an active leader in an evangelical church, was separated from his wife Joan and living with another woman. Joan wanted to save their marriage and, as it turns out, remained faithful and open to reconciliation for years. The pastor had talked with both Jeff and his wife on numerous occasions. In time, they did reunite and now have a happy and stable marriage.

> Dear Jeff,
>   I guess this letter has been months and months running through my mind. You and your family are on my mind daily. I trust

that what I will share with you will be helpful, for that's the deep desire of my life.

I remember the time when you were seeking God's best for your life. I saw this taking place in your home and in your work. When you decided to go into business for yourself we prayed together that God would direct you and lead you. God was your partner. You chose to make Him the director of your heart's desires.

All of us come to points in our lives when we are tempted. And except for the grace of God, any of us can be drawn away from our first love. It seems that you brought into your life, into your business and then into your family a person not of God's choosing but of your own willful choosing. She has brought nothing but heartache to you and to those who love you. I say it not in jest; I really look at Mona as the "Jonah" in your life. She has caused you to forfeit the things in your own life that you knew to be right. She has also caused you to draw around you other business people of like philosophy. Because you wanted to change your life-style you began to employ people who also have low moral standards and have no thought of being faithful to their own wives, to their job or to their families. God has been speaking to you about it and yet you have continued now for years to rationalize around the real problem in your life.

Just as in biblical times, when it was important to throw Jonah overboard before the ship could safely reach its destiny, so you also need to get rid of your Jonah if you

ever expect God to be your partner again,
helping you in your family, in your business
and in your personal life most of all. Jeff, my
heart bleeds for you as I've seen you suffer
for many months. You've become a proud
and self-willed man, so much so that you
look to others who are not seeking God's
best to base decisions in life. At the present
time you find yourself turning on your wife
and your two oldest sons. The reason you
turn on them is because they understand the
life that you're living and they convict you
just by their very presence.

Over many months I have heard Joan
share that you have taken a position that
God forgives divorce. Your trend of thought
seems to conclude that you could divorce
Joan, desert your family, marry someone
else and then get right with God. However,
may I remind you that God is not dumb. He
knows when we play games with Him. The
Scripture says that God is not mocked—that
what a man sows, he reaps. Presumptuous
sinning is not taken lightly by Him. He is
very explicit about the importance of
faithfulness in our marriage vows.

God, by His Spirit, has been tugging at
your heart over many, many months. You
have chosen not to heed the wooings of His
Spirit. May I ask you: What makes you think
that if you continually resist the wooing of
God's Spirit now that you would ever find
the place of true repentance and follow His
will after you involve yourself with another
wife? Do you *really* believe that she is
interested in repentance and finding God's

will? Her actions totally indicate otherwise.

You see, the folly of thinking that we can play games with the eternal God and still be righteous in His eyes is quite foolish.

Remember, God will let you play the game your way. But please don't forget that He has set the rules as to the outcome of disobedience.

The thought has gone through my mind often, *Where's the Jeff Green that I used to know? Where's the Jeff Green that God loves so much and has in the past and would like to today bless so abundantly?*

Jeff, does it embarrass you when I tell you that I love you? Is it possible for you to understand that God's people are not laughing up their sleeves or rejoicing in any sense at your present heartache? God wants so very much for you to find the place of repentance and to find newness of life in Him. My prayer for you, Jeff, is that you will be willing to come to the cross of Jesus Christ and there know His cleansing, His peace, His joy and His purpose—which is the finest thing that any man can have and know. Remember these words, "Just as I am and waiting not to rid my soul of one dark blot, to Thee whose blood can cleanse each spot, O Lamb of God I come! I come! Just as I am thou wilt receive, wilt welcome, pardon, cleanse, relieve, Because Thy promise I believe, O Lamb of God I come, I come."[1]

Jeff, will you believe God's promise? He said that if we confess our sin, He is faithful and just to forgive us and to cleanse us from all unrighteousness. Would you join me as a

cleansed sinner whom God loves? I really
think that's what you want to do. May God
give you the courage to do it, now.

Sincerely,

P.S. I will continue to pray for you and would
be happy to pray with you.

The letter made an impact on Jeff. He did not immediately
return to Joan but eventually he did go home for good.

Key Questions for the Sinning Christian
The same pastor also wrote to Mona, the other woman,
while the adulterous affair was still going on. As the letter suggests, Mona claimed that she herself belonged to Jesus Christ.

Dear Mona,
   It's me again. Would you please consider
the following questions and insights?
1. Is Joan interested in rebuilding her
   marriage with Jeff?
2. Do you really love Jeff? Genuine love
   causes an individual to work for the
   benefit of the one they love, not for their
   own gain.
3. Have you encouraged Jeff and made every
   attempt to convince him that he should
   be reconciled to Joan? The lack of such
   encouragement on your part would
   certainly indicate a lack of genuine love
   for Jeff, Joan and their four children.
4. Do you recall the strong judgment on the
   husband if he initiates a divorce? Read
   Malachi 2:13-16 and 1 Peter 3:7.

5. Would you think less or more of your
   father if, when you were a teenager, he
   had and continued a relationship similar
   to yours?

6. One of the most important marks of
   leadership in a husband is to be a one-
   woman man, not letting another woman
   meet his needs. Are you doing everything
   within your power to help Jeff fulfill this
   role? "Therefore shall a man leave his
   father and his mother, and shall cleave
   unto his wife: and they shall be one flesh"
   (Gen. 2:24, KJV). This is God's best for
   Jeff and Joan.

7. How does God want you to serve Him
   with your life? It is essential for every
   person to first find his/her place of
   service for God and then determine how
   marriage will influence that service. It
   seems that an improper marriage
   relationship has become first in your life,
   Mona.

8. Marriage is a human object lesson of a
   divine relationship. God has special
   consequences for any who damage this
   object lesson. Read Proverbs 6:32-33.

9. Is your family and Jeff's family fully in
   harmony with this relationship? God will
   often use the basic wishes of parents and
   family members as further warnings not
   to proceed with a wrong relationship.
   Agreement of parents doesn't establish
   the rightness of a relationship, but their
   disapproval does establish the wrongness
   of it. Read Proverbs 10:17.

10. I am aware that you and Jeff speak often

of your "feeling" for one another. And you even consider this some kind of problem other than spiritual. It would be very helpful I suppose if that were true. However, when you respond correctly to God's truth, you can count on your feelings; they will straighten out too.

11. You are doing yourself and Jeff a great disservice. I appeal to you to do the right thing by encouraging Jeff to reconcile with Joan and show genuine love by breaking off this destroying relationship.

Consider these steps:

1. Humble yourself.
   Result: Grace—the desire and power to do God's will. Read James 4:10.
2. Resist the devil. Find a new job and remove yourself from the daily temptation.
   Result: He will flee from you.
3. Come close to God.
   Result: Your "hands" will be clean and your conscience clear.
4. Realize how you have sinned.
   Result: Your motives will be pure once again.

Discern who you are really serving and look to God *only* for approval. May God help you take the steps necessary to be *His* woman.

Sincerely,

P.S. *Now* is always the right time to do what
is right.

A Son Appeals to His Father

The next letter was written by a man who works for a corporation as a scientist. The words, with only minor exceptions, are his. It is a powerful appeal from the oldest son in a family who is now grown and has children of his own. His dad's reply follows the letter.

Dear Mom and Dad,
This letter is written to both of you and I
request that you read it together. Please read
it very slowly, very carefully, and, under no
circumstances, should you insert meanings
or implications that aren't there.

On History
Dad, you have been accused of having an
extramarital affair of long standing. Fred (a
brother) says you told him personally and
have refused to discuss it since. You have yet
to approach me, even though you must have
known for some time now that Mom called
me.
Mom, you said that you felt that we knew
of your problems before you called and
wondered if Aunt Emma told us. Yes, we
knew; no, she didn't tell us. No mortal told
us. We didn't have the particulars, but we
knew there was serious trouble. We sensed it
each time we talked to you on the phone.

On Wrongdoing and Love
You are my parents and words cannot

adequately express how much I love you.
Furthermore, you are my mother and my
father and as such, I shall forever honor you
both, not only because the Bible says I
should, but because I love you. As a child I
put you both through some pretty rough
times. Yet, I have no doubts whatsoever that
there was nothing I could have done that
would have caused you to reject me or to
stop loving me. You too must know that
there is nothing, absolutely nothing that you
could ever do that could alter my love for
you. Nothing past, nothing present, nothing
future. I LOVE YOU.

And so it is with God. There is no wrong,
no matter how dastardly, that can alter His
love for us. The Bible is replete with
examples of God's perfect separation of the
sinner from his sin and God's limitless love
for the sinner, even when unrepentant.

On Sin, Repentance and Forgiveness

God's forgiveness is easily obtainable. All
He asks is that the sinner repent of his sins
(see Mark 11:26). David sinned greatly
when he violated Bathsheba and murdered
Uriah, her husband. "But the thing that
David had done displeased the Lord" (2 Sam.
11:27). However, was he forever
condemned? No! When confronted with his
sin by Nathan the prophet, David did the
only thing that has to be done to obtain
forgiveness—he admitted his guilt, repented
and was forgiven. "Then David said to
Nathan, 'I have sinned against the Lord.'
And Nathan said to David, 'The Lord also has

taken away your sin; you shall not die'" (2 Sam. 12:13, *NASB*). And David lived to a ripe, old age.

The lesson is clear. "For the wages of sin is death." (Rom. 6:23). But God's forgiveness erases sin, and His forgiveness requires only repentance. To be repentant means you're sorry and you won't do it again. Repentance and forgiveness are the clue to the repair of your sinking ship.

But, remember that repentance is impossible without any admission of guilt. Try as I may, I cannot recall a single time that I ever heard Dad admit guilt, wrong, or even simple error.

Mom, in all gentleness, you have had a history of dogmatic religious beliefs and intolerance towards human sinful frailties. I do remember several times when Dad got the silent treatment for wayward actions. And not just for a day, but for up to two weeks at a stretch. The tension was so thick in that house you could cut it with a knife. Was that forgiveness? I have to believe that you have not been the easiest person to live with. Are you willing to accept that responsibility, and thoroughly address any and all corrective measures?

On Sin, Forgiveness and Punishment

When I was young, and living at home, I most certainly committed sins which demanded punishment. Though I may have been repentant, and though I may have been forgiven, still, the earned punishment was swift, and just as certain as the sin.

Forgiveness does not preclude punishment.
They are separate issues entirely.
Forgiveness is optional, being dependent on
the sinner's desire to repent. Punishment is
subject to no such option.

Despite their long service and devotion to
the Lord, neither Moses nor Aaron were
permitted to enter the Promised Land. Why?
Because they disobeyed the Lord at the
waters of Meribah Kadesh, and struck the
water-bearing rock instead of talking to it as
the Lord had commanded. Yet they died and
joined the Lord.

How about David? He was forgiven of his
grievous sin, and died and joined the Lord.
Did he escape punishment? No. He was
permitted to keep Bathsheba only because
he had killed her husband and fathered her
child. He had to support her. Other than
that, he fared very badly. His first son with
Bathsheba, conceived out of wedlock, died.
Absalom, David's second son, killed his
brother, conspired to kill David and make
himself king, and died by the sword. Prior to
his death, Absalom took David's concubines
and violated them in full sight of the nation.
All as promised. (See 2 Sam. 12:11.) David
suffered greatly for his sin, yet he took his
punishment, and joined the Lord.

On Dad and the Rest of This Letter

Dad, the rest of this letter is going to be
rough on you, so I'm giving you fair
warning. By doing so, I'm counting on the
fact that you love me as much as I love you.
That means that you'll hear me out,

knowing that I have nothing but love for the
both of you, and your best interests at heart.
I've never had to do anything like this
before. It's the hardest thing I've ever done,
and I hope and pray that I'll never have to
do it again.

On Repentance, Punishment and Pride

As I see it, right now another woman is
the stumbling block, at least the biggest one.
If you, Dad, have any intentions at all of
rectifying this great wrong, then you must
give her up, absolutely, completely, forever,
without further contact. You are permitted
one phone call, in Mom's presence, during
which you will dismiss this woman for good,
with no excuses other than that the
relationship is wrong. Furthermore, you will
not attend any function, or go anywhere, if
encountering her is even a possibility. You
must strike her existence from your life. If
you have to get an unlisted phone, then so be
it. If you have to leave the city, then so be it.
If you have to leave the state, then so be it.
You will have to do whatever is necessary to
escape her influence. That will probably
depend on how much hell she wants to raise
after giving up her own family and then
being scorned. The measure of the distress
she causes you may be the measure of the
punishment you have earned. That will be
up to God. But what is a bit of earthly
inconvenience compared to eternally losing
your relationship with God? Dad, are you
man enough to give up your home, your city,

and your state to escape a woman you can't
resist?

Are you going to take a lifetime of good
works and ruin it all at the end by thumbing
your nose at God?

On Happiness

I understand that, when confronted by
Mom, the other woman stated that she
thought she could make Dad happy. WRONG!
No one can make Dad happy but Dad. Dad
will find his happiness where he chooses to
seek it. Our forefathers knew this, when, in
the Declaration of Independence, they
declared every man's right to " ... Life,
Liberty, and the pursuit of Happiness."
Notice the last right is not to Happiness, but
to the Pursuit of happiness. We choose those
things which we pursue, if, indeed, we
choose to pursue anything at all. If Dad has
found happiness outside the home, then it is
because he looked for it there.

On Reasoning and Conduct

Here you are—throwing away a lifetime
of laudable accomplishments, and placing
your reputation in the hands of another
woman. Consider it carefully. Webster
defines a mistress as (among other things):
(1) a woman who has power, authority, or
ownership; as a woman who possesses or
controls something; (2) a woman with
whom a man habitually fornicates. In other
words, in exchange for an extramarital
relationship, you have permitted another
woman to gain power, authority, ownership,

possession, and control over your life. If you
want to deny that, then consider whether or
not, by broadcasting your infidelity in a
spiteful manner, she could completely
destroy your reputation, a reputation of
respect that you have spent a lifetime
building. Mom couldn't and wouldn't do that.
She is one with you, and can hardly attack
herself. You have turned over the control of
your destiny to another person, something
you have never done before, and the reasons
are totally irrelevant. It defies logic.

You taught us to be honest, sincere, that
a man's word was his bond, that
commitments were made to keep. You
taught us that infidelity was wrong, that
divorce was a sin, that the marriage vows
were an invoidable contract, an irrevocable
commitment, an eternal obligation.
Apparently you no longer consider that to be
true. Sorry, I can't agree with you. Not only
that, but either you were wrong then, or you
are wrong now. The two positions are in
direct opposition. You had better make up
your mind which is right. You are defying
reason.

You taught us that we should be honest
with our parents, that they are our best and
most trusted counsel. With them we should
share our joy, grief, and problems. Yet, it is
my understanding that your own mother
has not been told of your relationship with
the other woman. Why not? If you are so
sure that this relationship is the right thing
to do, then you should have been the first to
share your joy with her. That is what you

taught us. Could it be that, deep down inside, you know very well that you are wrong? Frankly, I don't blame you. If I were in your shoes I wouldn't have the guts to tell my mother either. Especially when she thinks she has such a fine, upstanding, Christian boy. You are letting her live that lie too. To deny this information to your own mother is to admit your guilt. Make up your mind what is right. You are defying reason.

On Dad's Opportunity

Dad, you are, of course, free to reject all of the above. But, if you do, and if you are thinking rationally, then you will have a clear, logical explanation as to why I am wrong and you are right. You will also have a clear, logical explanation as to why you were wrong about everything you taught me as a child, since your 180 degree shift has discounted all of that. You will then have a clear, logical, convincing explanation as to why I should believe you are right now, if everything you taught me before is now wrong.

On Dad's Danger

Dad, you are playing with fire, literally. If you are a Christian, you know that. If you are not a Christian, then you either don't know that, or you're not sure. The reason that I give a choice is because I'm not really sure if you are a Christian or not. I can't recall ever hearing you openly express your conviction one way or the other, and you certainly never assumed the proper

Christian role of the spiritual leader in our home.

If you reject Christianity altogether, and won't change, then you are lost. All we can do is pray for you and hope for the best.

If you are a Christian, or at least leaning that way, then don't pull the old trick of waiting until the last minute to try for a deathbed confession. You have no way of knowing when that time will be, and you might not make it to bed. While it is true that forgiveness is there for the asking, it is also true that Christ said, "So then, you will know them by their fruits. Not every one who says to Me, 'Lord, Lord,' will enter the kingdom of heaven; but he who does the will of My Father who is in heaven" (Matt. 7:20-21 *NASB*). You will have to do an awful lot of fast talking at the pearly gates to convince St. Peter that the fruits you are presently harvesting represent the will of the Father.

On Relationships, Can Do's and Can't Do's

Dad, your only hope is to stay in that house and knock off the extracurricular activities, unless you have to move to ensure a clean break. If you leave Mom and join the other woman, then you will burn your bridge behind you. If you persist in living with Mom, and "playing" at the same time, then you will come close to destroying my inherent faith that every man has endearing qualities somewhere (won't affect my love, though).

As long as you are still "playing," I might as well lay a few things on the line. You are forcing me to make some decisions that I would rather not have to make. Just as I love you and Mom, so do I have the capacity to love the other woman, just as I can love any child of God. However, I am under no conviction whatsoever to condone your relationship. It was born of evil. No matter what shall come to pass it will remain evil, and I hereby declare your relationship with that woman to be anathema. There is nothing you can do that is capable of legitimatizing your relationship with her.

Her name shall never be spoken in my house, nor will she ever be permitted entrance to it. Until they are of age, I will not permit your grandchildren near her. If we come to your town, and she appears, then we will leave, immediately. Should that happen, don't feel hurt. It will be your decision to cut yourself off from your family, not the other way around.

You made a lifetime commitment to my mother, and I am going to hold you to it. However, that commitment did not include your bringing daily torture on her by constantly exposing her to the ultimate form of disrespect. I don't care if Mom was hard to live with, what you are doing to her now is intolerable. The Bible may say that it is a wife's duty to obey her husband, but it also says that it is the husband's duty to love his wife as Christ loved the Church. That leaves no room for your present actions. Either return to her, totally, completely and absolutely, or quit the act and get out, totally, completely and absolutely. Choose one or the other, your wife or your mistress. You can't have both!

Mom, I have no way of knowing if Dad's heart is completely hardened or not. If it is, then let him go. If it isn't, then he may need some time to sort this letter out. Give him that time. Meanwhile, search your own heart for any and all previous actions on your part that served to separate you, or that were not designed to bring the two of you closer. Especially any actions that were capable of interfering with constant, continuous, intimate communication. Check your forgiveness quotient. I know that it is a lot better than it used to be, but is it as good as it can be? We are all sinners, and our forgiveness must be immediate and absolute.

Should Dad not turn around rather quickly, and see the error of his ways, and truly repent of his actions, and clearly and completely break from his playmate, then I feel that Grandma must be told—even if Dad doesn't have the courage to do it himself. We are talking about Dad's soul being lost. There can be no stronger petition brought before the Lord on his behalf than that of his mother. It won't kill her, unless it is her time anyway. It may keep her alive a while longer, since her prayers are a must right now. Please discuss this with Dad's sisters, if Dad won't do it. How can we stand back and not invoke the ultimate earthly strength available?

On Hope

For all the talk about alternatives, and

for all the raking over the coals that Dad has been through here, do not lose track of the fact that, until Dad is gone, signed, sealed and delivered, it is not too late. God can accomplish anything. No marriage or relationship is beyond His ability to repair. BUT, it takes two petitions, not just one. One party does not a marriage make.

I am including for each of you a copy of one of the best marriage books around. It's not long, and I appeal to you, I beg of you, especially Dad, to read it from cover to cover before you make any decisions. Dad, I'm your son—do not ignore me. Frankly, as I finish this letter, I have been typing continuously for 26 hours (just figured it out). Our whole Sunday School class prayed for you this morning, and for me as I sought the right words for you. If your marriage goes down the tubes, I am going to lose a lot more than a night's sleep. And, for what?

You know, Dad, I have yet to hear why you are doing what you are doing. Surely you have an opinion on your own actions. You've never lacked for opinions before. Why now? I love you, Dad. Why are you withdrawing your love from us? Is the dad I once knew still out there somewhere? Or has he gone away? I would love nothing better than to be told that this whole thing is just a bad dream. It is not happening. Would that someone show me that my own dad really isn't capable of doing what the reports say, that what I have heard isn't true, and that I just wasted 26 hours of typing. I would kiss them after I wake up sometime tomorrow.

Dear God, please help Mom and Dad.
Please help me, their son, to know what is
right to do. I am actually crying for the first
time in twenty years. Let my tears fall on
Dad's heart and soften it. Where is he, God?
Where did he go? Please bring my dad back
to me. Bring him back to us. Please.

Your loving son,

A Success Story

His dad responded with a short note that made his son's
heart sing.

Dear Son,
Thanks for your splendid research, your
contemplation, your time spent in typing,
your deep spiritual and filial concern, your
love and prayers.
God heard your prayers—this is *your* dad
"coming back to you."
I've sinned, I'm sorry, I've turned, I'm
forgiven, I'm *free.*
I'm terribly sorry for all the pain I've
caused so many people.
Please continue to pray for me to resist
Satan. I'm sure he will work on me harder
than ever.

With all my love to
my son,

Your dad

His dad kept the letter and read it over and over again during the following months.

Three years later the writer of this letter reports that his dad and mom are together and doing well. They resolved the crisis and saved their marriage.

AN INTERCESSORY PRAYER

Most of the written prayers in this book are patterned after those found in *The Adversary* and *Overcoming the Adversary* by Mark I. Bubeck. This one, written for a sinning friend, is especially effective. I encourage you to pray this prayer, replacing Fred Smith with the name of someone you are concerned about.

Heavenly Father, I bring before You and the Lord Jesus Christ one who is very dear to You and to me, Fred Smith. I have come to see that Satan is blinding and binding him in awful bondage. He is in such a condition that he cannot or will not come to You for help on his own. I stand in for him in intercessory prayer before Your throne. I draw upon the Person of the Holy Spirit that He may guide me to pray in wisdom, power, and understanding.

In the name of the Lord Jesus Christ, I loose Fred from the awful bondage the powers of darkness are putting upon him. I bind all powers of darkness set on destroying his life. I bind them aside in the name of the Lord Jesus Christ and forbid them to work. I bind up all powers of depression that are seeking to cut Fred off and imprison him in a tomb of despondency. I bring in prayer the focus of the Person and work of the Lord Jesus Christ directly upon Fred to his strengthening and help. I bring the mighty power of my Lord's incarnation, crucifixion, resurrection, ascension, and glorification directly against all forces of darkness seeking to destroy

Fred. I ask the Holy Spirit to apply all of the mighty work of the Lord Jesus Christ directly against all forces of darkness seeking to destroy Fred.

I pray, heavenly Father, that You may open Fred's eyes of understanding. Remove all blindness and spiritual deafness from his heart. As a priest of God in Fred's life, I plead Your mercy over his sins of failure and rebellion. I claim all of his life united together in obedient love and service to the Lord Jesus Christ. May the Spirit of the living God focus His mighty work upon Fred to grant him repentance and to set him completely free from all that binds him.

In the name of the Lord Jesus Christ, I thank You for Your answer. Grant me the grace to be persistent and faithful in my intercessions for Fred, that You may be glorified through this deliverance. Amen.[2]

The Joy of Pure Sex 7

Purity and passion make wonderful bedfellows. Cleansed from guilt and shame, pure sex brings delight to the human heart and honor to God. Sex as God intended it is fulfilling, satisfying and fun. Winning over sexual temptation is worth all the effort when one enters into the joy of pure sex. This delight, this sense of inner well-being is available in differing ways to Christian singles and marrieds alike.

By pure sex I mean what the scholars call sexual purity, fidelity or chastity. For Christian singles it means enjoying sexuality in every relationship without indulging in sexual sin. For married Christians it means enjoying the pleasure of becoming "one flesh" in body, soul and spirit without engaging in adultery. Forgiveness and cleansing from Christ purifies God-given sexuality, setting us free from selfish demands and self-destructive behavior. Married Christians soar to the heights of sexual pleasure and plummet the depths of quiet satisfaction. Both marrieds and singles can know peace and contentment in satisfying relationships.

LET'S CELEBRATE
I have often thought that John Gillespie Magee, Jr.'s sonnet,

"High Flight" is a wonderful metaphor of pure sex within marriage. Although he was describing the thrill of piloting his Spitfire airplane into the wild, blue yonder, his sense of freedom and joy reminds me of sexual love.

> Oh! I have slipped the surly bonds of earth,
> and danced the skies on laughter-silvered wings;
> Sunward I've climbed and joined the tumbling mirth
> of sunsplit clouds—and done a hundred things
> You have not dreamed of—wheeled and soared and
> swung—high in the sunlit silence.
> Hov'ring there, I've chased the shouting winds
> along,
> and flung my eager craft through footless halls of
> air.
> Up, up the long, delirious, burning blue, I've topped
> the windswept heights with easy grace.
> Where never lark or even eagle flew.
> And, while with silent, lifting mind I've trod the high
> Untrespassed sanctity of space,
> Put out my hand, and touched the face of God.[1]

In my opinion the best description of pure sex is the Song of Songs. So full of celebration, warmth, intimacy, desire and contentment is this series of love songs, that many Christians consider it an allegory of Christ and the Church. One thing is certain: pure sex and Christian spirituality are closely related.

> Lover: How beautiful you are, my darling!
> Oh, how beautiful!
> Your eyes behind your veil are doves.
> Your hair is like a flock of goats
> descending from Mount Gilead.
> Until the day breaks
> and the shadows flee,
> I will go to the mountain of myrrh

and to the hill of incense.
All beautiful you are, my darling;
there is no flaw in you.

You have stolen my heart, my sister, my
bride;
you have stolen my heart
with one glance of your eyes,
with one jewel of your necklace.
How delightful is your love, my sister, my
bride!
(Song of Sol. 4:1,6-7,9-10, *NIV*)

Beloved: Under the apple tree I roused you;
there your mother conceived you,
there she who was in labor gave you birth.

Place me like a seal over your heart,
like a seal over your arm;
for love is as strong as death,
its jealousy unyielding as the grave.
It burns like blazing fire,
like a mighty flame.

Many waters cannot quench love;
rivers cannot wash it away.
If one were to give
all the wealth of his house for love,
it would be utterly scorned.
I am a wall,
and my breasts are like towers.
Thus I have become in his eyes
like one bringing contentment.
(Song of Sol. 8:5-7,10, *NIV*)

THE REAL THING

The Bible is the most realistic book in the world. It records
the freedom of pure sex and the slavery of immoral sex. In her
excellent book, *Passion and Purity,* Elisabeth Elliot contrasts

the popular misconception of purity with the real thing.

> Purity, I fear, has gotten mixed up in people's minds
> with the caricature of Puritanism, which, in the pop-
> ular imagination, is a dour, brittle revolt against all
> the pleasures of the flesh. Puritans were in fact very
> earthy people, robust in their affirmation of life, not
> by any means "Victorian" (another word grossly
> misunderstood today in being made a synonym for all
> that is negative). Neither the concept of purity nor
> the doctrines of the Puritans deny life. Rather they
> refer back to the very Giver of Life Himself. Purity
> means freedom from contamination, from anything
> that would spoil the taste or the pleasure, reduce the
> power, or in any way adulterate what the thing was
> meant to be. It means cleanness, clearness—no
> additives, nothing artificial—in other words, "all nat-
> ural," in the sense in which the Original Designer
> designed it to be.[2]

Created in His Image

The Bible takes a positive view about sex as God intended it.
God's Word tells us that pure sex was part of God's original creation for husband and wife before the fall (see Gen. 2:24). Adam
and Eve enjoyed a perfect sexual relationship before disobeying
God. Even after the Fall, men and women of God in the Bible,
such as Abraham, Ruth, David and Esther, showed healthy sexual passion although sometimes they abused it. As a single,
Jesus demonstrated respect, purity and tenderness toward the
women who were close to Him. Paul taught that husbands and
wives have mutual responsibilities in satisfying each other's sexual desires (see 1 Cor. 7:3-5).

Review what the first chapter of the Bible says about male-
ness, femaleness and God's image.

> So God created man in his own image,

in the image of God he created him;
male and female he created them (Gen. 1:27, *NIV*).

How we understand what God says in the first chapters of Genesis makes a major impact on our Christian viewpoint of sexuality. Of course women and men hold different perspectives on God's original creation. Women say, "God created man. Then He looked at what He had fashioned and said, 'I can do better than that.' So He created woman!" Men see it in a different light. "God created man," they say, "and all was peaceful and quiet. Too quiet. So He created woman and neither God nor man has had peace and quiet ever since!" Neither viewpoint is quite biblical, of course!

More seriously, I like Richard J. Foster's summary:

> Our human sexuality, our maleness and femaleness, is not just an accidental arrangement of the human species, not just a convenient way to keep the human race going. No, it is at the center of our true humanity. We exist as male and female in relationship. Our sexualness, our capacity to love and be loved, is intimately related to our creation in the image of God. What a high view of human sexuality![3]

The Good News of Grace

Now for the bad news and the good news. The bad news, as everyone knows, is that pure sex did not stay pure. The fall of the human race into sin, and the individual choice of every person to go his own way, had a devastating effect. The image of God, including sexuality, was broken, warped, damaged, twisted and perverted. The good news is that the image of God cannot be totally destroyed—it can be redeemed. Jesus Christ alone reflects the full image of God and He has the power to restore a healthy self-image in others (see Col. 1:15; 2:9-10; 3:9-10 and Heb. 1:3). Some of the best news about Christianity is its power to renew the image of God in the sexual department of life. His redemption not only restores peace with God but also brings about a right relationship between male and female.

Reflect on what the image of God means in daily life as it relates to human sexuality.

- The image of God reveals that every person holds infinite worth and value. No one is worthless, disposable, beyond hope. This includes the worst sexual sinner and the most uptight Pharisee.
- The image of God shows us that every person holds the potential of an intimate union with the Creator and Redeemer. The intimate male-female relationship illustrates the closeness God desires with us.
- The indestructible nature of the image of God means that every person holds the potential of redemption and recovery from sin, including the sexual variety.
- As the image of God is progressively restored in Christ, His followers grow in their capacity to experience all that God intended. Every person redeemed by Christ holds the potential of enjoying the pure sex that God designed. Within marriage, Christians should be sexier than anyone.

The grace of God can transform anyone, including the judgmental person who rejects what the Lord created and who thinks sex is dirty. It is possible for a good person to be so severe that no one likes to be near him. Those around him may say, "If that is what sexual purity does to your personality, then 'no thanks.'" Instead, the wise Christian will let the indwelling Christ develop holy sexuality as part of the image of God. The simple result is that he will like himself and other people more than before.

The wonder is that the living power of Christ can cause a good man to become tender like Jesus and a bad man to become holy like Jesus. It even causes the two of them to become brothers in the Lord. No other force on earth has so much influence in changing our self-image for the better. No other person has so much power to release the potential within human sexuality for good. It can even help you and me when we feel disappointed with ourselves. And we in turn can help others when they struggle with low self-esteem or warped thinking about sex.

Are you ready to lighten up? Let your imagination run free as we indulge in a little toad talk.

Do you ever feel like a toad? Toads feel cold and clammy, ugly and lonely, ridiculed and rejected. How do I know? Would you believe one told me?

The toad feeling seeps in when you want to feel all together, but you are coming apart at the seams; when you want to feel cool and collected, but you are churning with anger; when you want to feel courageous, but you are scared to death; when you want to feel calm, but you are panic-stricken; when you want to feel elated, but you are so depressed you could die.

Yes, sooner or later each of us finds himself in the pits, sitting between a rock and a hard place, going nowhere in life. Feeling frustrated and desperate, and too toadish to jump.

Once upon a time there lived a toad, only he wasn't really a toad. He was a wonderful prince who felt and looked like a toad. Someone said a wicked witch had cast an evil spell on him. Only one thing would bring him back, the kiss of a beautiful maiden. But since when do charming princesses kiss toads? So there he sat, an unloved prince in toad form.

Yet miracles do happen. One day a good-looking maiden threw her arms around him and gave him a huge smooch. Whammy! Pow! Zing! There he stood, a charming prince. You can guess the rest of the story—they lived happily ever after.

So what's the task of the true Christian? Kissing toads, of course.

Sexual Sin and Self-Esteem

The toad feeling can come from many causes, but when it

comes from sexual sin it damages the self-image. Immoral sex warps healthy self-esteem into self-hatred and self-destruction (see Rom. 1:24-32; Deut. 28:58-59,65-67 and Prov. 6:25-29,32). Charles Colson relays a telling incident reported in *Psychology Today*. "A woman in her mid-20s is undergoing psychiatric treatment, her nerves shot from too many all-night parties and discos, her thoughts tangled by pot, booze and sex. 'Why don't you stop?' the therapist asks.

"Startled, she replies, 'You mean I really don't have to do what I want to do?'"

Charles Colson comments, "That insidious tendency toward self-destruction is a sure sign of judgment upon us. And the craving to destroy is voracious."[4]

It is my personal conviction that a basic cause-effect relationship exists between immoral sex and loss of self-esteem. The chain of events goes like this. The person who follows sexual immorality as a way of life begins to deny God or at least becomes agnostic. He somehow puts God far enough out of his thoughts that the Holy One no longer bothers his conscience. What comes next is a loss of self-control. He finds that at times he cannot control his impulses. Like a spider web wrapping strand after strand around its victim with each little indulgence, the hold of sexual sin grows stronger and stronger. The Bible warns that sin turns a valuable human being into a slave, a mere puppet strung up to the invisible hand of lust. Listen to one man's story.

> I learned quickly that lust, like physical sex, points in only one direction. You cannot go back to a lower level and stay satisfied. Always you want more. I've experienced enough of the unquenchable nature of sex to frighten me for good. Lust does not satisfy; it stirs up.[5]

The people who have gone to the extremes still want more. One of Satan's favorite traps is increasing sexual desires with decreasing satisfaction. The evil desires grow stronger, the appetite gets bigger, the lusts become more demanding while the actual experience gives less and less satisfaction. The person feels high for short periods but plunges into the depth of negative emotions between thrills. Sex sins seem so good at the moment, but turn out so bad later. With the loss of self-control comes low self-esteem. The individual who cannot control his impulses and yet despises their negative consequences no longer feels good about himself.

Contrast the toad feeling with the healthy sense of self-esteem that emerges from the image of God, including a right relationship between male and female. The people who reflect Christ's image by a life-style of holy living feel good about themselves. Far from hating discipline and self-control, they consider it essential to the best life. They like the results which most often follow: good mental health, enjoyable sexuality, good marriages and stable families. While not all attain this ideal, most come close enough that they improve their self-image. The fruit of their relationship with Christ is positive self-esteem.

PURE SEX WITHIN MARRIAGE

God created sex as a unifying, beautiful expression of married love. Through physical union husband and wife become "one flesh" and one in spirit. From this union of love comes the fruit of the womb, their own sons and daughters. In addition to the blessing of childbearing, the sexual relationship serves as a binding, soul-knitting experience. So precious in God's sight is this intimate oneness that He commands everyone not to spoil it by any use before or outside of the covenant of marriage. In a fascinating article entitled, "What the Bible Says About Sex," Billy Graham writes,

> One thing the Bible does not teach is that sex in itself is sin. Far from being prudish, the Bible celebrates sex and its proper use, presenting it as God-

created, God-ordained, God-blessed. It makes plain
that God himself implanted the physical magnetism
between the sexes for two reasons: for the propaga-
tion of the human race, and for the expression of that
kind of love between man and wife that makes for
true oneness. His command to the first man and
woman to be "one flesh" was as important as his
command to "be fruitful and multiply."[6]

Since God created sex, it seems that those who know Him
intimately might well enjoy it more than others. *Redbook* magazine once published a survey on female sexuality and in an amazing response, 100,000 mostly-married women unbuttoned their
intimate lives. What shocked a lot of people was that the more
religious a woman described herself, the happier she was about
her sex life and her marriage. The most religious in all age cate-
gories ranked the highest when describing their marriages and
sex life as good, discussing sex freely with their husbands, feeling satisfied with the frequency of intercourse and more consistently reaching orgasm.[7] Even taking into account that popular
surveys are not scientific samplings, the results were astounding
to the uninformed. As I recall the conversations among my
friends about that time, most committed Christian women were
not so surprised. They expected God's way to produce a happier
marriage and sex life.

All marriages, including Christian couples, experience times
of disillusionment and pain. Some bear up under sexual dysfunc-
tion for years. Others lapse into patterns of boredom or frustration. Fortunately, more help is available today than ever before.
Some Christian marriage therapists specialize in correcting
problems and teaching sexual enhancement within marriage.
Excellent books and tapes are also available in Christian bookstores.[8] Within a covenant of trust and commitment, sexual dys-
functions are most often overcome. Pure sex provides a commitment to work through problems and increase pleasure rather
than walk away from them. What are those to do who find no

solution? As trite as it sounds, and I say this with compassionate pain in my heart, those who find no relief from pressing problems and unresolved sexual needs can still rely on the God who cares (see Heb. 4:14-16 and 2 Cor. 12:7-10). God blesses faithfulness and obedience, sometimes in other ways. It may well be that those who benefit most from pure sex among married Christians are the children from these homes. Even if the parents consider it "a bad marriage" and yet stay faithful, the children benefit.

Check on it for yourself. Talk to the public school teachers whom you know. Ask them, "In your classroom, who would you say have the most learning handicaps and behavior problems? Would you say the children with the most problems come from broken homes or from homes with a 'bad marriage' where the parents are still together?" The school teachers I talk with reply with one voice that children from broken homes show the most problems at school. It follows that those from stable homes (including the ones with a bad marriage) have the least problems. Pure sex protects children in two ways—the stability of their homes and the examples of commitment and faithfulness for their own future marriages and families.

PURE SEX AND CHRISTIAN SINGLES

Many Christian singles burn with sexual passion. Many who reject the social life of the bars, resist explicit sexual stimuli and commit themselves to purity still find themselves aflame with desire. Single men (and some women) struggle with impulsive lust from a strong sex drive. Single women (and some men) crave emotional attention, sometimes (obviously) not of God's choice. They agree with the Bible's wisdom, "it is better to marry than to burn with passion" (1 Cor. 7:9, *NIV*). But for many a Christian marriage, however strongly desired, appears out of their reach for the foreseeable future.

A later chapter will address the issue of staying strong when emotions scream for the wrong. At this point turn your thoughts to singles who need help in recovering from sexual immorality.

Drake and Brenda's Story

Drake was single and never married, although he had lived with Brenda three different times. He thought of this attractive divorceé as his wife but she did not see it that way. Their adulterous affair had blown up each time with explosive anger. What seemed strange was that they both considered themselves Christians and in many other ways were trying to live out their beliefs. It was Drake who suggested they see a pastor for counseling. He wanted to know if there was any way to make this relationship work.

Brenda liked Drake but did not trust him. She was tired of his deceit. When they went to see the pastor they were dating again but not living together. They poured out their story of living double lives and yet wondered why it did not work. Theirs was a love-hate, hot-cold, on-again, off-again relationship. Was there any way to get it all together?

After listening to their stories the pastor made an appeal. He challenged both of them to make Jesus Christ Lord of their lives whether or not they ever proceeded toward marriage. Following Jesus as Lord, he explained, meant Christ was to become the boss, the master, the ruler of every part of their lives. This included sex, anger, money, relationships and everything else. Making this commitment involved a heart's intent to obey the Bible. It would become their standard and guide for life. All decisions, including whether or not they should marry, would bow before His Lordship.

Then he explained why their living together did not work. Their relationship looked like an upside down pyramid.

The part of Drake and Brenda's lives least able to bear the weight of an enduring relationship—genital sex—had become the foundation. Their capacities for character development (social) and Christian growth (spiritual) were out of balance. No one can build a house upside down and enjoy living in it forever. Sooner or later it will collapse. In Drake and Brenda's case, the

Spiritual Interests

Social Activities

Emotional Romance

Physical Sex

inevitable crash came—yet they still found themselves attracted to each other. How can someone unscramble an egg?

Beginning with the Lordship of Jesus Christ and the authority of the Word of God as their foundation, the pastor suggested that Drake and Brenda start over. If indeed the Lord Jesus should lead them together, and He might not, they would need to rebuild the pyramid of their lives right side up. Upon the spiritual foundation they both needed godly social values, character development and unselfish love. Emotional closeness might follow, but the physical relationship of sexual intercourse must wait until after marriage. A diagram of a solid, Christian relationship looks like a stable pyramid.

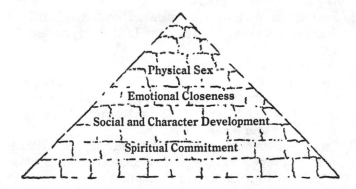

Physical Sex

Emotional Closeness

Social and Character Development

Spiritual Commitment

Dean's Story

Dean was preparing for the ministry and served well as an intern in a local church. He had the ability to build and sustain warm relationships with people of all ages. He was sensitive, flexible and a reconciler. All of this was in addition to his more obvious musical and speaking gifts. As a single, Dean dated a lot of different girls and only a few times entered into a relationship that lasted for a significant period of time. Yet he had many friends of both sexes and seemed the model of a likable Christian guy.

When Dean came to see me, he knew he had a problem. As he put it, "I do not have a pure heart." When his story came out, it became clear that he was not a one-woman sort of man. He had reverted into premarital sex again and again. In private, he would repent from his heart and then relapse. In fact, he became desperate enough about his struggle to issue an indirect call for help. The question now was what to do about it.

Dean's own suggestion was that he find a spiritual director and spend a year in discipleship and personal growth. I agreed, but added some steps for a program of self-imposed discipline.

1. Learn and practice the Spirit-controlled life.
2. Make spiritual warfare praying part of his daily devotional time.
3. Read the best Christian books available on the subject of winning over sexual temptation.
4. Read classics of Christian devotion and books on spiritual discipline as well as engage in intensive Bible study and discipleship.
5. Develop a powerful prayer life.
6. Find an experienced pastor who will serve as spiritual director, but do not stop there. Make a full confession to the elders of his church about past sins and ask for help in becoming a winner over sexual temptation.
7. Remain self-supporting and out of the ministry until this battle is won. Agree with the elders that the discipline is voluntary and can be terminated at any time. However, while

under their authority, make a pledge of absolute obedience to follow their direction and counsel (unless, of course, it contradicted Scripture in some way).

Burning with Unfulfilled Desire

God is right, of course, in limiting sexual intercourse to marriage. The one-flesh union is too life-linking, too binding to share outside the covenant of marriage. So what is the single to do when mind and body flame with sexual or emotional desire? The arsenal of weapons to develop a clean mind discussed elsewhere in this book will certainly help. Some honest self-talk may also change our perspective. *No one ever died for lack of sexual intercourse and neither will I. Christ will help me sublimate these desires into productive service for others.*

Sublimation is a healthy psychological principle for dealing with frustrated desires. Webster says that sublimate means "to divert the expression of (an instinctual desire or impulse) from its primitive form to one that is considered more socially or culturally acceptable." The spiritual equivalent of sublimation comes in Jesus' teaching: "Whoever finds his life will lose it, and whoever loses his life for my sake will find it" (Matt. 10:39, *NIV*). Sexual and emotional energy can be harnessed by Christ and directed toward His goals. Loving, serving and caring all take energy. So does using our abilities and gifts for the good of others.

Losing our life for Christ's sake does not mean that sexual temptation goes away. The Christian life is designed for battles, suffering and pain. The Holy Spirit does His best work in the face of weakness and discomfort. God is faithful to meet His struggling child at the point of greatest need. A Christian single woman struggled with selective lust, strong desires for male attention even when it clearly was not God's will. She wrote me a note about it.

There is a situation/relationship in my past— about 6-7 years ago—in which I allowed myself to

yield to the attention which I wanted and "needed"
so much even though I knew inside it wasn't really
God's way for me. There wasn't anything "wrong"
with the relationship, but that it was not God's
choice for me and I knew it.

I fooled myself into thinking that it was okay as
long as I didn't make any moves. I also could see
some ministry opportunity and I used that as an
excuse to deceive myself into justifying my involvement.

Later, when in a loving and sovereign way God
spoke strongly to me, I had to go through a great
deal of pain. It was a supernatural experience of having a vision (the only one in my life) which revealed,
in a way that I could not ignore, that I was not going
God's way, but my own. After deciding to obey the
Lord, I had a long, difficult road ahead of me to get
out of that detour. But by God's grace, all turned out
well and I learned *much* from it all.

Sexuality for Singles by Choice

While some are single against their will, others enjoy the
high calling of God to singleness (see 1 Cor. 7:25-40). Discerning Christians whom they trust confirm the Lord's leading in
their lives. They pour the time and energy normally spent in
marriage into pleasing Christ in a wide range of activities. While
the social pressure to marry seems relentless, the God-called
single can relax in the knowledge of God's approval. Both Jesus
and the apostle Paul were single and taught its benefits and limitations (see Matt. 19:12; 1 Cor. 7 and 1 Tim. 5:11-15).

Our Lord Jesus stands as the supreme example of pure sexuality in a man who chose to remain single. He maintained close
friendship and ministry relationships with women without the
slightest hint of immorality. He never denied His masculinity nor
did He ever put down femininity. He accepted the love of the
woman who poured expensive perfume on His head (see Matt.

26:6-10) and the one who anointed and kissed His feet (see Luke 7:36-50). The observers were scandalized but Jesus was not!

What Jesus demonstrates is that singles can enjoy emotional intimacy without sexual intercourse. Warm friendship, including touching, can express God-given sexuality without petting or stimulating erotic sensuality. Healthy passions can come under the Holy Spirit's control and unhealthy ones can be crucified with Christ. Pure sex for singles means valuing and enjoying the opposite sex in profound friendships and emotional closeness. What the Christian single must not do is deny his or her sexuality and live as an "it" rather than as he or she. A unisex society is too bland and boring for God's people.

Since premarital and extramarital sex violate God's absolute moral law, how much physical intimacy is too much for Christian singles? For those who make up their own morality and question the absolutes of God's law, I am reminded of a quote I once saw in the *Reader's Digest.* "If voluntary compliance worked, Moses would have come down from Mount Sinai with the Ten Guidelines."[9] This also reminds me of an old ditty I heard in high school:

> I slipped my fingers through her hair.
> What could I do but linger?
> And as my lips drew close to hers
> A cootie bit my finger.

Bad—I know. Not even funny. But seriously, how much physical contact is acceptable before marriage? Since dating was unknown in Bible times because marriages were arranged by parents, God's Word is silent about a custom that did not exist when it was written. The suggestion that increased intimacy must always be accompanied by additional commitment makes a lot of sense, but it is so easy to rationalize. Most people need definite decisions before the moment of passion arrives. While every Christian must seek guidance from the Holy Spirit, my specific counsel is this: keep your clothes on and your hands on the outside! ('Nuff said.)

PURE SEX AND SEEING GOD

What the unnamed writer in *Leadership Journal* confesses is shocking for anyone in full-time Christian ministry. What he tells about his war with hard-core lust is moving, personal and scary. Anyone who has fought the battle with lust can relate to his struggles, defeats and sense of despair. What makes the article of great value is not the detailed confession of his sin, but rather how God led him to lasting moral victory. The positive force that helped him become a winner is the beatitude, "Blessed are the pure in heart, for they will see God" (Matt. 5:8). Read his words with great care.

> Purity, says Mauriac (Francois Mauriac, author of *What I Believe*), is the condition for a higher love—for a possession superior to all possessions: God himself . . . We are the ones who suffer if we sin, by forfeiting the development of character and Christ-likeness that would have resulted if we had not sinned.
>
> The thought hit me like a bell rung, in a dark, silent hall. So far, none of the scary, negative arguments against lust had succeeded in keeping me from it. Fear and guilt simply did not give me resolve; they added self-hatred to my problems. But here was a description of what I was missing by continuing to harbor lust: I was limiting my own intimacy with God. The love he offers is so transcendent and possessing that it requires our faculties to be purified and cleansed before we can possibly contain it. Could he, in fact, substitute another thirst and another hunger for the one I had never filled? Would Living

Water somehow quench lust? That was the gamble of faith.

Perhaps, just perhaps, the discipline and commitment involved in somehow allowing God to purge out the impurities formed the *sine qua non,* the essential first step toward a relationship with God I had ever known."[10]

Before going on with his story, it is worthwhile to pause and look at what God's Word claims about purity as essential for intimacy with God. David asks in Psalm 24:3-5 *(NIV),* "Who may ascend the hill of the Lord? Who may stand in his holy place? [The answer is,] He who has clean hands and a pure heart." The Bible adds a promise, "He will receive blessing from the Lord and vindication from God His Savior." Purity of heart does indeed lead to intimacy with God. The experience of the *Leadership* writer in seeking purity and finding more of God is not an isolated accident. Rather it is one man's story of a basic Bible principle valid for all Christians everywhere.

God has kept his part of the bargain. In a way I had never known before, I have come to see God. At times (not so often, maybe once every couple of months), I have had an experience with God that has stunned me with its depth and intimacy, an experience of an order I did not even know existed before. Some of these moments have come during prayer and Bible reading, some during deep conversation with other people, and one, the most memorable of all because of my occupation, while I was speaking at a Christian conference. At such moments I have felt possessed, but this time joyfully so (demonic possession is a poor parody of the filling of the Spirit). They have left me shaken and humbled, renewed and cleansed. I had not known that level of mystical experience, had not, in fact, even sought it except in the general way of seeking purity. God has revealed himself to me.[11]

There is nothing better than the joy of seeing God in all the glorious splendor of His majesty. There is nothing worse than facing His angry judgment. (Contrast Matt. 5:8; Ps. 24:3-4; Heb. 12:14 and 1 John 3:2-3 with Rom. 1:18-32; 1 Cor. 6:9-10; Gal. 5:19,21; Eph. 5:5-6 and Col. 3:5-6.)

Prayer

Thank you, heavenly Father, for making us in your image, male and female. I rejoice in my God-given sexuality and that you made me very good. "I praise you because I am fearfully and wonderfully made; your works are wonderful, I know that full well" (Ps. 139:14, *NIV*). Thank you for the joy of pure sex. I praise you for the pattern of Christian living that leads to increasing satisfaction in body, mind and spirit.

I face up to the distortion in my sexuality brought by sin. I bring all the broken pieces to you. Renew my mind and remold my heart to heal the hurts and restore the damage in the sex department of my life. Thank you that the Lord Jesus Christ is the full image of God, and in Him I am complete, including my sexuality. Thank you that He is now restoring the image of God in my sexual attitudes and actions and will continue to do so until I meet you, heavenly Father, face to face. In the pure and holy name of Jesus, I pray. Amen.

"You Don't 8 Understand. I'm Different."

When it comes to sex, some people feel that every day is terrible, horrible, unbearable. Runaway passions rule their thinking and actions. Out-of-control sexual sins drive them down deviant back roads. They hate themselves for their practices of adultery, homosexual activity or incest—and yet they cannot stop. What started as intrigue and excitement turned into a nightmare of incredible pain. Only another sexual episode seems to give them a brief spurt of immoral pleasure before the depressing darkness returns. They feel hopeless, helpless and *misunderstood*.

Before we examine sexual practices in which some people feel *most* misunderstood, I would like to share with you a letter from a Friend—everybody's Friend. His love extends to us all:

Dear Friend,

How are you? I just had to send a note to tell you how much I love you and care for you.

I saw you yesterday as you were talking with your friends. I waited all day, hoping you would want to talk with me also. As evening drew near, I gave you a sunset to close your day and a cool breeze to rest you—and I waited. You never came. Yes, it did hurt me—but I still love you because I am your friend.

I saw you fall asleep last night and longed to touch your brow so I spilled moonlight upon your pillow and face. Again I waited, wanting to rush down so we could talk. I have so many gifts for you! You awakened late and rushed off to work. My tears were in the rain.

Today you looked so sad—so all alone. It makes my heart ache because I understand. My friends let me down and hurt me so many times, too, but I love you.

Oh! If you would only listen to me. I LOVE YOU! I try to tell you in the blue sky and in the quiet green grass. I whisper it through the leaves on the trees and breathe it in the colors of the flowers. I shout it to you in the mountain streams and give the birds love songs to sing to you. I clothe you with warm sunshine and perfume the air with nature's scents. My love for you is deeper than the oceans and bigger than the biggest want or need in your heart. Oh! If you only knew how much I want to help you. I want you to meet my Father. He wants to help you, too. My Father is that way, you know.

Just call me—ask me—talk with me. Oh! Please, please don't forget me. I have so much to share with you.

OK, I won't hassle you any further. You are free to choose me. It is your decision. I have chosen you, and, because of this, I will wait—because I LOVE YOU.

Your Friend,
Jesus[1]

Jesus Christ offers hope, intimacy and satisfaction to those who feel no one else cares. His powerful compassion gives Him a heart for those who are slaves of sexual perversion. Jesus loves those who cannot escape from the prisons of abnormal sexual activity, and He brings rescue and release. He understands the misunderstood.

"YOU DON'T UNDERSTAND.
WE WANT TO LIVE TOGETHER FIRST."

What a wonderful feeling it is to fall in love. Everything feels so good. Some couples follow the impulses of sexual attraction into premarital or extramarital sex and then begin living together without marriage. The well-known writer and philosopher, Dr. Elton Trueblood, sums up the current concepts held by many.

> The breakup of married couples is more than matched by the great and growing practice of men and women living together without marriage and often with no intention of marriage. In some parts of the culture this practice has become standard rather than exceptional. It is often assumed, without argument, and apparently without doubt, that fornication is not a sin and really nothing wrong at all. The invention of the pill having largely taken away the fear of unwanted pregnancy, there is now no reason for refusing to obey passing impulses. *This is because, for millions in the modern world, sexual experience is not looked upon as something involving principle* (italics are his).[2]

Christians know better. They believe the Bible and therefore look upon sexual experience as something involving God's revealed will. God's way is most often the opposite of our first human impulse:
- When we are mad, the human impulse is to strike out.
  Jesus says to turn the other cheek.
- When we are hurt, the human impulse is to blame someone.

The Bible says, forgive as Christ forgave you.
* When we see attractive material things, the human impulse is to get, get, get.
Christianity teaches us to give, give, give.
* The human impulse is sex first, marriage later.
God's Word teaches marriage first, sex later.

When so many marriages end in divorce, our human impulse is to live together before marriage to see if we are compatible. This human impulse sounds fine, looks good and seems to work at first—but couples find out later that living together before marriage is only a shortcut to disaster. Sex *before* marriage fouls up sex *after* marriage. Think about those couples who have lived together before marrying. It seems if anyone would have a dynamic sexual relationship, it would be those whose sexual experience led them to marry, right? Wrong. The couples who have premarital sex often develop not only severe sexual problems, but a high degree of misery in their whole relationship. The more physical intimacies are saved exclusively for marriage, the better sexual relationships will become after the wedding day.

In *Strike the Original Match,* a fine book on biblical principles for making a marriage better, Charles R. Swindoll makes some telling comments about the lasting effects of premarital sex.

> The young bride marries with disappointment over the violation done against her by her fiancé. She soon becomes dominant and aggressive, taking the role of leadership from her husband because of a mixture of resentment and anger. And the man? Well, he feels guilty, disappointed with himself, and ultimately becomes passive.
>
> She takes charge (and hates it) while he backs off (and feels miserable). All because their intimate relationship was incorrectly set in motion before marriage.

Of the hundreds of unhappy couples I have counseled who finally admitted to premarital promiscuity,
I can hardly recall an exception to this strange pattern.[3]

For some unknown reason, many a Christian woman feels
little guilt about a progressing physical relationship with the man
she loves. But later it all catches up with her. Often 10 or 15
years after she is married the guilt comes back to haunt her.
With a heart full of regrets, she believes her past experience is
hurting her present relationship with her husband. In response
to a magazine article I once wrote, a homemaker in her twenties
wrote to me.

I have been married for seven years and I surely
can say Amen to your advice for the unmarried.
Since I was a young child, I have always loved going
to church and hearing God's Word. My family was
always active in church activities. I never really
dated, as I went to an all girl Christian high school.
As soon as I graduated I met a young man who
had many personal and family problems. Since I was
involved in a young people's prayer group I invited
him to come along. He always went to all meetings
and outings faithfully, yet I always knew he went to
please me and not for the purpose of letting the Lord
Jesus come in and heal his wounds, yet I was satisfied because he was cooperative. In a short time he
made it known to me that his interest was in me.
And gradually throughout this time I had come to fall
in love with him. Before long we were sleeping
together.
Needless to say, my relationship with the Lord
went downhill, and I stopped attending church. After
two years I met a group of young Christians and

again my love for the Lord grew. Accordingly my conscience was pricked and I insisted we marry or break it off. He was glad to oblige and we were married in the church. He always dutifully attended, but always holding back. This past year he stopped attending and forbade me to attend also. I am so lonely without fellowship. Needless to say, our sex life is nil.

I wish I would have read your article seven years ago. I wish pastors wouldn't be afraid to speak out about subjects like these. I hope you can show my letter to a young girl that might be asking you what's the matter with premarital sex. I only wished that earlier in my life I learned to believe in the Lord's blood so after the first sexual encounter I could have run to the cleansing fountain instead of wallowing in guilt and continuing in this relationship thinking I was damned anyway so I might as well go on sinning.

Her letter reminds me of the Bible's wise counsel that Christians always marry "in the Lord" (see 1 Cor. 7:38 and 2 Cor. 6:14). "Love is blind" the old saying goes and those who date unbelievers run the high risk that emotional attachment will lead them to direct disobedience of God's revealed will. In his book on 1 John, Ray Stedman shares the following letter to God from a Christian about to marry an unbeliever:

Dear God, I can hardly believe that this is my wedding day. I know I haven't been able to spend much time with You lately, with all the rush of getting ready for today, and I'm sorry. I guess, too, that I feel a little guilty when I try to pray about all this, since Larry still isn't a Christian. But oh, Father, I love him so much, what else can I do? I just couldn't give him up. Oh, You must save him, some way, somehow.

You know how much I've prayed for him, and the way we've discussed the gospel together. I've tried not to appear too religious, I know, but that's because I didn't want to scare him off. Yet he isn't antagonistic and I can't understand why he hasn't responded. Oh, if he only were a Christian.

Dear Father, please bless our marriage. I don't want to disobey You, but I do love him and I want to be his wife, so please be with us and please don't spoil my wedding day.

That sounds like a sincere, earnest prayer, does it not? But if it is stripped of its fine, pious language, it is really saying something like this:

Dear Father, I don't want to disobey You, but I must have my own way at all costs. For I love what You do not love, and I want what You do not want. So please be a good God and deny Yourself, and move off Your throne, and let me take over. If You don't like this, then all I ask is that You bite Your tongue and say or do nothing that will spoil my plans, but let me enjoy myself.[4]

"YOU DON'T UNDERSTAND. I MASTURBATE."

Although our responses range from "So what?" to "That's awful," the Bible does not directly address the issue of masturbation. In the past, passages such as Leviticus 15:16, Deuteronomy 23:9-11 and Genesis 38:8-10 were thought to condemn it. Today, however, almost all evangelical scholars agree that these Scripture passages refer to other matters and do not even mention masturbation. Whatever direction the Bible gives comes from its teaching on related subjects such as lust and self-control. Medically speaking, authorities agree that the practice does no physical harm. The emotional effect, however, often depends on what a person was taught as a child and how he or she feels about it as an adult.

In my opinion, masturbation is not sinful in and of itself, but it is still a bad idea. It can easily become compulsive, or within marriage, a poor substitute for relational sex. The problem with masturbation is not the physical release of a self-stimulated orgasm. The problem is the lustful fantasies that often accompany it. Let me make it clear that not all sexual fantasies are sinful. Yet for those who struggle with sexual temptation, fantasy moves their innocent thoughts to sexual arousal, to out-of-control thinking to sinful lust. When the backwaters of imagination draw an individual into the raging current of mental adultery, then sin wins another victory.

Recall that the *intent of the heart* makes the difference between mental temptation and sinful thoughts (see Matt. 5:27-30). Lewis B. Smedes makes some helpful comments in trying to discern the difference between the two. "There is no way of defining lust exactly; we must take Jesus seriously without pinpointing the exact edge of the precipice. To lust after a person must have something to do with fanning desire into a flame of specific intent . . . . When the sense of excitement conceives a plan to use a person, when attraction turns into scheme, we have crossed beyond erotic excitement into spiritual adultery."⁵

The lustful fantasies that accompany masturbation sometimes turn into an obsession. Hours of wasted time, drained energies and outright disobedience to God are often the bitter fruit. To recommend masturbation and sexual fantasy to the person who already battles against runaway lust is like offering whiskey to a reformed alcoholic. Even a little sets off a chain reaction that the person cannot resist. Those who seldom struggle with sexual temptation will find this hard to understand because compulsive behavior always seems strange to the person who has never been there.

Breaking the Habit

What if a Christian wants to give up masturbation? What if he or she knows it is compulsive, is a substitute for relational sex within marriage, or is an integral part of sinful lust? How does he or she break the habit?

While all of the principles given in this book apply here, a few specific suggestions may also help.

1. *Become a tiger for God.* Go hard after Him and never let go. Make knowing Him the greatest passion of your life. Renew your efforts at daily Bible reading and prayer. Even the busiest and most committed Christians struggle to stay consistent in daily devotions. Those who enjoy this practice of time alone with God often find that such discipline spills over into other areas of their lives. Christ alone satisfies the deepest needs of our human heart.

2. *Daily give your body, including its genital parts, to the Holy Spirit as His temple.* Ask Him to dwell in all of you, including your imagination. Ask for the fruit of the Spirit that is self-control (see Gal. 5:22-23).

3. *Identify the behavior that precedes it.* What are your triggers? Loneliness? Pornography? Heavy petting? Most often a predictable chain of events comes before masturbation. Break the chain early and have backup stopping points if you miss the first one. Changing these habit patterns helps to break the habitual cycle.

4. *Develop an alternate plan.* Write down three behaviors to substitute for the masturbation. It may seem silly, like spinning around three times and leaving the room. If you still blow it, your alternate *plan* failed but *you* did not. You simply learned what did not work for you. Come up with another alternate plan.

5. *Assign rewards and punishments.* Every day that you succeed, enjoy something special (Keep it fun!). If you fail, take an appropriate punishment (Ouch!).

6. *Find a trusted Christian friend who will hold you accountable.* Check in with each other, even by phone, as often as nec-

essary. When compulsive masturbation escapes from secrecy much of its hold is broken.

7. *Fill your life with fresh challenges.* My grandmother used to quote the old folk saying, "Idleness is the devil's workshop." Develop a God-given ministry. Discover your spiritual gifts and use them. Become active in a small group of caring Christians who study the Bible and pray together.

8. *Consider reduction in the frequency of masturbation a victory.* Chart your progress. Rejoice when a daily habit becomes every other day, every third day, once a week. Once the practice loses its compulsive grip and lustful fantasy fades toward reality, the whole issue may seem less important.

9. *Do not be afraid to seek counseling from a trained Christian therapist.* Compulsive masturbation may signal a deeper problem. If it is a symptom of an obsession, the skilled counselor may help identify the underlying cause.

10. *Plan a celebration when you break the habit.* If you prefer, not everyone in on the celebration need know *why* you are rejoicing. A victory experience, however, is most helpful.

Programming for Wholesome Dreaming

The subject of fantasy raises questions about erotic dreams. A college student once asked me whether dreams about sexual sins qualify as lust. The discussion that followed led to a couple of helpful suggestions. Since dreams often build on material put in the mind during waking hours, guarding your mental intake may help. If you feed your inner self on everything wholesome, you are programming your brain for better dreams *and* better living!

Another idea is to pray just before going to sleep, asking the Holy Spirit to take charge of all dreams. Once you filter your mental intake and ask the Lord to guard your dreams, you can relax. You need not worry about them. Erotic dreams emerge from physiological urges as well as conscious impressions. Nowhere in the Bible does it say that God holds a person responsible to control his dreams! Since dream memories usually fade quickly after waking up, simply dismiss from thought any that might seem displeasing to Christ.

"YOU DON'T UNDERSTAND. I'M GAY."

The unexpected confession, "I'm gay," from a son or daughter sends shock waves through family members and friends. What does he or she mean? Before jumping to conclusions explore whether the person means fleeting temptations or habitual sexual sin. It may mean a confused sexual identity, a strong same-sex arousal, a one-time encounter or an active, often promiscuous life style.

Some individuals will discover that they are not homosexual due to a lack of a deep-rooted pattern of same-sex preference. Erotic arousal by someone of the same sex, an occasional homosexual encounter or even bisexual experience does not necessarily indicate a confirmed homosexual orientation. If you are a person in doubt you may want to ask, "What kind of sexual fantasies or dreams do you have? Are they most often about the opposite sex?" If this is the case, confirmed same-sex preference is in doubt.[6] "Social scientists tell us that about 5 percent of all males and about half that percentage of all females have a confirmed sexual drive toward persons of their own sex."[7]

More than any other group of people, homosexuals feel rejected by the Church of Jesus Christ. Somehow many Christians, and I am sometimes guilty, convey total rejection of not only their sins, but their personhood. Homosexuals rightly hate this double standard. I imagine these questions: "Why are we treated as lepers, untouchables, when other sexual sinners are loved, accepted and forgiven? Why are we treated as dirt—unwanted, unworthy and untouchable? Didn't the Lord Jesus die for us as homosexual sinners as well as all others? Didn't His resurrection provide power for release from our sins as well as others? Doesn't the Lord Jesus Christ have power to drive away our demons as well as others?" Jesus loves the homosexual but rejects *porneia*, which includes homosexual sin (see Matt.

15:19-20). Our attitude should be like His.

I have taken a strong stand against the sin of homosexual practice and its approval by the Church. The passages condemning homosexual activity are well-known to most informed Christians and the following verses are among the most explicit: Leviticus 18:22,24; Deuteronomy 23:17-18; Romans 1:18-27; 1 Corinthians 6:9-11 and 1 Timothy 1:10. God's original design in creation was for male and female to reflect His image (see Gen. 2:24). The high view of heterosexual marriage, the imagery of the Church as the bride of Christ and the consistent context of Scripture confirms that God's intent is union of male and female. Some Bible scholars have tried with considerable skill to reinterpret the Bible's condemnation of homosexual activity, but without success. The Scriptures make it undeniably clear that in God's eyes, homosexual activity always has been and always will be a sin.

The Facts of Science

"Once gay, always gay" is the big lie believed by many practicing homosexuals. Neither science nor human experience confirms it and the Bible absolutely refutes it. Scientific investigation is beginning to confirm that many homosexuals with preference only for the same sex can change. With Christ's help many can become heterosexual. In the *American Journal of Psychiatry,* E. Mansell Pattison and Myrna Loy Pattison write, "The data provides a substantial body of evidence for the plausibility of change from exclusive homosexuality to exclusive heterosexuality, which is in accordance with the Kinsey statistical probabilities for such change, the Masters and Johnson data, and the clinical or observational anecdotes of such change . . . . When homosexuality is defined as an immutable and fixed condition that must be accepted, the potential for change seems slim. In our study, however, when homosexuality was defined as a changeable condition, it appears that change was possible."[8]

Popular Christian psychologist James Dobson writes, "I would recommend that the homosexual enter into a therapeutic relationship with a *Christian* psychologist or psychiatrist who is equally committed to Christian virtues. This condition *can* be treated successfully when the individual wants to be helped, and when a knowledgeable professional is dedicated to the same goal. Some of my colleagues report better than a 70 percent "cure" rate when these conditions exist ("cure" being defined as the individual becoming comfortable in a heterosexual relationship and making at least a moderately successful adjustment to a non-homosexual life-style).[9]

Dr. Dobson wisely recommends only Christian professionals committed to biblical values as counselors for homosexuals who want to change. His obvious implication is that many non-Christian counselors only try to help a practicing homosexual reduce his guilt feelings and make a better adjustment to the sinful life-style.

Based on careful research, helpful treatment procedures for children who show marked confusion in their sexual identity is also now available to competent professionals. Dr. George Alan Rekers spent 10 years researching this subject with marked success in helping children with confused sexual identities. Although he has written numerous book chapters and technical articles, concerned parents may want to read his more popular books such as *Shaping Your Child's Sexual Identity* and *Growing Up Straight: What Every Family Should Know About Homosexuality.* Such competent Christian counsel and treatment can help a child develop a certain sexual identity and reduce the risk that he or she will move into an adult pattern of a practicing homosexual.

Is there such a thing as a physical predisposition to homosexual activity? Authorities sharply disagree and certainly more research will be done in the future. What seems clear is that some children, whether from physical, social or other causes, do indeed have extraordinary susceptibility to homosexual activity. For that matter, it may well be that every person has unusual susceptibility to some sin, just as alcoholics do toward drunkenness. One purpose of our Lord Jesus Christ coming to earth was not only to forgive our sins but also to set us free from our sins—especially the ones that we are most vulnerable to. (See Rom. 6:18 and 1 John 1:7.)

Through Jesus Christ a homosexual can find freedom from his lust and cease homosexual sin even if he never develops a heterosexual orientation. Clinical psychologist Earl D. Wilson is right when he writes, "Homosexual lust is basically no different from heterosexual lust. All lust is out-of-control thinking."[10] Those who work most with homosexuals stress that recovery and change is a process and seldom a quick fix. Instantaneous deliverance is rare. For many this is battleground experience. The power of redemption and the hope of recovery lies in the atonement of our Lord Jesus Christ on Calvary's cross for every sin. Power to live in "the obedience that comes from faith" (Romans 1:5) has its source in Christ's defeat of sin, Satan and selfishness.

After warning that the wicked will not inherit the Kingdom of God, the Bible offers hope to a long list of sinners (see 1 Cor. 6:9-11). Buried in the list along with the greedy and slanderers lie homosexual offenders and male prostitutes. Please note that no one kind of sin is singled out. Our hope comes in these words, "And that is what some of you were. But you were washed, you were sanctified, you were justified in the name of the Lord Jesus Christ and by the Spirit of our God" (1 Cor. 6:11, *NIV*). Formerly practicing homosexuals, along with other kinds of sinners, can be transformed by Christ and become active in the Church. Don Baker illuminates this passage in his heartrending and joyous book, *Beyond Rejection*.

> *It even records some of the steps out of homosexuality.* The words "you were washed" suggest cleansing. Cleansing always requires the active participation of the one being washed. A homosexual, like any other sinner, must admit to his need for cleansing and then submit to the process, no matter how long or how painful it may be.

The words "you were sanctified" speak to a homosexual's need for acceptance—one of the most powerful and universal needs among the homosexual community. To be sanctified means to be set apart for God, or to be God's property. God accepts completely and totally whatever is given to him. In sanctification God says, "You are mine."

The words "you were justified" deal with the crippling problem of self-image. A homosexual, like any other sinner who has accepted divine forgiveness, stands before God as one who has never sinned. He is no longer obsessed with his failure; he is aware that his former life is gone.

He is now a new person with new potentials and new desires. In justification God says, "You are all right."

It reveals the sources of help that are available. "In the name of the Lord Jesus Christ" draws our attention to the authority figure who is capable of rebuking and limiting the satanic or demonic forces that may be at work in the homosexual's body.

"In the Spirit of our God" places the focus on the indwelling companion who is able to provide such internal resources as spiritual energy, contentment, satisfaction, and peace. The Spirit of God is the one who changes attitudes and desires. He is the one who makes homosexuality repulsive and holiness attractive.

The act of homosexuality, its ensuing guilt, and its compelling habitual life-style are all dealt with in the redemptive work of Jesus Christ.

The emotional complications that a homosexual experiences may not disappear immediately, but the power to change is inherent in Jesus Christ.[11]

Please note what Pastor Baker says about "rebuking and

limiting the satanic or demonic forces." Much more research is needed in the relationship between demon activity and any kind of sexual sin. The danger remains great enough, however, that anyone wanting release from any compulsive sex sin, including a homosexual one, should constantly pray a warfare prayer such as the one I've included at that close of chapter 4. Reading excellent Christian books on the subject and finding a mature believer to pray with during the long process of deliverance and healing can also make a marked difference.

When it comes to human experience, a growing number of people report freedom through Jesus Christ and His understanding after years of homosexual activity. Just as practicing homosexuals have come out of the closet to make demands, so released homosexuals are now openly telling of Christ's deliverance. Joseph Miller writes:

> I have lived in homosexuality for thirty-eight of my forty-five years. Four and a half years I lived a blatant "Gay Life-Style."
>
> I was introduced to homosexual behavior at the age of six years. Childhood curiosity followed. Later it was preadolescence experimentation. In Jr. High I knew I was different from most boys. I prayed. I asked God to remove my strange desire. I had heterosexual urges and homosexual encounters during my high school years. College life found me frustrated and confused. Marriage, I thought, would cure my tendency repressed by evangelical doctrine and Biblical truth. I was fine for awhile.
>
> Repressed homosexual behavior surfaced in a closet-homosexual life. I embarked upon a double life-style with guilt, pain, frustration, disappointment and failure. A husband, a father, school teacher and a pastor, no one knew of the battle that raged within the real Joseph. My desire to live a holy life found me seeking and not finding deliverance from my on-

going bondage to homosexual behavior. Homosexuality fast became the focus of my thinking.

I came close to deliverance as I engaged in spiritual healing of the emotions. I agonized in prayer. I resorted to fasting and finally confessed to confident Christian friends that I was homosexual. I sought deliverance through the laying on of hands. Nothing worked! I was gay. I would die gay. This is the lie Satan had me believing. The repressed guilt and living a double life took its toll in the form of nervous breakdowns, heart disease and back surgery. Finally, the deterioration of a marriage.

The inevitable happened. I was "found out." It seemed the whole world knew I was gay. I was relieved. I did not have to live a lie anymore. I was alone now—free to choose the life I wanted to live.

Live I did! . . . I dove headlong into the promiscuous passion of alcohol, drugs and sex. I turned off God and lived for four and a half years as if I had no conscience. I was accepted for who I was in the gay community. It felt good. I had nothing to lose. The MCC church (gay church) received me with open arms. I threw my life into Satan's "gay" attractions. I went through jobs faster than I could spend the money.

It was apparent I was engaged in self-defeating behavior. As a result of wrong choices, rebellion and disobedience to God I found myself at the abyss of eternity: a night with no end; a darkness where there would never be light. Psychotherapy, three attempts at suicide, being incarcerated, broken relationships, I realized "Gay" life was not bringing me happiness. I was in bondage. I was a slave to my own selfish desires. I was unhappy! Where could I turn?

I remembered the prayers of a godly mother and

father. I remembered that in all my confusion I really did at one time KNOW my Heavenly Father. Within minutes, I left where I was living, taking only what I could carry in my arms. I left all and headed to my father and home. The prodigal was coming home. I did not know how I would ever be delivered from my homosexuality, but I knew I wanted Jesus more than anything. I had seen hell from afar and I did not want to go there.

Through the discernment of family members, we were led to "Exodus International," a referral agency of active ministries available for the homosexual. (A referral list of Christian ministries to homosexuals worldwide may be obtained from: Exodus International P.O. Box 14052 Las Vegas, Nevada 89114 *or* Exodus International P.O. Box 2121 San Rafael, Ca. 94912.) Through involvement in Homosexual Anonymous, growth classes, weekly counseling sessions and support groups, I have denounced my "Gay Life-Style." It has not been without struggle and failure. There has been much pain, rethinking, relearning and restoration. Through my desire, my determination, and the grace of God I have found freedom from homosexuality. I have found in Jesus the POWER to be kept and the FAITH to withstand the attacks of Satan upon my life. My life is not without temptation, but Jesus gives me strength to overcome.

The pro-gay movement says it is a cruel hoax! I say, it is a miracle. A deliverance from a lie. I am a creation of God. A heterosexual. God has called me to rediscover that identity in Him through Jesus Christ, My Lord, My Savior![12]

Testimonies of regenerated and released homosexuals are available from many places. One experienced agency with testimonies available is *Love in Action,* P.O. Box 2655, San Rafael, CA 94912. The phone number is (415) 454-0960.

The Bible's exhortation, "let us do good to all people" (see Gal. 6:10) may take on special meaning for the Christian who is acquainted with a practicing homosexual. Dennis Kinlaw, Methodist evangelist, shares a moving experience.

I have a friend who for most of his life was a practicing homosexual. Over a period of time, God wonderfully delivered him. Today he is an active Christian witness. And he's free. We are fairly close and so I have had an opportunity to watch his witness and ministry.

He learned about a young man who had AIDS. This young man and all his friends knew he was dying. He was confined to a hospital isolation room where no one could get near him without donning gown, mask and gloves. There he lay, separated from everyone.

My friend asked an acquaintance of the young man, "Do you think it would be possible for me to visit him?"

"I think it would," the acquaintance replied.

Before entering the hospital isolation room he was given a gown, cap, mask and gloves. Later he reported, "I was about half dressed when the Spirit of Jesus said to me, "I took your sin. Are you going to separate yourself from him?"

He turned to the doctor and said, "I don't want to wear this garb. May I go in without it?"

The doctor remonstrated, "It's deadly dangerous."

"But he's my brother!"

"It's your life," the doctor answered.

He took off the cap and gown, mask and gloves, walked in and laid his hand down on human flesh that had not had human flesh touch it since the identification of the disease.

"Friend," he said, "AIDS is not a judgment of God on you in which He is punishing you for your sin. AIDS is a consequence of our living against His loving patterns for us. God loves you, and I love you."

Kinlaw adds, "Now it's no accident that the patient with AIDS became a Christian. And I don't think that my friend was contaminated."[13] This man showed warm sensitivity and compassion while refusing to condone the sin. Kinlaw dates this incident in 1984. At the time of this writing some medical authorities are reporting that AIDS is not transmitted by simple touch but rather by the exchange of body fluids such as semen or blood. As this book goes to press intensive AIDS research is underway. We can all hope that a cure will be found.

"YOU DON'T UNDERSTAND. I WAS MOLESTED."

A resident counselor in a respected evangelical college was reporting to some of her superiors. Among the student group assigned to her, four of the young women revealed that they were molested during their growing up years. What was even more shocking was the fact that three of their fathers were pastors.

Incest is an unpleasant subject and it often leads to emotional devastation in its victims. Facing up to being molested as a child can do much to free a person from false guilt. Martha Janssen was a victim of incest. Her family was middle-class, educated and respectable. In her moving book, *Silent Scream,* she shares her pain and recovery. In this poem, entitled "Point of View," Martha lets us in on a little girl's feelings.

A grown woman
realizes what she did for years
to appease

and please her father.
Even though she's been told
and knows in her mind
that she had no choice
from early childhood—
she feels responsible
somehow at fault
or perhaps deserving.
Weak, disgraced, ashamed
her only hope is—
once she realizes and weeps,
she can start to recognize
it wasn't she who failed at all.
She is the victim
not the criminal.[14]

Victims of incest, rape or other sexual sins can benefit from a compassionate and committed Christian counselor. Surfacing old feelings, finding new ways of thinking about men and sex, and sometimes confronting the offender with a declaration that the act was wrong can all lead to a new sense of inner freedom. False forgiveness will never solve the victim's resulting problems. After all, false forgiveness is lip service, done in order to keep the peace in a family, protect a relative's sin or repress feelings of guilt and shame. David Augsburger states the issue of false forgiveness in a way that penetrates our emotions.

When "forgiveness"
distorts feelings by
denying that there was
hurt,
disconnecting from
feelings of pain
squelching the emotions
that rise,
pretending that all is

forgiven,
forgotten
forgone—
Don't trust it.
It's a mechanical trick.

When "forgiveness"
   denies
      that there is anger,
acts
   as if it never happened,
smiles
   as though it never hurt,
fakes
   as though it's all forgotten—
Don't offer it.
Don't trust it.
Don't depend on it.
It's not
   forgiveness
It's
   a magical fantasy.[15]

In families where incest is taking place, someone *must* blow
the whistle. Elizabeth Wainwright is a pastor's wife, a mother
and also a victim of incest. She writes, "For any healing to come
to an incestuous family, the secret must be broken, no matter
how much it hurts. In our family, I was the one who had to take
the responsibility of breaking the harmful silence, to risk opening
up old wounds—more than once—in order to bring healing to
my family. The healing began when I turned my life over to Jesus
Christ. He gave me the courage to tell my mother about my
relationship with my stepfather and to say no to Cal again and
again until he believed it was really over."[16]

In a special issue, *Family Life Today* magazine listed sources
of help for incest victims.[17] Your nearest Department of Social

Services will also provide valuable assistance. The following organizations may be of considerable help to you as well:

V.O.I.C.E., Inc. (Victims of Incest Can Emerge)
Grand Junction, CO 81501
(303) 241-2746

Child Sexual Abuse Treatment Program
Director: Henry Giaretto
467 S. Third Street
San Jose, CA 95110
(408) 300 0511

Parents United, Daughters and Sons United
(408) 280-5055

Child Help USA
Woodland Hills, CA 91370
(800) 4A CHILD

National Center for the Prevention of Child Abuse
and Neglect
P.O. Box 1182
Washington, D.C. 20013
(202) 245-2856

Don't Forget Those Healthy Touches

While Christian counseling can help victims and perpetrators, a word of guidance needs to be spoken to non-incestuous fathers. Many men fear incest so much that they never give any hugs or kisses to their adolescent daughters. Healthy touching between parents and children communicates love and affection and fathers who embrace their kids play an essential role in their healthy sexual development. Emotional warmth, including touch, helps their sons become virile men with normal desires.

Likewise with their daughters, a warm and proper relationship prepares the way for self-control in youth and sexual satisfaction in marriage.

An absence of healthy touching can cause emotional damage. Daisy became involved in an adulterous affair in adult life, although she never set out looking for one. After recovering from the disaster she reflected on what made her so vulnerable. "It all started back in my family as I was growing up. My father never hugged me. I guess his generation didn't do that. I grew up wondering if my father loved me. I doubted he did. He never told me that he loved me. I needed a man's affection. When a friend like my father would hug me, I liked it so much. I craved a man's affection and I wasn't getting it from my husband."

What Daisy reports rings true. Joanne Feldmeth writes, "Giving that 'safe' affection—healthy parental love—is one of the greatest joys of family. It is, however, a skill that is usually missing in incestuous homes. Incest is not the result of too much family warmth; therapists agree that it is more likely to occur in homes where children are hungry for affection."[18] One key to healthy touching seems to lie in keeping it open and spontaneous with a special sensitivity for the child's feelings. It is fondling in secret, not hugs in front of the family, that leads to trouble.

Warning Signals

Incestuous families often show a pattern of stress and severe conflict. Mother and daughter do not get along. Trouble in the marriage may mean the husband feels little, if any, sexual satisfaction. Such a man must beware that he never lets a daughter replace his wife's place, in his heart or in his arms. What marks incestuous fathers is a driving desire to satisfy their own sexual needs. These men seem blind to the damage they inflict on their daughters until it is too late. They may unwittingly drive their daughter into prostitution or sexual promiscuity.

Lack of healthy affection, and especially incest, stands as a major contributing factor in prostitution. In a well-researched, well-written editorial in *Christianity Today* magazine, Harold

Myra reports that "more than one study had indicated around 60 percent of young prostitutes are victims of incest."[19]

Incest victims almost always suffer from poor self-esteem. Some follow in their father's footsteps and live in sexual promiscuity. Many struggle with lack of sexual satisfaction in a marriage where a husband genuinely loves and respects them. The best hope lies in a husband's patient understanding, competent professional counseling and the healing power of our Lord Jesus Christ. The victim of incest can restore wholeness and sexual satisfaction to her life.

"YOU DON'T UNDERSTAND. I HAD AN ABORTION."

"Pastor, I've done something awful. I know God forgives me, but I'm having a hard time forgiving myself."

My heart goes out in compassion to the woman, often a Christian woman, who has undergone an abortion. Years later, it often happens: she feels guilt, remorse and regret. It is not uncommon that after finding Christ's forgiveness and cleansing (see 1 John 1:9), she still struggles to forgive herself. There may be exceptions to these painful emotions, but inner torment is a common pattern that sooner or later begins. Mildred Jefferson, M.D., speaks with compassion and power. The woman who has been through an abortion has, in Jefferson's words, "already paid the maximum penalty by allowing her body to be used as the death chamber for a child. You can't create a greater penalty. She has to live with it. She can suppress it for any number of years, but she's not going to suppress it forever. She lives with her own punishment."[20]

While many feel compassion for the woman, few understand what agony men go through as a result of abortion. True, some men are cold and uncaring, telling their girlfriends, "That's your problem." Underneath the surface, however, most men cannot suppress their guilt either. Sociologist Arthur Shostak spent almost 10 years studying the impact of abortion on men. His findings: "Abortion is a great, unrecognized trauma for males, perhaps the only major one that most men go through without help."[21] Although most men hide their emotions from everyone, including the woman involved, the inner pain does not go away. During interviews for the study, many men broke down and cried. Arnold Medvene, a psychologist at the University of Maryland Counseling Center, says, "Abortion is one of the major death experiences that men go through."[22]

As Christians we have the important role of offering Christ's compassion and caring for both women *and* men who have gone through abortion. The old saying, "Love the sinner, but hate the sin" fits well here. The Bible is absolutely clear that life begins in the womb, not after birth.

"For you created my inmost being; you knit me together in my mother's womb. I praise you because I am fearfully and wonderfully made; your works are wonderful, I know that full well. My frame was not hidden from you when I was made in the secret place. When I was woven together in the depths of the earth, your eyes saw my unformed body. All the days ordained for me were written in your book before one of them came to be" (Ps. 139:13-16, *NIV*).

What if the virgin Mary had conceived by the Holy Spirit during an age of rampant abortion? What if her parents had felt concerned with her mental health, her "delusions" of hearing voices and seeing angels? What if they had talked her into an abortion? If this seems as repulsive to you as it does to me, then please recall that every unborn baby is made in the image of God.

Even those who do not read the Bible know that life begins in the womb. Photographs of the unborn child in popular magazines are convincing enough. It is a scientific fact that the unique genetic pattern of each person begins at conception.

Let us be certain of our convictions. To destroy human life, to kill the unborn, is clearly wrong and sinful. Many Scriptures shed light on God's view of abortion and deserve careful reading and prayerful obedience: Genesis 1:27; 9:6; Exodus 20:13; 21:22-23; Numbers 35:33; Deuteronomy 5:17; Job 31:15; Psalm 106:38; Proverbs 6:16-19; 24:11-12; Ecclesiastes 11:5;

Isaiah 5:20-21; 49:1; Jeremiah 1:5; Matthew 19:14; Luke 1:41-44 and Galatians 1:15-16.

Interesting, isn't it, that when the unborn child is wanted, he/she is called "our baby." If she/he is unwanted then it is "just a fetus." A natural miscarriage, occurring when parents desire a child, is often lamented with the words, "We lost our baby." But a planned abortion bypasses the moral issue by calling it a "terminated pregnancy."

If there were ever a cause that all churches and all Christians should unite on, it is opposition to abortion. But let us never forget that we are less than fully Christian if we do not show compassion in the process. And I am encouraged to see this kind of practical caring beginning to happen. "Save-a-baby" clinics are emerging in some churches and communities. In fact, it is estimated that two million families in America want to adopt a child.

No matter what struggle or heartache you face, due to sexual misconduct, Jesus understands!

Prayer

Heavenly Father, you understand the scars on my soul from misused sex. "O Lord, hear my prayer, listen to my cry for mercy; in your faithfulness and righteousness come to my relief. Do not bring your servant into judgment, for no one living is righteous before you" (Ps. 143:1-2, *NIV*). Bring hope and help and healing into my life.

I affirm that it is your will that I should be holy in regard to sex, honesty and truth. Help me to drop my defenses before you and humbly follow your direction in finding expert Christian counsel. Teach me (and help me *learn*) to control my body in a way that is holy and honorable and not in passionate lust like the heathen who do not know God.

Where I have been victimized, I appeal to you as my strength. "Rescue me from my enemies, O Lord, for I hide myself in you" (Ps. 143:9, *NIV*).

Where I have victimized others, I honestly repent and actually turn from my sin. I trust you in simple and wholehearted faith, Lord Jesus. "Teach me to do your will, for you are my God; may your good Spirit lead me on level ground" (Ps. 143:10, *NIV*). In the mighty name of the Lord Jesus Christ I pray. Amen.

How Can I Forgive Myself? 9

Fifteen years after serving in army intelligence, a soldier was still struggling with regret for some of the things he had done, things far removed from the godly training his folks instilled in him during childhood. How could he forgive himself?

* * *

A woman who served with her husband as a career missionary fell into an adulterous affair. She broke it off and became faithful again. In deep remorse she repented and knew at once that God forgave her. What she found so difficult was forgiving herself. Her wounded conscience screamed with pain. Her guilt kept coming back to haunt her. The thoughts tumbling through her head seemed like a two-headed monster, at times condemning and at other times excusing her misdeeds.

* * *

A man recovering from homosexual activity wrote in a private letter, "I had already experienced God's forgiveness but it has been a real experience for me to see God's people express this forgiveness. The most difficult part has been learning to forgive myself."

* * *

Some hurts and regrets from our past do not keep bothering us. We seek God's forgiveness, then forgive and forget. No harm, no foul. Other memories keep on hurting us for a long time with stingers of guilt, regret or resentment. Some come from major sins, as human beings judge them: child abuse, rape or incest. Others of us struggle to forgive ourselves or someone else for a small matter that should not keep hurting, but it does.

By God's grace, forgiveness of oneself or others stands available to every child of God. Think now of your A, B, Cs.

A
ABOLISH EVERY BARRIER TO FORGIVENESS

Many Christians let the past control their present and manipulate their future. They never can forget. Tim Timmons and Stephen Arterburn in their book *Hooked on Life* compare this backward focus to driving in a car with an oversize rear-view mirror.[1] Imagine this mirror growing and enlarging until it blocks most of the view of the front windshield. Always looking back and seldom ahead means a crash is coming. Reviewing and rehearsing past failures and regrets sets us up for another crisis.

Rick Warren, pastor of Saddleback Community Church and to whom I am indebted for some of the ideas and phrasing in this chapter, once preached, "The Siamese twins of misery are Regrets and Resentments. Regrets come because of what I have done to others; Resentments because of what they have done to me."[2] These life-choking feelings wreck health, ruin happiness, damage marriages, cause depression and sap energy. Barriers to forgiveness are no fun! Why not give them up and enjoy life?

People have been resisting forgiveness for a long time. My friend, psychologist Dan Smith, once commented to me, "In 10 years of practice, I have never heard a professional paper on forgiveness." George Alan Rekers writes, "I'm painfully aware as a psychologist that the modern solution to shame over sexual sin rarely involves any recognition of the need for forgiveness or healing of moral guilt."[3] Putting up barriers to forgiveness has been going on long before modern psychology; in fact, ever since Adam and Eve. God gave them total freedom except for one restriction. "You are free to eat from any tree in the garden; but you must not eat from the tree of the knowledge of good and evil, for when you eat of it you will surely die" (Gen. 2:16-17, *NIV*).

What did Adam and Eve do? The same thing we do when warned never to disobey God. They listened to the crafty serpent's deceiving talk and deliberately sinned against God. At once their eyes were opened to their shattered sexuality. "They realized they were naked; so they sewed fig leaves together and made coverings for themselves" (Gen. 3:7, *NIV*).

In the cool of the day the Lord God came walking in the garden and called out, "Where are you?" The Lord, of course, knew where Adam and Eve were. But Adam and Eve did not know where Adam and Eve were. Their instant response to God's approaching presence was that they felt afraid, full of guilt and shame and they hid themselves. (See Gen. 3:10.)

When confronted by the Lord God, Eve blamed the serpent. Adam took it like a man and blamed his wife. He even blamed God for putting a woman in his life. (See Gen. 3:12.) In his best-selling book, *Healing for Damaged Emotions*, David A. Seamands said, "The reason some people have never been able to forgive is that if they forgave, the last rug would be pulled out from under them and they would have no one to blame."[4] When shame and blame enter the personality, up go the defense mechanisms. Fear, guilt and shame raise barriers to forgiveness. Other barriers include bargaining with God, running away, fighting back, rationalizing, giving up and getting depressed. Abolish any and all of these to discover that forgiveness is real.

When one person hurts another, the victim most often feels angry. Then the anger subsides into resentment. If not resolved the resentment settles into underlying bitterness. With a root of bitterness in the heart, the wounded victim begins to build walls around himself. The next step may well be to reject what he/she needs most—the love of another person and the love of God. The crying need is to forgive the one who did the damage in the first place.

Your Attention, Please!

The Bible singles out one barrier for special attention: the refusal to forgive others. The individual who will not forgive the one who hurt him finds that he cannot forgive himself. "He who cannot forgive others breaks the bridge over which he must pass himself."[5]

Jesus stressed the need to forgive and outlined the worst possible consequences for refusing it. Following the Lord's Prayer, He asserted that the heavenly Father refuses to forgive the sins of anyone who will not forgive others (see Matt. 6:14-15). He told Peter that he must forgive his brother not seven times, but seventy-times-seven (see Matt. 18:22, *KJV*). He also taught repeated forgiveness for multiple offenses (see Luke 17:3-4). In the parable of the unmerciful servant Jesus warned that torture will come to the person who refuses to forgive another from his heart (see Matt. 18:23-35). Without forgiving others no one can experience the peace that God intends.

One of the smartest things anyone can do is to forgive others even before they ask for it. "Even before they apologize?" you ask. Imagine this conversation between Debbie and our Lord.

"Yes, Debbie, take the first step toward reconciliation."

"Even if they don't know I feel resentful?" questioned Debbie.

"Yes. The Holy Spirit will give direction as to whether or not you should tell them."

"Who should I forgive?" asked Debbie, even though she had a feeling what the answer would be.

"It may be a parent, a spouse, a boss, a pastor or a former lover," cautioned our Lord.

A face flashed into her mind and Debbie *knew* who she should forgive.

"Will you explain why this forgiveness is so important?"

"Forgiveness," the Lord replied, "frees you up to face the future. Recall the enlarged rearview mirror that keeps so many of you focused on the past? Forgiveness reduces it back to normal size. It opens your eyes to the best of life that lies ahead. For your own sake, Debbie, offer forgiveness. It makes you unhappy when you don't. When you do, it may well provide the key to forgiving yourself."

Tip of the Iceberg?

Dr. Henry Brandt, Christian psychologist, author and lecturer, applies basic principles of biblical psychology to everyday life with humor and insight. While driving him to the Los Angeles International Airport after a conference, I asked, "What do you say to the person who says, 'I can't forgive myself?'"

With typical humor he replied, "Go ahead and ache." After the chuckles he shared a helpful pointer. "The focal point of attention, what a person cannot forgive, may be but the tip of the iceberg. Sometimes a look under the surface reveals other problems that must be resolved first. Then forgiveness becomes possible." Those who cannot forgive may derive great benefit from a skilled Christian counselor or simply a good friend.

Healing power flows from confessing a troubling sin to a trusted Christian friend. "A generalized confession may save us from humiliation and shame, but it does not ignite inner healing," writes Richard J. Foster.[6] Pouring out the truth about a specific sin, without shameful details, has a powerful effect. It drags the wrong out of the dark and into the open, crushing pride in its path. God promises special grace and healing to those who humble themselves before a fellow Christian (see 1 Peter 5:5 and Jas. 5:16). Hearing a man or woman of God say that Christ's forgiveness now applies to this sin gives wonderful release. Discerning prayer then brings about a supernatural change for the better.

B
BELIEVE THAT FORGIVENESS IS REAL

After abolishing the barriers, meditate on Ephesians 4:32 *(NIV)*: "Be kind and compassionate to one another, forgiving each other, just as *in Christ God forgave you*" (italics mine). Recall three wonderful truths from the Old Testament.

1. The heavenly Father puts your sins *out of sight.* Isaiah 38:17 *(NIV)* says, "You have put all my sins behind your back."

2. The Lord God puts your sins *out of reach.* Psalm 103:12 *(NIV)* promises, "As far as the east is from the west, so far has he removed our transgressions from us." You can go to the north pole or the south pole, but you cannot travel to an east pole or west pole. East and west keep going, out of reach from each other.

3. Jeremiah 31:34 *(NIV)* may be the best of all: "I . . . will remember their sins no more." He puts your sins *out of memory.* If God forgets your sins, mistakes and failures, shouldn't you?

Many Christians believe God forgives and forgets, but they cannot. Although they confess their sins, repenting and forsaking them, they still feel guilty every time they think about the past. Christian psychologists call this false guilt because it never comes from God. False guilt always comes from within a person, or from the devil, and never from a loving heavenly Father. In his well-written book *Bouncing Back* William L. Coleman writes, "A great stumbling block is carrying too much luggage from the past. We have real and imagined regrets. The ghosts of yesteryear shackle us. We rattle through life dragging the chains of mistakes. These manacles hold us down and create pain for decades. But if we refuse to forget the past we sacrifice the present and the future."[7] With the help of the Holy Spirit, a Christian can eliminate false guilt that comes from within the human personality, if he is patient.

Let Your Emotions Catch Up
Self-forgiveness begins with God and significant others, but

it takes time for the emotions to heal. And the emotion of guilt hangs around for a long time. Following any major trauma our emotions will cycle. Sometimes we will feel fine; at other times guilt, depression and even despair may flood our personality. We will find it necessary to forgive ourselves and others over and over. This is a normal part of healing, not abnormal. Repeating the process allows enough time for the emotions to catch up with the mind and the will.

Understanding Your Conscience

Forgiving oneself often takes a long time because of the power of the conscience. Please note these facts about this most morally sensitive part of our human personality:

- Everyone in the world has one
- No two are exactly alike
- It sounds an alarm when we step out of bounds
- It can be programmed in a child and conditioned in an adult
- It can make us feel confident or guilty
- It can build or destroy our self-esteem.

In spite of the fine benefits of a healthy conscience, it is not uncommon for a deformity to develop. Unhealthy consciences may be described as faulty, weak, defiled, wounded, corrupted or seared. A damaging side effect sometimes produced by an unhealthy conscience is false guilt. Dr. Paul Brand and Philip Yancey eloquently illustrate its effects.

> Amputees often experience some sensation of a phantom limb. Somewhere, locked in their brains, a memory lingers of the nonexistent hand or leg. Invisible toes curl, imaginary hands grasp things, a "leg" feels so sturdy a patient may try to stand on it.
>
> For a few, the experience includes pain. Doctors watch helplessly, for the part of the body screaming for attention does not exist.
>
> One such patient was my medical school administrator, Mr. Barwick, who had a serious and painful

circulation problem in his leg but refused to allow the recommended amputation.

As the pain grew worse, Barwick grew bitter.

"I hate it! I hate it!" he would mutter about the leg. At last he relented and told the doctor, "I can't stand it anymore. I'm through with that leg. Take it off." Surgery was scheduled immediately.

Before the operation, however, Barwick asked the doctor, "What do you do with legs after they're removed?"

"We may take a biopsy or explore them a bit but afterwards we incinerate them," the doctor replied.

Barwick proceeded with a bizarre request. "I would like you to preserve my leg in a pickling jar. I will install it on my mantle shelf. Then, as I sit in my armchair, I will taunt that leg, 'Hah! You can't hurt me anymore!'"

Ultimately, he got his wish. But the despised leg had the last laugh.

Barwick suffered phantom limb pain of the worst degree. The wound healed, but he could feel the torturous pressure of the swelling as the muscles cramped, and he had no prospect of relief. He had hated the leg with such intensity that the pain had unaccountably lodged permanently in his brain.

To me, phantom limb pain provides wonderful insight into the phenomenon of false guilt.

Christians can be obsessed by the memory of some sin committed years ago. It never leaves them, crippling their ministry, their devotional life, their relationships with others. They live in fear that someone will discover their past. They work overtime trying to prove to God they're truly repentant. They erect barriers against the enveloping, loving grace of God.

Unless they experience the truth in 1 John 3:19-

20 that "God is greater than our heart," they become as pitiful as poor Mr. Barwick, shaking his fist in fury at the pickled leg on the mantle.[8]

Anyone who struggles with feeling guilty, even after asking forgiveness, might want to take a hard look at Colossians 2:13-14 *(NIV)*: "Christ . . . forgave us all our sins, having canceled the written code, with its regulations, that was against us and that stood opposed to us; he took it away, nailing it to the cross." The Bible here compares the old ways of defeat to a certificate of debt. Every sin seemed to increase the list of what God and other people held against us. It was like receiving a credit card bill for things charged but with no money to pay. The situation was so desperate that only Christ could cancel the debt, pay the bill and remove the relentless guilt of being delinquent.

Picture God's Truth

Here is a way that helped me to release my guilt feelings. I used my imagination in meditating on Colossians 2:14 in prayer. The goal was to visualize God's truth until it became vivid in my mind and precious to my heart. In my mind's eye I saw my every sin written on a long list. (I made it specific, such as every lustful thought.) God the Father rolled up this certificate and took it to the cross. I imagined strong hands driving large nails into the list, fastening it to Christ's cross. I listened to six or seven loud thuds of a huge hammer hitting the nails.

God the Father stood back, His task completed. He refused to let anyone interfere with what happened next. The blood of God's Son shed on that cross began to soak into the list, covering the handwriting. In a miracle beyond my understanding, it wiped the list clean. My sins vanished forever. I never had to face them again, nor the guilt feelings that went with them. Christ's death paid the bill and removed the penalty of every sin.

Remember the Spiritual Warfare Tactics

When false guilt comes from Satan, rather than the human

psyche alone, the believer must engage in the spiritual warfare described earlier. As a brief reminder, the Bible says, "Resist the devil, and he will flee from you" (Jas. 4:7, *NIV*). The growing Christian will learn how to pray:

> Heavenly Father, I bring all the nature and work of the Lord Jesus Christ against Satan and the false guilt feelings he brings to my mind and emotions. I bring to bear against the devil all the work of our Lord Jesus Christ in His incarnation, His crucifixion, His burial and resurrection, His ascension, His session (being seated in authority at the right hand of the heavenly Father with all "authorities" and evil "powers" under His feet). I claim all the power of Pentecost and the outpouring of the Holy Spirit in my life. I bring to bear against the deceiver all the work of Christ's intercession, His headship of the Church, His rule and reign in the universe. I bring to bear against Satan all the victory of Christ's second coming.

When you are on the run and need a shorthand prayer, just say, "I bring against the devil the shed blood of our Lord Jesus Christ." It works.

By his nature Satan lies and deceives. Before a person commits a sin the tempter minimizes it. He makes it look attractive, offering pleasure, profit or power. He whispers in a person's thoughts, *Hey, it's no big deal. Everybody's doing it. Why shouldn't I? It's such a tiny sin that it doesn't make any difference. What's wrong with it anyway?*

After committing the sin the accuser blows it all out of proportion. Especially with sexual sins he screams, *What? You did that? You have committed the unpardonable sin! You can never forgive yourself. It's hopeless. You're no good anyway, nothing but a failure. God is finished with you. Something terrible will happen to you or someone you love before long. It serves you right—just what you deserve!*

Wait a minute! The devil makes no sense at all! Before the sin he convinced you it did not matter. After the sin he made you feel worthless and wasted, a hopeless failure. Stop listening to him! He is a liar. He is also cruel and treacherous, wanting to use, abuse and dispose of his victims. If possible, he wants to kill every believer.

Listen to Jesus instead! The Lord Jesus Christ cares. He loves, understands and rebuilds. On the cross with outstretched arms he cried, "It is finished!" In the original Greek the sentence, "It is finished" is all one word, *tetelestai.* I have heard that officials stamped *tetelestai* on the papers of prisoners released from jail when their sentence was completed. Creditors marked bills *tetelestai* when the debt was paid in full.

May I ask a simple question? How long do you worry about last month's utility bills that are already paid? Not a minute, I'm sure. Jesus already paid the bill for every sin. He became the substitute, the atoning sacrifice. He took all the punishment that the worst sinner deserves. He cancels the penalty of every sin, stamping it "paid in full!" To pay the bill it cost the heavenly Father the highest possible price, His Son.

With the price paid, He sets free those who deserve death. Anyone can receive all the benefit of Jesus Christ's payment for sin by coming to Him in repentance and faith. Repentance involves turning from our self-destructive thoughts and deeds. We must forsake our sins and trust Jesus Christ in childlike faith. We then receive Christ as Lord and Saviour, master and leader, submitting to His authority and accepting His reign and rule in our daily lives. The astonishing result is this: we will find ourselves liberated. "You have been set free from sin" (Rom. 6:18, *NIV*).

Although Gregg trusted Christ and His finished atonement on the cross as a college student, he later fell into premarital sex sin. Feeling deeply sorry, he broke off the wrong relationship and repented before God, earnestly praying for Christ's forgiveness. Looking back, he wondered if he had really become a Christian in the first place and if he really belonged to Jesus Christ now. When it comes to sex sins, nagging guilt keeps pestering a person for a long time. It sometimes takes special effort to overcome this inner sense of uneasiness. Some Christian friends encouraged him to claim God's promise of forgiveness in 1 John 1:9 *(KJV)*: "If we confess our sins, he is faithful and just to forgive us *our* sins, and to cleanse us from all unrighteousness."

A famous story also helped Gregg. Once there was a farmer who questioned his salvation. The devil was driving him crazy with doubts. Then he hit upon an idea that gave him inner assurance for the rest of his life. Going out behind his haystack, he drove a stake into the ground. Beside the stake, he knelt and prayed something like this.

> Dear heavenly Father, I'm not sure whether or not Christ has really come into my life. So right now I'm inviting Him to come in once and for all. Please forgive all my sins. I forsake them. Thank you for sending Jesus Christ into my heart. I give myself fully to Him. By faith I believe He has come into my heart. Thank you, Lord Jesus, for coming in and taking control. Amen.

Then he wrote the date on the stake. From that day on whenever the question of his salvation came up he took a little walk behind the haystack. Pointing to the stake, he would say, "On that day I fully gave my life to Christ. Read it for yourself, Satan."

Believe That God's People Forgive

The most loving thing that a Christian who feels no guilt can do is accept, forgive and care for the one who does. Recall the soldier mentioned at the beginning of this chapter? His actual name is John B. Aker.

Fifteen years later, after serving in army intelligence and struggling with remorse for some of the things I had done—things far removed from the godly traits my folks tried to instill—I made a special trip home to visit Dad. On a walk I shall never forget, I poured out what I was afraid and ashamed to say to anyone else. Right there, in the middle of Barker Drive, he turned to me and said, "There's nothing you could do that would ever interrupt my relationship with you. I will never be ashamed to call you my son, and I don't ever want you to hesitate to call me Dad." He threw his arms around me and pulled me close as if to never let go. All the affirmation a child could want was expressed in that embrace.[9]

John Aker forgave himself because God *and his dad* forgave him.

Remember the career missionary that I mentioned at the beginning of this chapter who fell into adultery? Although not their real names, think of this married couple as Ron and Marie. In a well-written letter, Marie shares how she was finally able to forgive herself.

When I asked forgiveness from God, I could accept His forgiveness immediately. I knew it was real and complete and final. When Ron forgave me, I knew he meant it, too, and his constant reassurance of forgiveness and the fact that he never dug it up again to throw at me really clinched it for me that his forgiveness was real.

When it came to forgiving myself, it took a little longer for that forgiveness to seem real and complete. It was more of a process than a one-time act.

As I told you, the key to my being able to forgive myself was in Ron's forgiveness. I was much harder on myself. I couldn't believe I could have fallen so deep into Satan's pit. That was not my nature at all. I've loved the Lord since I was a little girl. Ron was my first love. I never *dreamed* I'd one day be unfaithful to him.

I remember now how I finally was really able to forgive myself. It was like I stepped back out of the picture and I reviewed my whole life as I would review the life of another. I saw all the hurts and insecurity and the trauma of my circumstances, everything. I looked at "this person's" life from childhood to the present. And as I tried to see everything from the outside looking in, I had compassion on her and could understand how and why she fell, never deliberately intending to let Satan get control of her life. Looking at myself that way, I was able to see how Jesus and Ron could have compassion on me and forgive me, and then I, too, was able to completely forgive myself.

Does that make any sense to you at all? I'm free from the terrible guilt because of forgiveness and I praise God for His loving grace. Although I'll always regret that it happened, I don't have to walk around in sackcloth and ashes for the rest of my life. I'm free!

Marie forgave herself through a loving God, a forgiving husband *and a fresh perspective of herself*. Good system. In his award-winning book *Forgive and Forget* Lewis B. Smedes uses colorful language to also explain how a fresh perspective of the past changes the present.

When you forgive yourself, you rewrite your script. What you are in your present scene is not tied down to what you did in an earlier scene. The bad guy you played in Act One is eliminated and you play Act Two as a good guy.

> You release yourself today from yesterday's scenario. You walk into tomorrow, guilt gone.[10]

A conversation with this delightful couple shed more light on the dynamics of forgiveness and rebuilding a marriage following adultery. "When Ron forgave me, he really forgave me. His love made it possible for me to forgive myself," Marie said with real gratitude in her voice. Ron understood that forgiveness meant never bringing the adultery up again to use against her as a weapon. They did talk together about it when the need arose, but never to damage one another.

It helped Ron to understand his wife's point of view about where he had gone wrong as a husband. "I wanted to be first in Ron's life, but I wasn't. I guess he always loved me, but not in a way that I could feel it. I felt so lonely before, but he would go back to work in the evenings and leave me alone."

"I was married to my job," Ron admitted. Then he added perceptively, "It helps a husband to forgive when he realizes the shared guilt."

Marie continued her story. "This man, a mutual friend, started coming by to talk while my husband was at work. It was only friendship. In fact, at first I kept wondering why he kept coming over so much. It irritated me that he just talked and talked. But then as the friendship formed, I began to like it."

"This man and I had a good relationship, I *thought*," Ron added. "Then I found out he was doing this behind my back . . . ." He let the sentence trail off, the silence speaking louder than any words.

"Then we had our own marriage encounter," Ron said forcefully. "We went to the organized Marriage Encounter a few weeks later and it was almost an anticlimax."

"Ron began to fill the void that I felt and meet my emotional needs," Marie added with a smile. "Our marriage is so happy now. I didn't think it was possible to have a happy marriage with Ron. I thought that when you were married the romance left after awhile. Then you just had to put up with it. Now I don't see how our marriage could be better!"

Ron's final comment came with a smile and a sideways glance at his now-happy wife. "I decided I had a jewel."

Marie was fortunate indeed to have a forgiving husband who knew how to put his words into action. Elizabeth was not so lucky. Her husband retaliated with several affairs of his own. To the very end of their marriage and beyond, he clung to her adultery as *carte blanche* for his own actions. Years later he said, "I will never forgive you." Today he is married to someone else and Elizabeth is alone.

In spite of his refusal to forgive, she learned to forgive herself. For Elizabeth, the route of inner forgiveness came through a church of caring people. They loved, accepted and counseled her. The more she learned of the Bible and of Christ's love through His people, the more she experienced God's forgiving grace. God's people put up with her foibles and faults until she approached maturity in Christ. With rebuilt self-esteem, she learned to forgive herself and now faces the future with confidence.

C
CELEBRATE THE NEW FREEDOM

A forgiven and cleansed sinner can celebrate freedom from guilt and resentment. "There is now no condemnation for those who are in Christ Jesus" (Rom. 8:1). Celebration happens best in public worship or joyful fellowship with other people but it does not stop there. A significant part of rejoicing and praise takes place in a person's own thoughts and feelings. "Rejoice in the Lord always. I will say it again: Rejoice!" (Phil. 4:4).

A Christian feels forgiven when he can look back on a painful memory and the stinger is gone. When the Moravian missionaries first went to Alaska, they found no word in the Eskimo language for forgiveness. To express the idea they built a 24-letter composite word, *issumagijoujungnainermik,* meaning, "not-being-able-to-think-about-it-anymore."[11] When a person can think back to an old hurt without fresh pain, he understands forgiveness.

Celebration becomes a way of life as a Christian learns to talk to himself in the right way. In his mental self-talk, he no longer says, *"If only* but instead, *Next time.* He refuses to tell himself, *I'm terrible, no good, rotten.* Instead he thinks, *By God's grace I'm becoming a better person, a little wiser and a little smarter for the next battle.* He refuses to think, *It's awful; I can't stand it.* But instead thinks, *I'm forgiving and growing.* He never thinks, *I can't forgive myself* but rather, *I can—I can do everything through Him who gives me strength.* (See Phil. 4:13.) *Christ gives me power to obey His commands.*

Celebration may come through music unto the Lord. It may come through laughter, playing in athletics or cheering on those who do. Some people celebrate through their creativity—serious poems, fun skits or moving drama. When it comes from a heart set free, celebration pleases God. The Bible says, "They will celebrate your abundant goodness and joyfully sing of your righteousness" (Ps. 145:7, *NIV*).

A Cleansing Exercise

For some people, a structured exercise helps to release guilt feeling and deal with authentic guilt. Begin by getting alone with God for a minimum of one hour. This gives time to let each step of the exercise sink deep into the spirit. Come with a heart and mind prepared to meet with the Lord Himself, and to respond to Him in obedience. Bring a Bible and pen and paper to record any significant impressions. Approach this time with a spirit of anticipation and expectancy.

Take a seat in a comfortable place with both feet on the floor. Wait silently before the Lord until your own mind is quiet and you sense His caring presence. Take a moment to claim the shed blood of our Lord Jesus Christ for protection from any wrong impressions or tempting thoughts from the devil. It may help to read a favorite Psalm or sing a much-loved hymn. Once you sense that your whole being is focused on the heavenly Father, you are ready to begin the exercise. Do not hurry through it. Let each part serve as a stimulus to prayer, meditation and quiet waiting before the Lord.

In faith, call upon the Lord with this prayer.

> I'm thankful, heavenly Father, that when I was dead in transgressions and sins, you made me alive with Christ. Thank you for forgiving all my sins. As an act of faith I now forgive others just as in Christ you forgave me. Please bring any name or face to my mind whom I need to forgive at this moment.
>
> Thank you for canceling any man-made regulations that contradict your inspired, written Word, and restrict God-given freedom in Christ. Thank you for disarming the principalities, powers, authorities and evil forces of darkness. Thank you for making a public spectacle of them, triumphing over them by the cross. I acknowledge that Jesus is triumphant over all demons and evil forces. With the fullness of Christ you have given authority over them and place them under my feet.

(Say out loud) In the name and by the authority of Jesus Christ, I forgive myself. Amen.

Face up. Begin by facing up to your own sin and your personal part in it. Tell the Lord, preferably out loud or in writing, exactly what you did to offend Him. Confess your sin, agreeing with Him about it. Hate it as He hates it. Grieve over it as He grieves. Turn from it as He turns from it. Forsake it completely.

Read Psalm 32 again and again. Ask the Holy Spirit to guide your thoughts as you identify with each section of it. Concentrate especially on verse five:

> Then I acknowledged my sin to you
> and did not cover up my iniquity.

> I said, "I will confess
>   my transgressions to the Lord"—
> and you forgave
>   the guilt of my sin.

Name the specific sin, iniquity and transgression that the Holy Spirit brings to mind. Admit your guilt without any excuses or rationalization. Face up to it. As Lewis B. Smedes writes, "You must call your own bluff: precisely, what is it that you need forgiveness for? For being unfaithful to your spouse last year? Good, you can work on that. For being an evil sort of person? No, that is too much, you cannot swallow yourself whole."[12]

Face down. Physically turn your face down in godly sorrow. Feel a genuine sense of remorse. Tell the Lord Jesus that you are sorry, deeply sorry. Say, out loud, "I was wrong. You were right. Please forgive me. Take away the guilt of my sin. Cleanse my motives, my desires, my thoughts, my words, my actions, my heart, soul and spirit from all unrighteousness." Meditate on Psalm 51:1-9, thinking about what it means to you.

Ask the Holy Spirit a simple question, "What's wrong with me?" Take a few moments to listen for His quiet inner voice in response. As necessary, start over in the exercise, facing up to these newly-uncovered sins and then facing down again in the godly sorrow that produces repentance. Turn from each sin in horror and disgust. Do not meditate at all on sensual or sordid details, but view only the offense against God and the pain in His heart. If you feel like weeping, go ahead and weep. Pray in the words of Psalm 51:1-9 again, this time from the depth of your emotions.

Hands down. Lift your hands off your knees keeping the palms turned downward. Release all the bitter feelings and resentment connected with your past sins. Visualize the faces of those who deceived, manipulated, victimized or hurt you. Naming them one by one, say, "I forgive (name) as you, Lord Jesus, have forgiven me." Turn to Ephesians 4:31-32, *(NIV)*, "Get rid of all bitterness, rage and anger, brawling and slander, along with every form of malice. Be kind and compassionate to one another, forgiving each other, just as in Christ God forgave you." Release all your negative feelings, shaking your hands as if these emotions were sticking to you.

David Augsburger wrote a fascinating book on true and false forgiveness. In *Caring Enough to Forgive* he says, "Letting go is relaxing one's grip on pain. Most human pain is caused by holding on or holding back. Holding on to the past is like attaching one's nerve endings to an object outside oneself which is stuck, stationary. One must either stay with it to avoid pain, or feel one's nerve fibers slowly drawn into wire-like threads of torture. But since time moves inexorably forward, one cannot stay with the past. Pain results."[13]

Do not hurry through this stage. Picturing specific people in your mind who have damaged you, or whom you have damaged, may seem so painful. Make notes on your paper of those whom you should say, "I forgive you as Christ has forgiven me." The Holy Spirit may direct you not to say anything to others. Either way, listen for His direction.

On another sheet write names of those whom you believe God wants you to approach and say, "I have come to understand that I was wrong in *(name the basic offense, not the details)*. Will you please forgive me?" If this is a person involved in a sexual sin with you, it is most wise *not* to meet him or her alone. Take along your spouse, if married, or a mature Christian friend. A letter may accomplish the same purpose.

Hands up. Turn the palms of your hands upward, resting the backs of them on your knees or in some comfortable position. Expect to receive all that the Holy Spirit has for you. Read Psalm 51:10-19 slowly and prayerfully. Ask the Lord to fill you afresh and anew with the fullness of His Holy Spirit. Read also Luke 11:11-13 and Ephesians 5:18. Tell Him that you accept the lasting consequences that follow your sins as purifying agents. Treat these as reminders of the importance of holy living from the hands of a loving God.

Ask the Lord for the fruit of positive character qualities in your life. Meditate on Galatians 5:22-25 and Colossians 3:12-14. Underline the character qualities that you most want the Lord to build into your life in the next three years. Focus on one of these as an immediate item for prayer. Commit yourself to practice this characteristic on a daily basis and remember that you are launching on a permanent way of life, not simply seeking the experience of the moment. As my pastor C. W. Perry once put it, "The Christian life is a cross-country run, not a 100-yard dash."

Face up again. Finally, turn your face up to God in joy, praise and worship. Thank Him for forgiving your sin and purging your guilt. Rejoice that Jesus Christ is your personal Saviour and Lord. Worship the Lord for His compassion toward you and mighty acts on your behalf. Turn to Psalm 103 and use it as a guide for thanksgiving and praise. Ask the Holy Spirit to rivet specific truths into your mind from this psalm that will drive away any remnants of guilt. As you worship Him from your heart, His Spirit transforms your spirit and sets you free.

Because emotions cycle, including guilt feelings, you may need to repeat this entire exercise on other occasions. In all probability you will find that it takes less time than before. The reason is that the real guilt is cleansed and gone. Only false guilt remains. Each time you repeat the exercise the time may shorten and the feelings of guilt may fade more quickly. Some will benefit from the understanding and discernment of a Christian brother or sister, pastor or counselor. Whatever it takes, through Christ you can forgive yourself.

Prayer

Heavenly Father, I thank you for providing everything I need to forgive others and for my own forgiveness through the atoning death of our Lord Jesus Christ on Calvary's cross. Thank you that what I owe for my sin is paid in full. I praise you for putting my sins out of sight, out of reach, out of memory.

Right now bring to my mind the faces or names of anyone and everyone whom I need to forgive. With the love and power of the Holy Spirit I now forgive them. Lead me to reconcile the shattered relationships that are within your will.

By faith I forgive myself and accept your healing of my emotions, memories and resentments. I give you my full permission to rebuild my self-esteem in the image of our Lord Jesus Christ. Help me to act out this truth even when my emotions cycle and tempt me to believe the same old lies. Thank you for setting me free. In Jesus' name. Amen.

Staying Strong When Your Emotions Scream for the Wrong

10

While I was writing this book my wife Nancy was reading the early chapters. "There's something that has been bothering me for a long time," she said. Whatever was coming next, I knew it was important. "Why didn't you tell me about your struggles years ago? We could have helped each other." Nancy was speaking from her heart, for she does not struggle with sexual temptation but fights constantly, and wins, in the battle with weight control.

"I guess I was too ashamed," was my feeble reply. Shame, or was it pride, kept me from maximizing the help of my finest human ally, my wife. She would have understood! And, she implied, my confession of weakness would have helped her. Why is it that I most often identify with others' weaknesses and yet want to share only my strengths? Why is it so helpful to hear of the Lord's healing in someone else's life and so threatening to share the progress in mine? In this situation, was it because I knew that I wasn't healed yet?

DAMAGED EMOTIONS

Everyone has some kind of weakness and some live with damaged emotions. Abuse or neglect in childhood coupled with responses of shame, fear, guilt, greed, selfish ambition, jealousy, rage or low self-esteem sometimes produce crippled emotions. According to David A. Seamands, "The two major causes of most emotional problems among evangelical Christians are these: the failure to understand, receive and live out God's unconditional grace and forgiveness; and the failure to give out that unconditional love, forgiveness and grace to other people."[1]

Damaged emotions seem hard to bear. Prayer and all of the disciplines of the Christian life bring no quick relief. Obsessions and compulsive behavior come easy and lead to an emotional high, followed by a crash with more misery than ever. Short periods of inner quiet never seem to last. It reminds me of the man in the lion's cage who saw the beast bow down and close his eyes. "At last I've conquered you," cried the man. To his surprise the lion answered, "Not so fast—I was just saying grace before my meal."

The Bible tells us that God understands and cares about human weaknesses—that middle ground somewhere between strengths and sins. Certainly this includes the flaws in our emotional pattern. Remember Christ's promises: "The Spirit helps us in our weakness" (Rom. 8:26, *NIV*) and "My grace is sufficient for you, for my power is made perfect in weakness" (2 Cor. 12:9, *NIV*). The Lord Jesus Christ, our great high priest, has a tender heart toward our greatest weakness, even if it is a sexual obsession.

CHRISTIAN ACCEPTANCE

Sometimes reckless words bruise the raw nerves of emotional pain. I know of a woman whose husband left her, turning from his Christian convictions to open adultery. Her embarrassment was magnified because he was well known in their community. Then a rumor started. The gossip was that she was cold and unresponsive to him during their married years. "It sure wasn't *all* his fault," the scandalmongers whispered. Along with the shock of screaming emotions, this Christian woman faced disgrace based on painful rumors.

Then another woman who suffered from the gossips' tongues years before came to her aid. She stuck up for her friend and defended her character. She stood by her, listened, cared and comforted. She put her scriptural convictions about love and mercy into action and refused to feel guilty for befriending the one whom others were putting down. She fleshed out the command of Psalm 82:4 *(NIV)*, "Rescue the weak and needy; deliver them from the hand of the wicked."

Christ's love, acceptance and forgiveness give a fresh start to every struggler who turns to Him. Yet the issue of *acceptance* is a tough one for many Christians. I know. It's a tough one for me.

Love and forgiveness, from Christ and from His people, we understand quite well. But acceptance means something different for the Christian than in the world system. In the world system acceptance means I will be tolerant of you no matter what. It often leads to putting a stamp of approval on a harmful or sinful life-style. Acceptance for the Christian means I will care for you as a person with wonderful potential. I will help you find solutions and point you to the Saviour.

The rub comes when the person, often a family member, has hurt me over and over again. This one may be an alcoholic, a drug abuser, someone who runs up my bills and refuses to pay or a spouse who is having an affair. How does the Christian love, accept and forgive the perennial offender, especially the one close to him? Why not think in terms of being responsible or irresponsible?

- I will *let* you be responsible. And I will not knowingly contribute to your being irresponsible.
- I will not try to force you to be responsible by nagging, condemning, scolding, moralizing.

- I will not knowingly let you be irresponsible by removing the consequences when you do what is wrong.
- I will stand by you, care for you, cry with you; but I will not bail you out time after time after time.
- I will not personally judge you, pretending I am your judge instead of God.
- Neither will I personally provide a shelter for your sin, pretending I am your Saviour instead of Christ.
- I will love you, accept you, forgive you and give you a fresh start whenever you ask for it.

It's refreshing to share in a fellowship of Christians who love, accept and forgive in the Spirit of Christ! When emotions scream for the wrong the easiest thing in the world is to find someone who will accept the sin and approve the harmful life-style. Like putting a Band-Aid over cancer, seeking out the wrong friends only covers over the cause of the problem. It brings no healing. When emotions cry out everyone wants relief, wants the pain to stop now. At that precise moment run to the heavenly Father. There is a permanent refuge in Jesus and in a loving group of Christian friends.

A friend of mine explained his way to become a winner. "Overcoming temptation prior to becoming a Christian was difficult and I generally gave in. Since becoming a Christian I find it extremely important always to say a prayer quickly or call a Christian person immediately. It's important for me because I don't generally like myself after I give in."

A HIGH GOAL

The conscious intent to live a life pleasing to Jesus Christ is essential for the one who wants to stay strong. This does not mean acting like a perfectionist, but rather staying in the flow of His grace. Some slip into obsessive thinking about sex, or some other sin, because they never made a conscious effort *not* to. Make it your goal, then, not to sin at all. (I am talking about known, deliberate, willful sin.) Such a high aim, along with the abundance of Christ's grace and forgiveness, is the consistent teaching of the New Testament. "My dear children, I write this to you so that you will not sin. But if anybody does sin, we have one who speaks to the Father in our defense—Jesus Christ, the Righteous One" (1 John 2:1, *NIV*). Paul also said, "Shall we go on sinning so that grace may increase? By no means! We died to sin; how can we live in it any longer?" (Rom. 6:1-2, *NIV*).

In his challenging book entitled *The Pursuit of Holiness,* Jerry Bridges tells of meditating on 1 John 2:1. "I realized that my personal life's objective regarding holiness was less than that of John's. He was saying, in effect, 'Make it your aim *not* to sin.' As I thought about this, I realized that deep within my heart my real aim was not to sin *very much.*"[2] No pilot flies his airplane with the intent of not crashing very often. No musician performs with the goal of hitting only a few wrong notes. No runner enters a race with the intent of not reaching the finish line every time.

> Can you imagine a soldier going into battle with the aim of "not getting hit very much"? The very suggestion is ridiculous. His aim is not to get hit at all! Yet if we have not made a commitment to holiness without exception, we are like a soldier going into battle with the aim of not getting hit very much. We can be sure if that is our aim, we will be hit—not with bullets, but with temptation over and over again.[3]

Not to sin at all? For the person in emotional pain, this sounds impossible, even ridiculous. It is like telling someone who seldom jogs to train for a marathon. Exactly! The part-time jogger will never become a marathoner unless he intends to! True, his training must increase little by little by adding more distance each day and gradually picking up speed. The same principle applies to a career, marriage and a Christian life. The only people who get good at it are the ones who make it their goal. Not every person has the potential of running a marathon, but because of Christ every Christian *can* live a life pleasing to God. "And we pray this in order that you may live a life worthy of the Lord and may please him in every way" (Col. 1:10, *NIV*).

A SURE CONFIDENCE

No Christian starts from scratch in this business of holy living. He always starts with Jesus Christ already living within. Tremendous confidence comes from this fact. "He who began a good work in you will carry it on to completion until the day of Christ Jesus" (Phil. 1:6, *NIV*). What Christ starts, He finishes! He is no quitter; He intends for you to win over sexual temptation and gives Himself to you to insure your success. Christ is at work within you! Never forget it!

When your inner feelings start longing for a wrong relationship, a little lust or some illicit sex, remember that God will finish what He started in your life. When the sensual longings first begin, turn your focus on Christ. As the pressure builds up, quote Scripture and turn on some inspiring Christian music. As your feelings cry out for the old, cheap substitutes for satisfaction, call out to Jesus Christ for help and change your activity. As the pain reaches the unbearable point, take charge of your emotions.

Negative feelings act like a naughty child throwing a temper tantrum. Invite the Holy Spirit to correct them like a loving parent. Isolate them from the rest of you until they calm down, ("Go to your room") and then soothe them with His comforting presence ("I love you"). This is not repressing negative emotions. It is acknowledging them openly and then dealing with them. The psychological term is suppression (not repression) and it is good for you.

When it comes to sexual temptation, little victories lead to big wins. Little defeats lead to big losses. Some losers have an easy answer, "Surrender!" In time, however, they do not like the consequences. So they attempt another approach and try to get away with it. In the long run, nobody does. Nobody gets away with it, not before God. "Do not be deceived: God cannot be mocked. A man reaps what he sows" (Gal. 6:7, *NIV*).

STRONG CONVICTIONS

Conquering temptation begins with definite commitments and strong convictions before the alluring moment strikes. J. Allan Petersen tells of a friend who stuck to his convictions when the pressure was on.

> A Christian salesman friend was attending a dealer's convention in New York City. On a free evening he was waiting for a car with others to see some of the city's sights. But he got into the wrong car. These salesmen were not headed for the tourist attractions but for a famous swinging bar. Before my friend knew his mistake, they were on the way with no turning back. Upon entering the bar, each man was immediately joined by a girl who took him by the arm and led him to a table. His girl was saucy, pert, dressed seductively. "As the evening continued, the temptation was like a steamroller," he told me later. "This girl was luscious. I had all I could do to keep from grabbing her impulsively and taking her to one of the back rooms. But the thing that held me and protected me—the only thing—was that before I had left home, I had told my wife that I was hers alone, and that regardless of any enticements, we belonged to each other and we would be praying for each other." His decision ahead of time saved him.[4]

To stay strong and build a pattern of consistent winning over temptation, check this list for reminders. Just possibly you might find a new idea or two that will help in the moment of greatest stress.

20 Tips to Conquer Temptation

1. Begin the day with a prayer of total commitment. Read Matthew 6:13.
2. Ask to be filled with the Holy Spirit afresh and anew. Read Ephesians 5:18.
3. Make no provision for the sinful nature—the lust of the flesh. Read Romans 13:14 and 1 John 2:15-17.
4. Pray, "Lord Jesus, protect me by your blood," when confronted by temptations. Expect immediate protection. Read 1 Corinthians 10:13.
5. Learn to hate sin like God hates it. Consider yourself dead to sin. Read Romans 6:12-14.
6. Fear the consequences of yielding to sexual temptation. Read Exodus 20:5 and 34:7.
7. Fill your mind with the best possible thoughts. Read Philippians 4:8 and James 1:12-16.
8. Fellowship with Christians and witness to non-Christians. Build your closest friendships among Christians. Read John 17:15-18.
9. Memorize Scripture and use it in spiritual battle. Read Matthew 4:1-11 and Luke 4:1-13.
10. Flee youthful lusts and change your activity. Read 2 Timothy 2:22.
11. Know your besetting sin and especially stay on guard against that kind of temptation. Read Hebrews 12:1 and 1 Peter 5:8-9.
12. Ask the Lord to take away the sinful desire or the part of the desire that is wrong. Read Matthew 18:8-9.
13. Draw near to God and resist the devil and he will flee from you. Read James 4:7-10.
14. Arm yourself for spiritual battle. Read Ephesians 6:11-18.
15. Stay alert to avoid temptation. Read Matthew 26:41.
16. Order Satan away in Jesus' name. Read Matthew 4:10 and James 4:7.
17. Make your stand for Christ clear. Let others know how you

shun sinful practices. Read Matthew 18:8-9.
18. Maintain your self-respect as a member of Christ's family. Remember who you are. Read 1 Corinthians 10:31 and James 1:2-4.
19. Set an example for those whom you love and those who love you. Read 1 Timothy 4:12 and Exodus 20:6.
20. Focus on the presence and power of our Lord Jesus Christ. Read Hebrews 2:18.

A HEALTHY CONSCIENCE

In an earlier chapter I wrote about the problem of an unhealthy conscience producing false guilt. A healthy conscience, on the other hand, is a wonderful asset in staying strong. I like this pun: "Conscience: something that no's what's wrong."[5]

Writing in *U.S. News and World Report,* psychiatrist Dr. Willard Gaylin of Columbia University's College of Physicians and Surgeons says, "The emotion of guilt has been given a bum rap." He believes "the guilt mechanism is central to our conscience" and that a true sense of guilt is good for children and adults alike. His comments make a lot of sense.

When you have actually done something morally wrong, it is always good to experience guilt—always. We do not knock down old ladies to beat them to cabs merely because it is against the law to do so but because most of us, feeling that we had violated our own standards of decency, would feel guilty and ashamed. The kind of person who does not experience guilt in that situation is not a specimen to be admired in our society.

Although Dr. Gaylin does not apply his comments directly to sexual behavior, the principle fits all moral actions.

When we examine either the behavior on our public streets or the moral behavior of many of our public officials, we begin to sense that the problem of our time is not an overwhelming sense of guilt but an underdeveloped one. When you do bad, feel guilty. It is good for you and for the rest of us who share your environment.[6]

Compare a court of law to conscience, the judiciary system of the inner person. It cannot write laws, for setting standards of conduct is the function of an inner legislature made up of God, society, parents and peers. It can, however, cross-examine one's actions and even his motives. It can hand down judgments on cases of personal conduct brought before it.[7] The verdict of a clear conscience brings joy. As Benjamin Franklin once quipped, "A good conscience is a continual Christmas."[8]

Consider a couple of benefits that make it well worthwhile to build a healthy friendship with your conscience.

1. *A good conscience gives courage when others question your motives or actions.* (See 1 Peter 3:16; Acts 23:1, 24:16 and 1 Tim. 1:5, 3:9.) Whether it is the apostle Paul on trial before Governor Felix, Timothy standing against divisive teachers or a person today falsely accused of a sexual sin, the result is the same. A clear conscience means a person has nothing to hide. So he displays an open and courageous attitude toward false accusers.

One pastor told me about a woman who left his church mad. He is a genuine, warm and loving personality. She was attractive—and attracted to him.

She phoned him one day. "My husband can't get off work to take me to the doctor. Could you give me a ride, please?" This pastor's wife worked and so she was not available to go along.

He replied, "I don't operate a taxi service, but since you're in a bind I'll take you this once." He failed to take anyone else along which turned out to be his first mistake.

On the way she began to tell him how much she loved him as

her pastor—and gave him enough signals to let him know she was interested in something more than a spiritual relationship.

He called her hand and confronted her with it. "I sense that you want something more than the love I give to all our people. But the only woman in my life is my wife."

It became stony silent in the car. She did not deny it. She only said, "When my love is rejected, I can be devastating." It was a veiled threat.

Sometime later she told her husband that the pastor had made a pass at her. The pastor responded to the accusation by going to talk with her husband about it. The accusing wife was present, too.

The pastor told his story. "I'm not going to be run off easily by lies. If you spread this false rumor to anyone in the church I'll call for a full investigation of my past and yours, since becoming a Christian. I'll call in officials from our denomination to study the entire matter." As a one-woman sort of man, he knew his moral record was one of being faithful to his wife. He also knew her record in the church was far from spotless—he was not the first man with whom she had been suggestive.

The woman became furious. "You're no preacher and I'm not getting fed from God's Word in this church!" she sneered. "I'm going to change churches to one where I can get a lot more out of it!" She intended to leave the church with or without her husband.

Her husband loved their church and did not want to leave. The wise pastor said to him, "If you want to save your marriage, go with her." He did.

So the church lost a family but guess what happened? The pastor reported that the Lord sent seven families to take their place.

2. *A strong conscience builds an inner sense of freedom about what is right and wrong.* (See 1 Cor. 8:7-13.) "A sensitive conscience speaks with a voice of authority. The more we submit in obedience to this voice, the clearer and more distinct will be its directives and the more effective its influence over our own will.

If we are guided by an alert conscience, our daily struggle becomes easier, not only in avoiding evil but also in doing that which is good."[9]

A healthy conscience can alert you to avoid temptation, just as the following note from a friend of mine suggests.

> The best way for me to resist temptation in everyday life is to remember that God is there and knows what I am doing, thinking and saying and I don't want to disappoint Him, nor do I want Him to be ashamed of me. I have a *very active* conscience and this often keeps me from yielding to temptation.

A word of caution seems necessary here. Conscience is a human part of our system, not an infallible source of moral truth. God never intended for it to become a substitute for His written Word. Some sex offenders commit terrible crimes in direct disobedience to the Bible. Their conscience never seems to bother them at all. A lack of guilt never gives permission to disobey God.

The conscience functions like a computerized alarm system. It warns a person not to violate his own values and makes him feel guilty when he does. It must never become confused with the Holy Spirit or the power of God. It can make a person want relief from wrong actions, but it holds no power to deliver him from sin. A woman once caught in the snare of an affair said, "I felt like I was in a deep, dark pit that had slippery sides. I couldn't get out of it. I couldn't. My conscience did not give me the power to break the evil."

CHRIST'S POWER

The power source for staying strong is not conscience but the Spirit of Christ. Far from calling attention to Himself, the Holy Spirit directs a person to our Lord Jesus. He especially helps the Christian grasp the inner meaning of the cross, our

Lord's death and resurrection. As I write these words, it is the Saturday between Good Friday and Easter Sunday. What a wonderful time to reflect on what Christ did for me and you in His death and resurrection.

- Jesus died for our sins and not ours only, but also the sins of the whole world. Read 1 John 2:2.
- Christ died to purchase each one of us, so that our bodies no longer belong to ourselves but to Him. Read 1 Corinthians 6:18-20; Galatians 2:20 and Romans 12:1-2.
- As His slaves, Jesus has the right to set us free from the power and dominion of sin, including the sexual variety. Read Romans 6:15-23; 8:2 and 1 Corinthians 6:9-20. Our gracious Lord no longer calls us slaves but friends (read John 15:14-15).
- We are now dead to sin and selfish desires and united with the crucified and risen Lord. Read Romans 6:1-14.
- We can live in the power of His death and resurrection, overcoming specific acts of sin and even rendering powerless the sin nature itself. Read Romans 6:6 and Galatians 2:20.
- As Jesus rose from the dead, so we also rise to a new life of love, joy, peace and holy living with Him. Read Ephesians 2:6-10 and Colossians 3:1-12.
- The Spirit of Jesus, the Holy Spirit, lives within us to give us freedom and power to do good things, even greater things than Jesus did while He was on earth. Read Romans 8:1-17; Galatians 5:13-26; Ephesians 2:8-10; 3:16-21 and John 14:12.
- One day Jesus Christ will come again to earth to claim us as His own and we will forever enjoy a resurrected body in the new heavens and new earth. Read John 14:3; 1 Thessalonians 4:13-18; 1 Corinthians 15 and Revelation 21:1-8.

The reality of every believer being crucified, buried and raised with Christ is one of the most powerful truths in the New Testament (see Col. 2:12-13). Elisabeth Elliott applies the cross of Christ to the most intimate relationships. "Until the will and affections are brought under the authority of Christ, we have not begun to understand, let alone to accept, His lordship. The Cross, as it enters the love life, will reveal the heart's truth."[10] Once crucified with Christ, you can be confident that the same power that raised Jesus Christ from the dead is capable of changing any sinful habit or practice.

Do you believe that Christ's power is available to you in staying strong when your emotions scream for the wrong? The Bible's answer is yes. Tell yourself the honest truth, *God made me alive with Christ, in Him I have staying power.*

When with all your heart you desire more of God and more of His grace in your life, it can be yours. The danger is to settle for too little—just enough to keep you comfortable, to get you into heaven and escape the worst miseries of earth. Some people want far too little, as Wilbur Rees suggests.

> I would like to buy $3 worth of God, please, not enough to explode my soul or disturb my sleep, but just enough to equal a cup of warm milk or a snooze in the sunshine. I don't want enough of Him to make me love a black man or pick beets with a migrant. I want ecstasy, not transformation; I want the warmth of the womb, not a new birth. I want a pound of the Eternal in a paper sack. I would like to buy $3 worth of God, please.[11]

GRACE AND DISCIPLINE

The winners in the Christian life learn how to balance grace and discipline. Grace is what God has already done for us in Jesus Christ; discipline is what the caring Christian will do in response. "Continue to work out your salvation with fear and trembling, for it is God who works in you to will and to act according to his good purpose" (Phil. 2:12-13, *NIV*). This is no magic cure, no instant solution. The way of grace and discipline seems hard to bear at first, but gets easier and better as you keep going.

My good friend Ray Ortlund once compared the Christian life to a funnel. The world system suggests instant gratification of every sexual urge like dropping you into the wide end of the funnel. As you swirl downward your life becomes more and more cramped and plagued with painful consequences. The Christian way starts with grace and discipline lifting you through the narrow end of the funnel. As you rise through it, your life opens up into wider and wider vistas of fun, freedom and joy. Soon you can agree with the apostle John, "This is love for God: to obey his commands. And his commands are not burdensome, for everyone born of God overcomes the world" (1 John 5:3-4, *NIV*).

All of the Christian life is a balance between grace and discipline. Grace is what God has done and continues to do for us through Jesus Christ. Discipline is what we must do in response. In the grammar of the Greek New Testament, Christ's provision of grace most often appears in the indicative mood, indicating our present possession as Christians. The call for discipline appears in the imperative mood, commanding us to respond in obedience. Note Colossians 3:1 *(NIV)* as a working example. "Since, then, you have been raised [indicative = grace] with Christ, set [imperative = discipline] your hearts on things above, where Christ is seated at the right hand of God." Think about these contrasts:

- *Grace* is your present possession in Christ. *Discipline* releases your potential with Christ.
- *Grace* comes from receiving Christ's conquest. *Discipline* comes by obeying Christ's command.
- *Grace* results from what Christ has done in the cross and resurrection. *Discipline* calls for what you must do in the power of the Holy Spirit.

A mouse and an elephant loved to travel together. One day they crossed an old bridge across a deep ravine. "Wow!" exclaimed the mouse, "We really made that old bridge shake!" In this little parable, grace is the elephant, the mover and shaker.

Discipline is the mouse that goes along. The mouse must hold on tight, however, to cross to the other side.

All of this sounds easy enough, but there is a snag. The Bible calls it "the flesh" or "the sinful nature." (See Rom. 8:4 and Gal. 5:16-18.) William Barclay gives a clear, easy-to-understand explanation of what the Bible means.

> When Paul uses the word flesh in this way he really means human nature in all its weakness, its impotence and its helplessness. He means human nature in its vulnerability to sin and to temptation. He means that part of man which gives sin its chance and its bridgehead. He means sinful human nature, apart from Christ and apart from God. He means everything that attaches a man to the world instead of to God. To live according to the flesh is to live a worldly life, to live life dominated by the dictates and desires of sinful human nature instead of a life dominated by the dictates and the love of God. The flesh is the lower side of man's nature.*

The flesh, the sinful nature, makes the temptations of the world system around us seem alluring and attractive. When indulged, the flesh gives Satan a foothold to exercise increasing control beyond the power of our own wills to overcome.

Some Christians end up in failure because they try to make the best of living with both the Spirit and the flesh. They serve God with much of their time and energy, but they also cherish a hidden idol. They make tiny compromises to pamper the flesh. They indulge in little surrenders to fulfill their lusts. One day they wake up to the fact that one room of their life is sealed off from the Lord Jesus Christ. They pray with fervor for Him to come in and clean up this room. Yet they never give Him the key or unlock the door.

*William Barclay, *Romans* in *The Daily Bible Study Series* (Philadelphia: Westminster Press, 1957), p. 108. Used by permission.

Read how one man describes his "sealed-room" experience.

> Lust became the one corner of my life that God
> could not enter. I welcomed him into the area of per-
> sonal finance, which he revolutionized as I awakened
> to world needs. He cleaned up many of my personal
> relationships. He gave stirrings of life to the devo-
> tional area and my sense of personal communion
> with him. But lust was sealed off, a forbidden room.
> How can I reconcile that statement with my earlier
> protestations that I often cried out for deliverance? I
> do not know. I felt both sensations: an overwhelming
> desire to be cleansed and an overwhelming desire to
> cling to the exotic pleasures of lust.[12]

In this corner of your life the sinful nature, the flesh, reigns
supreme. In this room you do not worship Christ, but rather
bow before pleasure, power, ego-satisfaction or some other
false god. In this room, every attempt is made to keep the sinful
nature under control, but not to execute it. A good friend of
mine, Lanette De Buhr, put the tension between flesh and Spirit
into graphic verse.

> Just as I am Lord,
> Nothing more, nothing less
> you've waited so patiently
> with loving open arms.
>
> And yet, a part of me
> had been hidden away
> Saying, you can have most all of me
> But this part I'll keep.
>
> I'll tuck it away, for no one to see—
> Surely Lord, you won't look for it,
> and when the guilt comes and the

shame is made clear,
It will know right where to go,
in that little black hole.

What do you mean you want all of me?
Don't you understand?
There are parts of me that no one would want!
What's that you're saying?
"Child, that's why I died
Not for the best part of you, but for that little
Black hole."

What Lanette De Buhr describes as a little black hole is the same reality as an inner room sealed off from Christ. Somewhere in your life you hold a hidden key to this sealed room of a compulsive habit or sin you cannot conquer. This hidden key will turn the lock of brokenhearted confession and wholehearted repentance. The key may be the willingness to confess openly and brokenly to a wife or husband or respected Christian friend about a struggle with this certain sin. The key may be in seeking forgiveness for shattered relationships and building a new intimacy on a Christlike foundation. The key may be an all-out commitment to trust and obey Christ every day. The key may be in asking God to reduce your sex drive.

Always, always your key will feel like death. It will seem repulsive, unbearable, unthinkable. When you use the key, something within you will die. That something is the flesh, the sinful nature. Executions are never pleasant, but there is no other way. Neither torture nor deprivation will fulfill the command of God's Word. "Put to death, therefore, whatever belongs to your earthly nature: sexual immorality, impurity, lust, evil desires and greed, which is idolatry" (Col. 3:5, *NIV*).

Based on what Jesus Christ has already done for us (grace), every Christian is commanded (discipline) to put to death the sinful nature, the flesh. (See Col. 3:5-10 and Rom. 6:11, 8:13.) Compulsive habits, burning temptations, impulsive lust—all lose their power when the flesh is put to death. For staying strong in regard to driving temptation, a decisive death must take place. It is a smiling execution because following this death real health returns.

Not every key will fit the lock to your sealed room. Yet if you ask, seek and knock at the door of heaven (see Matt. 7:7-8), the Holy Spirit is faithful to reveal where your particular key is hidden. When you give Him the key, you surrender totally. He then releases more grace and you have added power to exercise discipline. You use the key, open the door and execute the sinful nature.

One final word of instruction. When you unlock the door and open the sealed room, clean it out completely. Like clearing cancer out of the body, you have to get it all or it will metastasize and spread again. Once cleaned out, fill your inner room with the Holy Spirit and the good things He provides. Leave the room full of fragrance pleasing to God. Then you can live the Christian life with joy! (See Phil. 1:4-6.) My friend Richard J. Foster is right when he gives this reminder.

> *Joy, not grit, is the hallmark of holy obedience.* We need to be *lighthearted* in what we do to avoid taking ourselves too seriously. It is a cheerful revolt against self and pride. Our work is jubilant, carefree, merry. Utter abandonment to God is done freely and with celebration. And so I urge you to enjoy this ministry of self-surrender. Don't push too hard. Hold this work lightly, joyfully.[13]

RENEWED SELF-ESTEEM

What if your self-esteem from past failures is so low that you feel like it is all over? You have lost the moral battle again and again. You feel hopeless to the point of depression, even despair. Here is good news for you. It is never too late for the man or woman who trusts Christ and receives His resurrection power.

In light of this transforming relationship with Jesus, the task now is to let the Holy Spirit renew your self-image. Every promise of the Bible is at your disposal. "The Lord is faithful to all his promises and loving toward all he has made. The Lord upholds all who fall and lifts up all who are bowed down" (Ps. 145:13-14, *NIV*).

In their helpful book, *Telling Yourself the Truth,* William Backus and Marie Chapian show how everyone has unseen, mental self-talk. When self-talk turns positive, honest and faith-filled, it leads to incredible changes for the better. When this inner conversation is negative, lying or excuse-making, you will find yourself swamped with problems. Many of these evil thoughts are outright lies from the devil. Affirm in your thoughts what Christ can do within you and deny the wrong ideas that lead to defeat. Identifying wrong beliefs helps you to ferret out bad ideas that damage a healthy self-image. Here are some mistaken beliefs related to lack of self-control from Backus and Chapian's list:

> If you want something you should have it—no matter what considerations are involved.
>
> You cannot control your strong desires. They are "needs" and you can't stand it when they are not satisfied. Any time you have to spend being frustrated or ungratified is unendurable.
>
> You can't fight your desires—they're much too strong for you to expect yourself to handle them.
>
> You can't quit because you're too weak and besides, even though X is bad for you, it meets your need for gratification. (X stands for whatever habit happens to be the problem.)
>
> You're entitled to inflict your demands upon others.[14]

Why not check off the items on the list that seem to fit? Then ask the Lord to call it to your attention whenever you tell yourself one of these lies in your self-talk. As soon as you catch it, change the inner thought to the truth from Christ's point of view. Most often the truth is just the opposite of the misbelief. For example, change your thought of *I can't stand failure of any kind* to its opposite. Tell yourself, *Christ uses my failure to teach me to depend on Him for success in my Christian life.* Apply the same process to each wrong belief until the Holy Spirit renews your mind.

Let me tell you a story based on a Norwegian folktale. A boy snatched an egg from an eagle's nest. Taking it home to his farm, he put it in with the eggs of their tame goose. Although the baby eagle hatched along with the little goslings, he was always a misfit. Day after day he hobbled around the barnyard scratching for food because he simply could not learn to swim. He thought to himself, *It's hopeless!*

Then one day a majestic eagle soaring in giant circles in the sky swept low over the farm. The funny "goose" with a life of past failure fixed his eye on the marvel overhead. He began to run and flap his wings as hard as he could. Rising into the air, an updraft caught him, lifting him high into the sky. He found a new life, the one he was intended for. He was dead to his old life as a goose and alive to his new life as an eagle.

Like eagles, Christians are meant to soar. In Christ, you are more like a high-flying eagle than a barnyard goose. The Holy Spirit sweeps in to teach you to fly. With your heart and mind fixed on Christ your renewed self-image will wing its way to the heights instead of scratching in the dirt.[15]

Prayer

Heavenly Father, I praise you for promising to finish the good work that you started in me. Build within me a humble, submissive, cooperative spirit intent on obeying you in everything. Thank you for caring about my weaknesses, my flaws, my emotional damage. Just as I am, I give myself to please you, holy Father, and take your hand so that I may walk in the light as you are in the light. In fellowship with other Christians I joyfully praise Jesus Christ for cleansing and purifying me from all sin.

Intensify my godly passion for holiness until I honestly desire not to sin at all.

I invite you to search out my life for an inner room sealed off from your control. I ask, seek, knock for the hidden key to unlock the door, pry open the room and empty the little black hole. Once you place the key in my hand, give me no peace until I use it. Empower me to smile as I execute the sinful nature, the flesh, with its evil passions and desires. Help me to smash the idols in my heart and cast out the deceitful foe. Clean out the filth within me and heal the hurt left behind. Fill the empty spaces with the Lord Jesus Christ. I determine not to think about how to gratify the desires of the sinful nature, but rather to keep in step with the Holy Spirit.

I pray in the name of Jesus Christ who died for me while I was yet powerless and ungodly, and who reconciled me to God by His atoning death and powerful resurrection. Amen.

When the Church Must Get Tough

11

SOPHIE AND SAM'S STORY

The pain of separation from her husband brought Sophie back to church. It was like walking out of the bitter cold into a warm room. Friendship and love greeted her with open arms. The people in the church took her in as part of their extended family. Before long she even found herself teaching Sunday School. It felt so good to fellowship with the family of God.

In no way was Sophie looking for male companionship. It just seemed to happen. This man at church named Sam was going through the same stage of separation that she was. He seemed to like her and understood firsthand her frustration, anger and loneliness. They found themselves talking often and comforting each other with a listening ear. Their friendship soon became special and it seemed natural to start dating.

Before long the pastor and a likable elder asked to meet with them. The problem was that both she and Sam were separated but not divorced. As might be expected, their loving counsel was not to date, at least until both divorces were final. Sophie and Sam listened, nodded politely and kept going out together to dinner, church and a variety of activities. Before too many weeks several of their close friends also discouraged them from dating. A few others in the church, however, invited them to dinner as a couple, giving a measure of social approval. Mixed signals are hard to read so Sam and Sophie rationalized their actions and got together more often than before.

As if to dispel the myth of a platonic relationship in the minds of some people, Sophie became pregnant. She and Sam broke the news to the pastor, dismissing its seriousness by announcing that they were planning to get married after their divorces were final anyway. As the word of her pregnancy spread, people in the church felt alarmed, concerned, caring. Two of Sophie's closest friends offered her free room and board so she would not continue to live in sexual immorality. She said, "Thanks for the offer," turned them down and moved in with Sam.

The committed Christians in the church could not follow the logic of Sophie's do-it-yourself morality. And Sophie knew their actions were wrong in God's sight and the church's eyes, but because she and Sam were in this circumstance, living together seemed okay. Sam was more blunt. "It may be wrong but I don't really care. I feel far from God." He seemed proud of the fact that the baby was his and refused to face up to any wrongdoing. They kept going to worship together. Sam had never involved himself in other activities but Sophie kept teaching Sunday School as if nothing were wrong. Within the church their private affair turned into a public scandal.

Something had to be done. If this church was going to practice what it preached, it had to get tough. Yet they all loved Sophie and Sam, and wanted to stay tender in their attitudes. After a series of discussions and seeking God's will, the elders removed Sophie from her Sunday School teaching position and all ministry activities. Neither she nor Sam had formally joined the church so the elders did not deal with the matter of membership. With compassion they also appealed to them to refrain from further adultery. They did, however, allow Sophie and Sam to attend worship, reasoning that even flagrant sinners have an open invitation to hear the message of Jesus.

Sophie seemed shaken. At times she even felt broken with the thought of her sin and indicated that she might break off the adulterous relationship with Sam. "I'm just not sure that I can give him up," she sighed. Sam remained as defensive as ever and did everything in his power to hold on to Sophie. It was like a tug-of-war with the church's love on one side and Sam's lust on the other. The discerning members sensed a spiritual battle raging beneath the surface. Unfortunately more foolish choices occurred and Sophie did not move out.

Tension mounted in the church. Some of the people felt that any discipline was unloving and judgmental. Others felt that even their attending worship was hypocrisy of the worst sort and a public disgrace to the gospel of Jesus Christ. In an official session, the church body met to take disciplinary action. The elders explained their decision to suspend them from *any* leadership positions. Neither Sam nor Sophie attended the meeting for discipline. They were not repentant nor did they give any hint of turning from their adultery. After some discussion the church body also agreed to support the action taken by the elders earlier.

Even after the baby was born, Sam and Sophie, still unmarried, kept attending worship. They seemed blind to the gravity of their sin. Then came the annual Promotion Day for all the children. The printed program named every child, including the babies in the nursery. Since Sam and Sophie were not married (and Sophie was not even divorced yet), the bulletin listed their baby by Sophie's last name only. Sam was infuriated at the church's "insensitivity" in refusing to recognize him as the father. Sam took Sophie and the baby out the door that Sunday, saying they would never return.

Oh, the perplexities of church discipline! Some felt Sam and Sophie should have been banned from worship long before they walked out. Others preferred to ignore the whole issue. What seems clear is that the church had the courage to do *something* about sexual immorality in its midst. In spite of disagreements, even threats by some of Sophie's friends to leave the church, the believers stood together in the hour of crisis. With patience and compassion they tried to restore gently those who were caught in a sin (see Gal. 6:1).

Today the church is healthy and growing. A sense of unity prevails. An honest respect for God's truth walks hand in hand with an open sense of joy in worship. God's Spirit was not grieved by tolerating open sin in their fellowship (see Rev. 2:14,20-23). Far from alienating them from Christ forever, Sam and Sophie did eventually marry and started attending another church. Like surgery, even painful discipline has its benefits.

THE CHURCH MUST GET TOUGH

You may question the wisdom or even the validity of church discipline. In fact, for a number of years many churches considered such action archaic, a relic of the past. Then came the tragedy of Jim Jones and the mass suicide at Jonestown. When this "pastor" asked all his church members to drink Kool Aid laced with cyanide, and they along with their children followed him in this fatal act, the whole world knew something was wrong. Church leaders everywhere began to ask about corrective church discipline and investigations showed that adultery, false teaching, disorderly conduct and abusive speech were *all* a part of Jim Jones's practice. Why had no one taken official action before it was too late?[1]

When Christians, especially those in high profile positions, persist in sexual immorality, the Church must get tough. Moral failures allowed to run rampant cause havoc in a Christian fellowship. As Mel White points out, open sexual sin puts the future of the Church in jeopardy.[2] When all else fails, church discipline remains essential. Likewise Christian organizations must take measures to discipline or remove employees who live a double life. Far from being harsh or judgmental, discipline calls the offender to return to holy living, warns the unwary and checks the spread of spiritual cancer.

A VARIETY OF CASES

The Babe in Christ

Common sense tells us that not all sexual offenders should be treated in precisely the same way. The pastor of a congregation holds greater responsibility for his personal conduct than a new convert fresh out of a pagan life-style. The confused newcomer may need time and patience for the Holy Spirit to do His sanctifying work. The important question to ask is whether this person is moving toward Christ or away from Him. After teaching, exhortation, rebuke and encouragement, is there any difference in the life that is emerging?

The Mature Christian

The doubleminded church member of long standing requires more careful action. This individual knows what the Bible teaches and most often feels he is violating his own moral principles. Guilt, deceit and rationalization color his outlook. Harsh or vindictive action or any obvious mistake in procedure may lead to political manipulation on the part of the sinful person entrenched in the church. Following the specified church polity (governmental procedures) for discipline becomes highly important. Hasty action or cowardly inaction can both harm the local church for years to come. Much of the spiritual battle must be won in prayer and the greatest wisdom is needed every step of the way.

The Staff Member

The unrepentant pastor, leader or staff member in a Christian school or organization is the most pathetic of all. Satan zeroes in on these leaders as his special targets. When a church leader indulges in sexual sin and then remains unrepentant (with or without disciplinary action), he causes confusion and division beyond belief. Sometimes the tragedy of tragedies occurs: many Christians use the leader's sin as an excuse for their own disobedience. But worse yet, it confirms Satan's old lie, "The church is full of hypocrites." Non-Christians pounce on this excuse for rejecting Jesus Christ.

For the unrepentant paid leader, sure evidence and quick dismissal is the best route to go. Stating the reasons publicly, tactfully and truthfully remains both necessary and wise. Where the evidence is uncertain, the official action must depend upon discernment and good judgment. Sometimes it means releasing the person quietly or asking for a resignation. At other times a "wait and see" posture seems best. It is vital to honor scriptural counsel that no action is taken without two or three witnesses (see Deut. 19:15 and Matt. 18:16). Today it seems far too easy for one disgruntled person to frame an innocent man or woman.

Some wonderful Christian ministers have faced *false* accusations, either from malice or out of ignorance. Frank, a minister of Christian education in a church with an excellent preschool was accused of child molesting. Laws designed to protect children from painful memories made it impossible to cross-examine the child. Frank, although innocent, was caught in a cross fire between angry parents, detectives, lie detector specialists, the church staff and its attorney. After 11 painful days he was cleared, but the damage to his reputation was incredible. Although immensely capable in working with children, he later resigned from the church and pursued a degree in counseling.

His pastor wrote an insightful article that all church staffs with preschools should read. Because of the intense suspicion of the present climate, he suggests that men never work alone with children. If false charges begin he recommends expert legal counsel. "Few things produce stronger emotions than thinking your own child was molested, on one hand—or being falsely accused of sexually molesting a child on the other. And the police, being human with their own emotions, bring to the investigation their own agendas and dreams of promotion. Our experience taught us the value of the best possible lawyer of criminal justice, since this is a felony accusation. The cost of legal counsel is well worth the expense."[3]

Our High Calling: Public or Private?

The high calling of those in authority is to balance compassion and conviction when dealing with offenders. No one likes this messy business. Tensions always rise between keeping matters confidential or making them public. The old rule that the confession should go as far as the sin and no further, most often proves valid. For example, a pastor who has a one-night-stand never to be repeated is in a different category from the one who has a history of sexual affairs with counselees. A discerning group of elders who study the Scriptures can learn of the wisest course of action.

Most discipline within a church goes on in private. Pastors confront sexual immorality more often than their church members ever dream. Again and again ministers make appeals to the conscience behind closed doors, sometimes with wonderful results. This is the way it should be. Public church discipline is reserved for public sins that scandalize the heavenly Father's reputation. As Don Baker wisely puts it, "Corrective church discipline is designed for sins of such a nature that they obscure the purposes of God."[4]

Ken L. Bemis, pastor at North Community Evangelical Free Church in Brea, California made a scriptural list of such public sins. They include disorderly conduct, divisiveness, sexual immorality, false teaching, drunkenness, abusive speech, swindling and idolatry (2 Thess. 3:6-15; Rom. 16:17-18; 1 Tim. 1:20; 2 Tim. 2:17-18; Rev. 2:14-16 and 1 Cor. 6:9-11). In what he calls "The Reconciliation-Discipline Process" (and what *I* will call the Bemis Scale), Pastor Bemis has designed a helpful chart to explain the steps toward restoration.[5]

Understanding the Bemis Scale

Following these scriptural steps with prayer and discernment prevents hasty judgment on the one hand or utter neglect on the other. The Bemis Scale is a highly useful tool for churches and Christian organizations everywhere and some amplification on the chart may help.

The Bemis Scale

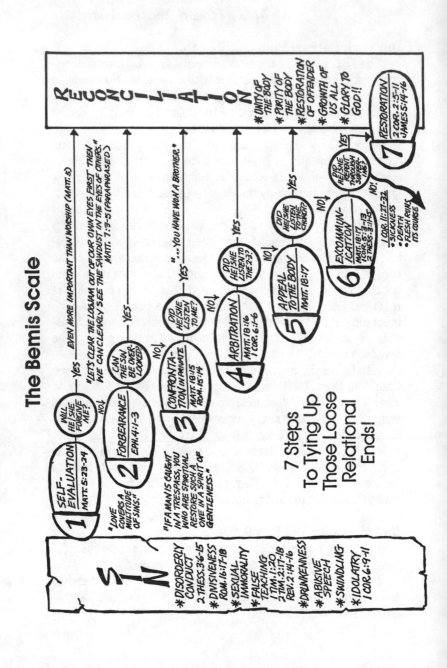

7 Steps To Tying Up Those Loose Relational Ends!

RECONCILIATION

* UNITY OF THE BODY
* PURITY OF THE BODY
* RESTORATION OF OFFENDER
* GROWTH OF US ALL
* GLORY TO GOD!!

1 SELF-EVALUATION
MATT. 5:23-24

WILL HE/SHE FORGIVE ME? — Yes — EVEN MORE IMPORTANT THAN WORSHIP (MATT. 5)

"LET'S CLEAR THE LOGJAM OUT OF OUR OWN EYES FIRST, THEN WE CAN CLEARLY SEE THE SAWDUST IN THE EYES OF OTHERS." MATT. 7:3-5 (PARAPHRASED)

NO↓

2 FORBEARANCE
EPH. 4:1-3

CAN THE SIN BE OVER-LOOKED? — YES

"LOVE COVERS A MULTITUDE OF SINS."

NO↓

3 CONFRONTA-TION IN PRIVATE
MATT. 18:15
ROM. 15:14

"IF A MAN IS CAUGHT IN A TRESPASS, YOU WHO ARE SPIRITUAL RESTORE SUCH A ONE IN A SPIRIT OF GENTLENESS."

DID HE/SHE LISTEN TO ME? — YES — "... YOU HAVE WON A BROTHER."

NO↓

4 ARBITRATION
MATT. 18:16
1 COR. 6:1-6

DID HE/SHE LISTEN TO THE 2-3? — YES

NO↓

5 APPEAL TO THE BODY
MATT. 18:17

DID HE/SHE LISTEN TO THE CHURCH? — YES

NO↓

6 EXCOMMUN-ICATION
MATT. 18:17
1 COR. 5:3-13
2 THESS. 3:14-15

DID HE/SHE REPENT THROUGH SUFFERING? — YES

NO↓
1 COR. 11:27-32
• SICKNESS
• DEATH
• FLESH RUNS ITS COURSE

7 RESTORATION
2 COR. 2:5-11
JAMES 5:14-16

SIN
* DISORDERLY CONDUCT
2 THESS. 3:6-15
* DIVISIVENESS
ROM. 16:17-18
* SEXUAL IMMORALITY
* FALSE TEACHING
1 TIM. 1:20
2 TIM. 2:17-18
REV. 2:14-16
* DRUNKENNESS
* ABUSIVE SPEECH
* SWINDLING
* IDOLATRY
1 COR. 6:9-11

1. Self-evaluation. In the Sermon on the Mount Jesus counsels His disciples to leave their gift on the Temple altar if they know that anyone holds something against them. "First go and be reconciled to your brother; then come and offer your gift" (Matt. 5:24, *NIV*). Reconciliation takes priority, even over one's worship. Anyone who works with people knows that every conflict has two or more viewpoints. Heart-searching for our own wrongdoing *always* comes first. Prayer and fasting often help to humble a person before God, lower defenses and bring about the attitude of a learner. Even if 95 percent of the wrongdoing lies on the other side, seeking forgiveness for one's own wrong remains the proper starting point.

The important question in the self-evaluation step is, "Will he/she forgive me?" If the individual does, reconciliation takes place. If not, move on to step two.

2. Forbearance. "Fools rush in where angels fear to tread," the old saying goes. The Bible points to forbearing attitudes also. "Be patient, bearing with one another in love. Make every effort to keep the unity of the Spirit through the bond of peace" (Eph. 4:2-3, *NIV*). Sometimes the most loving thing a person can do is look the other way. (See Prov. 10:12 and 1 Pet. 4:8.) If the sin is not so serious as to require a private confrontation, then the best thing to do is to put up with this person in love. *You* forgive and forget. The question to ask is, "Can this sin be overlooked?" If not, proceed to step three.

3. Confrontation in Private. Jesus gives precise instructions. "If your brother sins against you, go and show him his fault, just between the two of you. If he listens to you, you have won your brother over" (Matt. 18:15, *NIV*). "Listen" in the Hebrew way of thinking means to hear and respond in obedience to God. The goal is to win the offender over—to convince him, persuade him and bring him around. It is never to condemn, devastate or destroy. It is worth repeating here that this meeting is one-on-one, eyeball-to-eyeball, in private and in confidence. The last thing to do is to talk to everyone else about the problem. The good news is that private confrontation often leads to major change. If the person persists in sexual sin or any wrongdoing, move to step four.

4. Arbitration. "But if he will not listen, take one or two others along, so that 'every matter may be established by the testimony of two or three witnesses,'" says Jesus (Matt. 18:16, *NIV*). Do not take along Mr. Blistertongue or Mrs. Scandalmonger. Find respected people with good judgment and spiritual insight. The value of one or two discerning witnesses is that it leaves no room for hearsay. A factual approach and a gentle spirit go a long way toward restoring someone caught in a sin (see Gal. 6:1). If this step fails to bring about reconciliation, then it is time to consider official action by the church or Christian organization.

5. Appeal to the Body. "If he refuses to listen to them, tell it to the church" (Matt. 18:17, *NIV*). *This* is the time to go public and not before. In most local churches the place to begin is with the elders and pastors, official church board or functional equivalent. To bypass those in authority is ecclesiastical suicide. A few official bodies will refuse to act, preferring to sweep it under the rug, hush it up and make no waves. Even so, respect and obedience to those in authority is always appropriate (see 1 Thess. 5:12-13 and Heb. 13:17). When two or three respected people make an appeal to the official church body within their organizational guidelines, *something* will happen. Most churches or the official body within them will do what they believe is best to restore the person. If the offender resists the counsel of the official church body, proceed to the next step.

6. Excommunication. Churches and Christians who intend to obey the Bible will take the following passages about excommunication seriously.

> And if he refuses to listen even to the church, treat him as you would a pagan or a tax collector (Matt. 18:17, *NIV*).

> I have written you in my letter not to associate with

sexually immoral people—not at all meaning the people of this world who are immoral, or the greedy and swindlers, or idolaters. In that case you would have to leave this world. But now I am writing you that you must not associate with anyone who calls himself a brother but is sexually immoral or greedy, an idolater or a slanderer, a drunkard or a swindler. With such a man do not even eat. What business is it of mine to judge those outside the church? Are you not to judge those inside? God will judge those outside. "Expel the wicked man from among you" (1 Cor. 5:9-13, *NIV*).

If anyone does not obey our instruction in this letter, take special note of him. Do not associate with him, in order that he may feel ashamed. Yet do not regard him as an enemy, but warn him as a brother (2 Thess. 3:14-15, *NIV*).

7. Restoration. Excommunication is never an end in itself. It is a necessary means toward the goal of restoring the offender (see 2 Cor. 2:5-11). Excommunication may mean a ban on all participation including Sunday morning worship. Some churches, however, see the worship hour as a time of preaching the gospel with the intent of winning the lost and restoring those who go astray. "Pagans and tax collectors" are especially welcome at this hour. The one under discipline is simply banned from any ordinances. Each church will make its own decision based on its interpretation of Scripture and its own stated procedures.

GENERAL PRINCIPLES FOR EFFECTIVE CHURCH DISCIPLINE

When the Church moves in official action to deal with an offender in a matter of discipline, heaven takes note. This is serious business with more binding power than any human court. Immediately following Jesus' teaching in Matthew 18:17 about excommunication, our Lord says, "I tell you the truth, whatever you bind on earth will be bound in heaven, and whatever you loose on earth will be loosed in heaven" (Matt. 18:18, *NIV*). The apostle Paul speaks of a temporary handing over to Satan of certain ones disciplined by the church (see 1 Cor. 5:5 and 1 Tim. 1:20). Paul's wording makes it certain that he expected them to come back to the Lord. Satan causes torment and misery, sometimes sickness and death. By way of contrast, returning to full fellowship with Christ and His Church brings joy and peace, health and life (see Jas. 5:14-16). The Church has the authority to *do something* about defiant sexual sin.

Whenever reconciliation takes place it brings glory to God. Open, loving Church discipline contributes to unity and purity of the Body of Christ. The process is never easy and seldom as ideal as the clear principles of the Bemis scale. The next chapter will tell a true story of church discipline in action. But before moving on, I want to ask and answer a couple of questions. What summary guidelines can help a church regarding discipline? What general principles will make it more effective? Let me suggest five guidelines that may prove helpful.

Educate the Church in Advance

Most people reject anything strange or not well understood. In one church I know of an elder who teaches the Bemis Scale to each adult Sunday School class for a single hour. This sets the biblical framework for church discipline before it ever becomes necessary. When church leaders suggest and practice loving confrontation in small conflicts, it builds confidence in the power of private discipline. When someone complains about a fellow Christian simply ask, "Have you talked to him or her about it? I really think you should." If he resists, simply add, "I'll be seeing him soon and I'll tell him that you want to talk." Experience in settling small disagreements in a spirit of love paves the way for dealing with major offenses.

Balance Compassion and Conviction
Every Step of the Way

The dilemma most Christians face in church discipline is the teeter-totter between loving acceptance and caring confrontation, between compassion and conviction, between being tender and being tough. The danger is that feelings of resentment, even animosity, will intensify. No one can control the attitudes of the offenders, but the church leaders hold a special responsibility to show Christ's compassion while obeying His commands. The insightful words of Jesus make a lot of sense in such a time. "Do good to those who hate you, bless those who curse you, pray for those who mistreat you" (Luke 6:27-28, *NIV*).

Depend on the Holy Spirit for Guidance

Long before corrective discipline nears the public stage, the church leaders will want to spend extended time in prayer and fasting. One to three days in fasting with extra time given to prayer does much to humble those involved. It also opens them to fresh insights into the Scripture and fine-tuning to the inner voice of the Holy Spirit. When their motives remain cleansed and loving, their actions hold more power and effectiveness. Those with the spiritual gift of discernment deserve a special hearing in such a painful hour.

The great call today is for those with the courage of leadership who will humbly obey God's Word. "My brothers, if one of you should wander from the truth and someone should bring him back, remember this: Whoever turns a sinner from the error of his way will save him from death and cover over a multitude of sins" (Jas. 5:19-20, *NIV*).

Follow Biblical Procedures
Coupled with Your Own Polity

When faithfulness to God, the Scripture and the Lord's people requires a church to go public with a rebuke or excommunication, then the process becomes of vital importance. The wise pastor or elders will consult the Bible and the established procedures for discipline set up by his church. Anyone who violates these steps can expect frustration and embarrassment. It may also lead to a backlash from those who know how to use the official power in a church system to retaliate. Jesus taught that His disciples should "be as shrewd as snakes and as innocent as doves" (Matt. 10:16, *NIV*). This must be our aim also.

The smart church leader will not go it alone. He will consult with the wisest Christians he knows. This most often brings about prudent counsel and good sense. When the Lord brings a group of discerning elders or church leaders to a sense of unity, He is adding wisdom to power. If the group cannot reach unity, then a brief delay may seem best. God is never confused. Waiting, praying and a covenant of fasting may bring clarity and conviction about His will.

The binding power which God uses in church discipline is aimed most often at our sense of belonging to a primary group. The approval or disapproval of this group, made up of intimate family members, relatives, close friends and church family, where we feel that we are an integral part make a powerful impact upon us. Secondary groups such as employers, business associates and the government must rely on dismissal or the legal system for enforcing the law. Even outside the church structure, however, we must not discount the influence of appeal to conscience or the power of praying friends who really love a person. Christian discipline is effective because the Holy Spirit honors the action of His people who care enough to confront in love.

Use Discretion in Public Censure
Or Excommunication Proceedings

Wisdom, tact and sensitivity are key words. The church must never discipline in order to destroy, but only to correct and restore. Anything bordering on slander or libel is strictly out of place. If the offender remains unrepentant and angry, then greater caution is necessary. Although traditionally civil courts refuse to hear cases involving internal church disputes, a few recent suits indicate that the courts *may* interfere if slander, libel or invasion of privacy is involved. While God's people have always faced persecution in some form, they seldom want to make themselves vulnerable to charges of defamation.

Written letters and documents open a church up to court investigation. Unless the offender writes the letter, it seems better to keep the communication verbal and positive. If church polity calls for a written statement or for recording of official minutes, then the wording becomes of utmost importance. It even makes sense to have a Christian attorney read over the proposed wording in advance. Here is an example.

It has come to the attention of (the elders or whatever official body) that one of the members of (church name) has violated the rules for voluntary membership and the standards of Scripture. All of the facts of the case are confirmed by two or more witnesses. Careful discussion with (name) has been undertaken to bring about reconciliation and restoration, but without success. Therefore, according to our stated procedures, (name) has been dropped from membership (or the proper body recommends that he/she be removed from membership) until these differences can be reconciled. This means that the disciplined member will not be allowed to participate in any way except (spell out any exceptions such as attendance at worship). We earnestly ask that this action not become a matter for personal offense or private gossip. If any members have questions, the pastor and elders are willing to answer them in private.

Prayer

Our Father in heaven, hallowed be your name. We worship you and desire that your name be kept holy among us. Open our eyes to the damage that public sin in our midst causes to your name and your Church. We gladly confess that our Lord Jesus Christ is head of the Church universal and this local church in particular. We submit to Him as members of His Body and ask that we may become responsive to His direction.

May your Holy Spirit take charge of our thinking and discussion. Reveal the mind of Christ to us through your written Word. Bring us to one mind, united in heart and spirit, about what you want us to do in this particular case. Give us discernment to perceive the truth from two or three witnesses. Bring into the light of Christ all the truth that we should know at this moment. Guide us to take the best possible action in order to warn, correct and restore an offender, and to bring purity and unity to your Church.

In humility we claim the authority as a church that you have put into our hands, Lord Jesus. Our desire is to please you and to obey your commands. Teach us to practice sound doctrine with hearts full of love for everyone involved in this conflict. Show us how to speak the truth in love to the right people at the right time. Grant us grace to act with courage and compassion.

May all that is said and done, however difficult, bring honor to our Lord Jesus Christ and glory to God. In the powerful name of Jesus, we pray. Amen.

It's Too Late for Me— Or Is It? 12

Like a pied piper, Mac had a winning way with high schoolers at Community Church. As youth pastor, his love toward them just did not stop. His capacity for compassion was evident to all. The students responded with enthusiasm, sharing their best times with him. As a single, Mac gave his energy, heart and soul to these high schoolers. Ministry opportunities and social activities filled his days and nights.

Christian parents felt pleased that their high schoolers were active in such fine, Christian activities. Pastor Rob liked Mac's understanding of the unchurched young person. He always seemed to know if he or she were into drugs or booze. Trying to deceive Mac was like an alcoholic trying to lie to a recovered one. It just did not work. Mac had been there just a few years before. He understood and he cared. And he could not be fooled.

Mac had one weakness and he knew it. You see, before becoming a Christian Mac was a very streetwise young man. Barnyard immorality was a matter of pride with him and was a part of his macho image. He played the tough kid, big-gun role to the hilt—and liked it. He felt a sense of power over the people he exploited and his attractive personality and passionate heart lured several of the young women at work—both married and unmarried—to bed with him.

Mac loved none of these girls, except one. She captured his heart as well as his body. Then she became pregnant. The abortion that followed left a scar on Mac's soul, for he had a part in ending the life of his own unborn child and he did not like it. In the deepest part of his spirit, he cried. From then on he felt he owed somebody something. He acted as though he was always trying to prove himself.

When Mac found Jesus Christ as Lord and Saviour, his life changed from darkness to light. For a couple of years he stayed away from sexual sin without a problem. His holy-ground experience with God was strong and vivid, and it kept him going. Then the enticement of lust began to lure his mind once again. The hardest part of the old life to shake off was his memory of the old exploits. He fed his lust with picture-perfect recall and before long he relapsed into sexual sin.

At this point in time Mac was meeting with Grant, a church staff member who was discipling him. At least he was honest enough not to hide his sin. Grant responded by confronting Mac in love, telling him he was throwing away everything he was learning about the Christian life. Mac repented and determined to follow Jesus with renewed vigor. Yet somehow his old friends and habit patterns at work acted like a whirlpool, spinning him downward into foul language and one-night stands. Grant insisted he change jobs and as the two prayed about it, an unexpected transfer to another store in the area came through. He made a fresh start.

Mac also came clean. The old life-style gave way to the freedom of self-control. In time his transformed life and extraordinary leadership ability won him a place on the church staff. This time he moved into the fast lane of Christian activity, giving himself to the high schoolers with abandon. In fact, he allowed for too little personal time for himself.

Along with the fact pace came stress which began to build up in Mac's system. He knew enough to draw closer to Christ when the pressure was mounting, but he did not listen to the Spirit's inner voice. Instead, a series of compromises crisscrossed his inner soul. It all started with fudging on his time management. When the choices had to be made between hard study for speaking to the youth group or some spontaneous fun with a few high schoolers, he took the easy road. Before long he was spending less and less time in the Bible and in prayer. His personal devotions ground to a halt.

On the outside Mac kept his life above reproach, yet in the inner rooms of his mind the battle raged. He somehow found enough time alone to read some porno and add some R-rated movies to his schedule. His emotions began to churn like a washing machine. For awhile he would deny his sexuality and repress his normal feelings. Then a few days later he would recall with sensual pleasure his past sex exploits and feed his mind on the lust of his sin. Both offbeat extremes made him miserable.

As if a hidden choreographer were staging the scene, a series of blows intensified his stress and left Mac vulnerable. First, his parents were about to separate and this hurt his sensitive spirit. Second, he was struggling with Greek in seminary and his grades declined to the point where he was placed on probation. Third, although Pastor Rob was like a father to him, Mac felt embarrassed about bringing up the subjects of his masturbation and viewing of dirty movies. Finally, with the heavy petting going on during his dates, a predictable relationship crisis with a girl he liked took place.

Mac was experiencing wrenching guilt before his Lord during this time. He began telling himself, *I don't care what God will do to me.* He was running away from Jesus Christ inwardly while preaching about Him outwardly. A hidden rebel spirit captured his mind. Some call it backsliding, some call it stressed-out. But whatever the name, Mac was easy prey for what happened next.

A new girl from outside the church showed up at the high school group meeting one evening. She used some drugs but was not a heavy abuser. Without even wondering, Mac knew she was promiscuous. The two began making moves—subtle, hidden, flattering passes at first. But before long it was just like the old days. She was "madly in love" with Mac and his lust was inflamed for her. He had it planned the night it happened. She was the last one to drive home after a youth event and he knew exactly where he was taking her.

Within a few weeks she phoned to let him know she was pregnant—at least she thought so. As Mac puts it, "all hell broke loose" within him. He told her that abortion was not the way to go and that they should wait and see if she were pregnant for sure. He assumed she was and he did not want to be around when the dike broke open. *Things are going to get pretty mean,* he thought. *She was under age, a minor. Also, how could he face her parents, Pastor Rob, the inevitable church board and his personal friends? How could he, as a minister of the gospel, have done such a terrible thing?*

Deep depression settled in. He quit going to classes, withdrew from people and isolated himself as much as possible. Panic also added its stress to his enormous inner pressure. Mac spent time crying, praying, confessing to God—and thinking about suicide. Pent up in him were a lot of things to say, but he did not feel like saying anything to anyone. He felt exhausted, worn out, tired. Even TV commercials triggered memories that started him crying again. Mac was at the breaking point.

He borrowed a gun from his brother, a .357 magnum, and lied about wanting to do some target shooting. He locked it in his cupboard and started planning his death. In his confused mind he thought, *God would never forgive me for what I've done, but He could forgive me for shooting myself.* Mac wondered if it were better to kill himself at night on the church's back lawn, or fill his car with gas and go out of state first. A couple of days later he took out the gun, loaded it and hid it in a backpack with a few clothes in his office. That morning he planned to drive out of state. *It'll take a few days before anyone finds my body and notifies anyone,* he thought.

Shortly before he left the church his friend Grant unexpectedly walked into his office. "How come you're not in class?" he probed. The look on Mac's face alarmed him. "Hey, something's wrong, isn't it?" Without warning Mac began to sob.

"I went to bed with this girl. She's under age . . . " and he poured out his painful story.

Together Mac and Grant walked over to Pastor Rob's office. One look at Mac's face and in a flash of insight the pastor knew what was coming next. He listened with compassion to the whole confession that he already knew in his spirit was going to come forth. After Mac spilled out the sad account of his sin and suicidal depression, the pastor simply said, "Let's get the gun." They brought it back from the office, unloaded it and Pastor Rob kept it. "Commitment in love doesn't lead us to blow our brains out and leave our friends with questions and no answers," Pastor Rob counseled. With the secrecy gone, Mac's obsession with suicide evaporated. To stay on the safe side, however, Mac spent the day with Grant and some other church staff members.

Pastor Rob faced an agonizing decision. Should he dismiss Mac quietly and get him out of town? If so, would he repeat his sex sins in the next church? With his love for youth ministry, it was highly unlikely he would change vocations. Should he start some kind of church-wide discipline and take the risk of keeping Mac around? How would the other parents respond? He phoned several Bible expositors whose wisdom he respected. The same counsel came back from every source: without church discipline the problem will never stop and the people of God will suffer incredible damage.

Pastor Rob called an emergency meeting that included the elders and a denominational official. He did not want to walk alone along this treacherous path. They all agreed that they would try to avoid the obvious dangers of playing blind on the one hand or making a scandal out of Mac's sin on the other. Open, restorative discipline looked like a slippery tightrope but Pastor Rob knew it was the best way. In his compassionate heart he believed it was a severe mercy. Maybe, just maybe, they could reclaim Mac and pull the church together at the same time.

After breaking the sad news of what happened to the assembled group, they prayed together for wisdom. Then Pastor Rob invited Mac in to make his confession firsthand. Mac seemed broken and humbled as he poured out his story of what he had done and the pressures behind it. He assured them that this was a one-time, isolated incident and that no other girls in the youth group had ever had sexual intercourse with him. They believed Mac and began searching the Scriptures for God's direction.

Together the pastors and elders reviewed various passages where the Bible speaks about church discipline and about the standards of conduct for Christian leaders. In his powerful little volume *Beyond Forgiveness,* Don Baker gives a fine summary.

> *Matthew 18:15-20* teaches that a sinning brother is to be (1) confronted, (2) reproved, and (3) excluded from the church if he refuses to repent.
>
> *Acts 5:1-11* illustrates (1) the seriousness of sin within the church, (2) the sensitivity of the Holy Spirit to sin, and (3) the quick judgment of God upon sin.
>
> *First Corinthians 5:1-5* teaches that in the event of persistent, unrepentant sin, the church is to (1) grieve, (2) deliberate, (3) judge the sin, and (4) exclude the unrepentant.
>
> *First Thessalonians 5:14* commands us to warn the disobedient and the disorderly.
>
> *Second Thessalonians 3:6-15* teaches us to (1) warn the undisciplined brother and (2) withdraw from him.
>
> *First Timothy 5:20* tells us to rebuke persistent sin publicly.
>
> *Titus 1:13* says to severely reprove those who teach untruth.

Titus 3:10 commands us to withdraw from one who causes divisions, but only after adequate warning.

Revelation 2 and 3 call the churches to repentance and warn of impending discipline if they refuse.

In these passages, God makes it clear that He intends the church to take corrective measures in the event its members persist in the practice of sin.[1]

The elders shared several passages with one another that touched on the issue of church discipline. In Mac's case, the requirement for an elder to be "above reproach" was convincing (see 1 Tim. 3:2). Everyone loved Mac but he was no longer above reproach. It took some time before they came to agreement on starting church discipline, for it was not their custom in this church. It was something they had never done before. Before the evening was over the elders reached agreement about what to do. They outlined some immediate steps of action for Mac, the church and themselves.

1. Beginning immediately Mac was put on vacation. This was to last until the full congregation could be called together for a meeting for discipline.
2. Mac was to write a letter of resignation stating the facts in a tactful but honest way. Pastor Rob would help him rewrite the letter if necessary.
3. At the church business session involving the whole congregation, Mac was to share personally his problem and confess that he was involved in sexual sin.
4. He was then to read his letter of resignation and remove himself from his youth ministry position. The church would keep the letter on file to dispel any rumors that might follow the confession.

5. Pastor Rob and others were then to state the limitations on Mac's ministry and the responsibility of the congregation in the process of restoring him. These were:
   a. No ministry opportunities without the approval of the pastor and elders. All teaching and youth leadership roles were suspended.
   b. Commitment to personal discipleship with one or two of the elders in the coming year.
   c. Accountability of his time and activities.
   d. Periodic meetings with the denominational official with the goal of a future ministry on a career basis.
   e. A desire to bring about full restoration.

It was tough medicine and Mac hated the thought of it. He humbly protested the idea of making a public confession before the whole church. He had never heard of such a thing. But nobody budged. His choice was clear: either confess or run. Mac chose to swallow the bitter pill and get better. What really captured his heart was the willingness of the pastor and elders to restore him within this Body of Christ rather than just send him away from the people he knew and loved.

The Sunday for public discipline seemed like it would never come. Mac dreaded it and so did Pastor Rob and the elders. Everyone wanted to get it over and no one knew quite what to expect. Finally, the dreaded day arrived.

Pastor Rob preached on forgiveness on that memorable Sunday. From the passage about Jesus and the woman taken in adultery (see John 8:1-11), he encouraged the people to use their "first stones" for paperweights. Then he asked the members and regular attenders to stay for a scheduled business meeting of the church, especially those in the youth department and their parents. Mac had told some of his friends that "something heavy was coming down." Others sensed something awful had transpired. Almost everyone stayed afterward to see what was happening.

The atmosphere felt heavy with apprehension. The tense congregation bowed for prayer and then Pastor Rob cleared his throat as he began. "In the past few days certain information has come to us regarding one of our staff which of necessity has to come to the entire Body of believers. It is so important that we listen and support this person." He paused. Eyes searched the room to see which staff member would stand up. "Mac, will you come to the platform and share your heart with us?"

Everyone's attention was riveted on Mac as he began to speak. Quietly at first, but then with incredible power from the Lord, Mac confessed his sin of sexual involvement. He asked for the people's forgiveness and appealed for understanding. But he did more. He humbly requested the opportunity to be restored as a Christian in good standing within this congregation. He was willing to pay the price of church discipline if the people would love, accept and forgive him. He then read his letter of resignation.

Dear friends in Christ,

As youth pastor at Community Church, I've had the privilege of ministering to the needs of God's people and this has given me a great deal of pleasure and honor. This ministry has been a source of great blessing and has contributed much to my spiritual growth.

In recent months a series of events developed which have caused me to reevaluate my role of formal leadership among you. Due to a period of moral laxity, I have fallen into sexual sin with a person outside the church. Because my leadership is public, I feel my confession must be public also. I ask for your forgiveness and the support of your prayers during my restoration.

Therefore, with deep sorrow and regret, I request that you accept my resignation as youth pastor. For now, it is in all of our best interests that I step aside and allow other leadership to be secured.

A man after God's own heart,

Mac

As Mac returned to his seat Jim, the chairman of the elders, stepped forward to outline the limits of Mac's leadership in the church. Then came the first surprise. A woman, moved deeply by Mac's speech interrupted and spoke of the need for compassion. She wanted the church to accept Mac's request for forgiveness. Her main point was that each person has his or her own problems for which he seeks, or should seek, forgiveness. The scene might have turned into a debate about the pros and cons of church discipline if Jim had hesitated. But with genuine warmth he simply said, "Thank you," and then continued to spell out the conditions of the discipline as outlined by the elders.

With a wonderful spirit, this man of God used the Scriptures to explain the elders' responsibility of discipline, restoration and forgiveness. From Galatians 6:1-6 he summarized the process of restoration in three phrases no one could forget:

1. Lift him up
2. Hold him up
3. Build him up.

Pastor Rob then came to the pulpit and began to speak. What he said convinced the people that they were on the right course. "It is with sadness that we accept your resignation. I want to say again, Mac, that no matter what happens, I love you and I believe this Body of Christ is going to keep on loving you.

"It's our hope, dream and prayer that this will be a once-in-the-lifetime-of-the-church experience. However, if ever in the future a similar occasion should present itself, we're prepared to follow the same procedure. It's never our desire to 'hurt people' but always our call to follow the biblical pattern.

"Mac has asked to remain in our fellowship and experience forgiveness and restoration. It is here that he can best be held accountable. He has asked to submit to our discipline and this means he is to be restricted in his leadership in and out of the church.

"I pose several questions which I have had to work through in my own life. These questions may weigh heavily on your mind as well." Pastor Rob had read *Beyond Forgiveness* and used author Don Baker's good questions, adapting them to their own pressing situation:[2]

1. Why do this so publicly? Shouldn't it be done in private? Why expose Mac to such embarrassment? The nature of this sin broke a public and corporate trust held by the whole church body. Scripture points the way to discipline and then encourages the Church to receive back into fellowship the one who repents and proves it over a period of time (see 1 Cor. 5:1-3 and 2 Cor. 2:5-11).

2. Is this problem so serious as to require this kind of meeting? Yes. From all the best writers and Bible scholars that I consulted with, the answer was unanimous. First Timothy 3:1-7 explains the necessary character qualities for elders which we apply to all staff members. Four of these standards have been ruptured. The command to rebuke publicly an elder who sins must be obeyed so that others may take warning (1 Tim. 5:17-21).

3. What do we do now? Exactly what Jesus said to do—forgive, restore and bring the fallen back to health (see Luke 17:3-4). Please do not avoid Mac. Receive and love and heal him.

4. If we are forgiving and restoring, why not allow him to remain in ministry leadership? Mac is wounded and needs time to heal. He feels embarrassed, ashamed and has recently been struggling with deep depression. He needs time to recover. He needs this time to rebuild his confidence in himself, his peers, his leaders—and they in him. Mac has followed our recommendation in sharing both his sin and his need for restoration with the elders and congregation. He already has a secular job and plans to remain a participant of this church.

5. How long? We don't know. How long does it take to restore a '32 Ford after a Mack truck hit it? It all depends on how much damage it suffered and how well you want the restoration done. Some would pry out the fenders so they no longer rub the tires and put it back on the road. We don't, and God doesn't, want a wreck on the road. We want a restored man. Our goal is for Mac to be restored to the extent that he can resume ministry here. It will take a year, maybe longer, to prove to himself, his family, his church and his God that he is spiritually mature enough to carry on a ministry in which he can honor Christ.

"Mac has asked us, and we have asked him, to remain right here and be restored. Someone said the church is the only army that shoots or deserts its wounded. By God's grace we will do neither. We will not desert him! Don't you agree?"

After a couple of spontaneous comments like, "Yes, that's right" and "No, we will not," the congregation broke into a loud and prolonged applause.

"One more thing," Pastor Rob added. "Everything that needs saying has been said. Nothing stops gossip like speaking the whole truth. All the questions about the moral problem that need to be asked have been answered. No reason exists to keep probing for details. Mac has confessed and asked forgiveness and his letter is on file. The kindest thing you can do for Mac is not to ask any more questions."

He dismissed the meeting with prayer and then moved quickly to Mac and embraced him. The people swarmed forward and hugged Mac, assuring him of their support.

"I'm sorry, Mac. I didn't pray for you like I should have."

"It took a lot of courage to do what you have done. I sure do respect you."

"I don't know what you are feeling inside but I'm backing you up all the way, no matter what!"

Some were weeping and smiling at the same time. It was a beautiful experience of caring, sharing and reconciliation. The healing had begun, the pastor knew, as many shared with him:

"I'm so proud to be a member of Community Church. You are courageous to do it God's way."

A high schooler added, "You did what you had to do, Pastor, and I respect you for it."

One dad said, "What happened here today is what happens in homes when the rules are violated. Sometimes you have to ask for the car keys and restrict the driving. This is okay."

"Pastor, I didn't think I could bear coming this morning because Mac shared with me last night what was to be done. But I saw the real church working here this morning. I could not imagine that much love being given in a time of correction. Thanks for loving all of us."

"Praise God for the courage you had today. Our job now is to restore a wonderful man's dignity."

The most telling comment of all came from Mac himself some time later. "What you asked of me, confession and resignation, is not the hardest thing you could have asked!"

Pastor Rob thought, *What could we have asked that would have been more difficult?*

"You could have asked me to leave. 'There is the door. Just go away.'"

As Pastor Rob reflected on Mac's words, he came to a stunning conclusion. "It is easier to bear the pain of correction than to bear the pain of rejection and noncorrection."

Days passed. The high school girl found out from her doctor that she was not pregnant after all. Her foster parents were Christians and insisted that she attend their own church from then on. Mac began the long journey back to Christian usefulness. He gave himself to Bible study and prayer and after some weeks his devotional times came alive. His joy in the Lord was evident for all to see.

Disappointments met him along the way. After the first flush of acceptance people settled back into their old routines. The elders, at least at first, did not make the extra time for him that he needed. Pastor Rob continued his support and a couple of others met with him on occasion. But Mac felt left out, bypassed, forgotten. Yet he persisted.

In time he was allowed to date and he kept the relationship pure. He also attended some stress management seminars that gave him a fresh perspective. Then came the break he really needed. Jim, the chairman of the elders, offered him a job. It threw the two of them together often with some special times to talk. And talk they did—about the Bible, dating, sex, becoming a one-woman man, marriage. Mac was gaining on the battleground, rebuilding the one part of his life that was his greatest struggle.

He kept his life open to the scrutiny of the church Body. He went back to school and made the honor roll. The hardest part was sitting on the shelf, unable to lead or teach as he loved to do. Community Church hired another youth pastor to fill his former position. He understood and was glad to see the man succeed. Yet it never seemed easy to stand back, sit down, stay out of the limelight. Waiting is the hardest lesson in God's book.

After five months the elders allowed him to begin ministering in limited ways. He held no regular responsibilities in the church but could occasionally lead some Bible studies, assist in some seminars or help a struggling youth group in another church. The taste of youth ministry was delicious to Mac, yet he sensed in his spirit that he was not yet ready for full re-entry. As the months wore on he began working on his time management, watching his diet and identifying his mood swings. He wanted to grow up on the inside and somehow the discipline felt good in his life.

Because Mac repented from his heart and submitted to church discipline, he brought encouragement to the whole church. Every time Satan is thwarted and a sexual sinner surrenders body and soul to the Lord Jesus Christ, the angels of heaven rejoice. So do His people on earth—and how much more oo when a strong leader returns to the ministry! Eleven months from the time Mac was placed on probation the church honored him in morning worship and put their full blessing on his future ministry.

Mac wrote about his progress in the restoration process.

> The greatest lesson I learned from the whole disciplinary period was one of submissive obedience, not only toward God but also to the church and its leadership. I had the deep desire to serve Christ but I wanted to do it my way. I learned that my desire to serve God in the role of ministry, in whatever capacity, could not supersede obeying His will according to the written Scripture. This is a very hard way to learn the truth of Scripture. But the hurt and embarrassment have served to bring healing and victory in an area of my life I've had the most struggle in.
>
> After a long 11 months God brought glory to Himself through this entire event. I'm glad I went this route versus running—happy not only for myself but for the entire church body. If I had to face the same choice all over again—church discipline or run—I would do it the exact same way.

The best news of all was that Mac was restored to ministry. He watches his steps closely these days. He feels more realistic about how much work load and time commitment he takes on. He still struggles some with lustful thoughts but they are not as enormous as before. He finds he must watch his mental intake minute by minute. In his own words, "I feel great now. I have seen God do some great things in answer to prayer—car, housing, school. The biggest breakthroughs have come in the spiritual area of my life."

Mac became a winner.

Notes

Preface

1. James C. Dobson, *What Wives Wish Their Husbands Knew About Women* (Wheaton, Illinois: Tyndale House Publishers, Inc., 1975), pp. 96-97.

Chapter 1

1. *Time* magazine, June 6, 1983, p. 48.
2. Technically, the woman did not ask Jesus for forgiveness, but Edith understood the heart of what Jesus meant.
3. Leon Morris, *The Gospel According to John,* NICNT series (Grand Rapids, Michigan: Wm. B. Eerdmans Pub. Co., 1971), pp. 890-891.
4. Arnold Lobel, "Cookies" in *Frog and Toad Together* (New York: Harper & Row, Publishers, 1972), quoted in Raymond C. Ortlund, *Be a New Christian All Your Life* (Old Tappan, New Jersey: Fleming H. Revell Company, 1983), pp. 43-45.

Chapter 2

1. Ella Wheeler Wilcox, "An Unfaithful Wife to Her Husband," *Whatever Is, Is Best: A Collection of Poems* (Boulder, Colorado: Blue Mountain Arts, Inc., 1975), pp. 62-63.
2. Excerpted with permission from *Guideposts Magazine.* Copyright © 1983 by Guideposts Associates, Inc., Carmel, New York 10512.

3. Bob Phillips, *The Last of the Good Clean Joke Books* (Eugene, Oregon: Harvest House Publishers, 1974), p. 48.
4. From: THE MYTH OF THE GREENER GRASS by J. Allan Petersen, Copyright © 1983. Used by permission Tyndale House Publishers, Inc.
5. Taken from *The Message of Galatians* by John R. W. Stott, © 1968 by John R.W. Stott and used by permission of InterVarsity Press, Downers Grove, IL 60515.
6. Joyce Mayhew, *Argonaut* quoted in Frank S. Mead, ed., *The Encyclopedia of Religious Quotations* (Old Tappan, New Jersey: Fleming H. Revell Company, 1965), p. 304.
7. Alan Loy McGinnis, "How to Stay Happily Married," *Good Housekeeping* (September, 1982), p. 194, adapted from *The Romance Factor* (San Francisco: Harper & Row, Publishers, 1982), p. 162.

Chapter 3

1. From: THE MYTH OF THE GREENER GRASS by J. Allan Petersen. Copyright © 1983. Used by permission Tyndale House Publishers, Inc.
2. Richard J. Foster, *Money, Sex and Power: The Challenge of the Disciplined Life* (San Francisco: Harper & Row, Publishers, 1985), p. 99.
3. Heini Arnold, *Freedom from Sinful Thoughts: Christ Alone Breaks the Curse* (Rifton, New York: Plough Publishing House, 1973), p. 19.
4. Erwin W. Lutzer, *How to Say No to a Stubborn Habit* (Wheaton, Illinois: Victor Books, 1979), p. 41.
5. Name Withheld, "The War Within: An Anatomy of Lust," *Leadership, A Practical Journal for Church Leaders* 3, no. 4 (Fall, 1982), p. 47. Used by permission.
6. From *Tough Truths for Today's Living* (formally *Now for Something Totally Different*), copyright © 1978; used by permission of Word Books, Publisher, Waco, Texas.
7. Taken from *Eros Defiled* by John White. © 1977 by Inter-Varsity Christian Fellowship of the USA and used by permission of InterVarsity Press, Downers Grove, Illinois 60515.
8. Richard J. Foster, *Money, Sex and Power,* p. 208.
9. Earl D. Wilson, *Sexual Sanity: Breaking Free from Uncontrolled Habits* (Downers Grove, Illinois: InterVarsity Press, 1984), p. 118.
10. John Blattner, "Secret Struggles," *Pastoral Renewal* 8, no. 11 (June, 1984), pp. 156-157.
11. Erwin W. Lutzer, *Living with Your Passions* (Wheaton, Illinois: Victor Books, 1983), p. 113.
12. Mel White, *The Other Side of Love: Bible Stories Not for Children* (Old Tappan, New Jersey: Fleming H. Revell Company, 1978), p. 191. Used by permission.

Chapter 4

1. Robert H. Schuller, *You Can Become the Person You Want to Be* (New York: Hawthorn Books, 1973), pp. 90-91.
2. The idea and some of the wording of this answer comes from Walter Tro-

bisch, *Living with Unfulfilled Desires* (Downers Grove, Illinois: InterVarsity Press, 1979), p. 21.

3. Source unknown.

4. Neil Anderson, personal interview with the author, 9-10-85.

5. From: *The Adversary*, by Mark I. Bubeck, Copyright 1975. Moody Press. Moody Bible Institute of Chicago. Used by permission. Also see Bubeck, *Overcoming the Adversary; Warfare Praying Against Demon Activity* (Chicago: Moody Press, 1984). German scholar Kurt Koch has written more technical books on the subject: *Between Christ and Satan*, 1962; *The Devil's Alphabet*, 1969; *Occult Bondage and Deliverance*, 1970 and *Christian Counseling and Occultism*, 1972. All are published by Grand Rapids, Michigan: Kregel Publications.

6. Martin Luther, "A Mighty Fortress Is Our God," *Hymns for the Family of God* (Nashville, Tennessee: Paragon Associates, Inc., 1976), #118. Also found in most Christian hymnals.

7. Several excellent warfare prayers and good explanations of doctrinal praying are found in Bubeck, *The Adversary* and *Overcoming the Adversary*.

8. No author listed, *Be Alert to Spiritual Danger* (Oak Brook, Illinois: Institute in Basic Youth Conflicts, 1979), p. 23.

Chapter 5

1. From *Funny, Funny World* as recorded in James S. Hewett, ed., *Parables, Etc.*, 4, no. 6 (August, 1984), p. 3.

2. Gary D. Chapman, *Hope for the Separated: Wounded Marriages Can Be Healed* (Chicago: Moody Press, 1982), p. 13.

3. James Dobson, *Love Must Be Tough: New Hope for Families in Crisis* (Waco, Texas: Word Books, 1983), pp. 35-37.

4. Nicholas, Herman of Lorraine (Brother Lawrence), *The Practice of the Presence of God, the Best Rule of a Holy Life* (NY: Fleming H. Revell Company, 1985), seventh letter, p. 34.

5. No author listed, *Rebuilder's Guide* (Oak Brook, Illinois: Institute in Basic Youth Conflicts, 1982), p. 119.

6. Dobson, *Love Must Be Tough*, pp. 47,67-68.

Chapter 6

1. Charlotte Elliott (1789-1871). Public domain.

2. From: *The Adversary*, by Mark I. Bubeck, Copyright 1975. Moody Press. Moody Bible Institute of Chicago. Used by permission.

Chapter 7

1. As quoted in Janet Dailey, *Silver Wings, Santiago Blue* (Poseidon Press, New York, 1984), p. 9. Used by permission.

2. Elisabeth Elliot, *Passion and Purity* (Old Tappan, New Jersey: Fleming H.

Revell Company, 1984), pp. 131-132. Used by permission.

3. Richard J. Foster, *Money, Sex and Power: The Challenge of the Disciplined Life* (San Francisco: Harper & Row, Publishers, 1985), p. 163.

4. Charles W. Colson, "The Most Fearsome Judgment," *Christianity Today* (August 6, 1982), p. 21.

5. Copyright 1982 LEADERSHIP Journal. Used by permission.

6. Billy Graham, "What the Bible Says About Sex," in J. Allan Petersen, ed., *The Marriage Affair* (Wheaton, Illinois: Tyndale House Publishers, Inc., 1971), p. 370.

7. Susan Sadd and Carol Tavris, *The Redbook Report on Female Sexuality* (New York: Delacorte, 1977), pp. 97-106.

8. A thorough book on sexual enhancement within marriage and a bibliography that includes problem resolution is Clifford and Joyce Penner, *The Gift of Love: A Christian Guide to Sexual Fulfillment* (Waco, Texas: Word Books, 1981). Also well worth reading are Tim and Beverly LaHaye, *The Act of Marriage: The Beauty of Sexual Love* (Grand Rapids, Michigan: Zondervan Publishing House, 1976) and Ed Wheat, *Intended for Pleasure* (Old Tappan, New Jersey: Fleming H. Revell Company, 1981).

9. William R. David in Three Forks, Montana *Herald*, quoted in *The Reader's Digest* (March, 1980), p. 250.

10. Copyright 1982 LEADERSHIP Journal. Used by permission.

11. *Ibid.*

Chapter 8

1. Author unknown.

2. D. Elton Trueblood, *Quarterly Yoke Letter*, 17, no. 4 (December, 1976). Used by permission.

3. Charles R. Swindoll, *Strike the Original Match: Rekindling and Preserving Your Marriage Fire* (Portland, Oregon: Multnomah Press, 1980), pp. 77-78. Used by permission.

4. Ray C. Stedman, *Life by the Son: Expository Studies in I John* (Waco, Texas: Word Books, 1980), p. 361. Used by permission.

5. Lewis B. Smedes, *Sex for Christians: The Limits and Liberties of Sexual Living* (Grand Rapids, Michigan: William B. Eerdmans Publishing Company, 1976), p. 210.

6. For a clear and helpful discussion see Earl D. Wilson, *Sexual Sanity: Breaking Free from Uncontrolled Habits* (Downers Grove, Illinois: InterVarsity Press, 1984), pp. 85-90.

7. Richard J. Foster, *Money, Sex and Power: The Challenge of the Disciplined Life* (San Francisco: Harper & Row, Publishers, 1985), p. 110.

8. E. Mansell Pattison and Myrna Loy Pattison, "'Ex-Gays': Religiously Mediated Change in Homosexuals," *American Journal of Psychiatry*, 167, no. 12 (December, 1980), p. 1553.

9. James Dobson, *Dr. Dobson Answers Your Questions* (Wheaton, Illinois: Tyndale House Publishers, Inc., 1982), p. 453.

10. Earl D. Wilson, *Sexual Sanity*, p. 84.

11. From the book BEYOND REJECTION by Don Baker, copyright 1985 by Don Baker. Published by Multnomah Press, Portland, Oregon 97266. Used by permission.

12. Joseph Miller, "Homosexuality: A Personal Christian Perspective," *The Aviso* (Canton, Ohio: Malone College: April 3, 1985), p. 3. Reprinted by permission.

13. Dennis Kinlaw, address given at Newberg Friends Church, Newberg, Oregon 97132 during the annual sessions of Northwest Yearly Meeting of Friends Church, July 31, 1985.

14. Martha Janssen, *Silent Scream* (Philadelphia: Fortress Press, 1983). Used by permission.

15. David Augsburger, *Caring Enough to Not Forgive: False Forgiveness* (Ventura, California: Regal Books, 1981), pp. 38,52. Used by permission.

16. Elizabeth Wainwright, "Can You Ever Forgive Incest?" *Family Life Today,* 10, no. 5 (May, 1984), p. 35.

17. Clif Cartland, ed., *Family Life Today,* 10, no. 5 (May, 1984).

18. Joanne Feldmeth, "Encouraging Healthy Affection Between Parent and Child," *Family Life Today* (10, no. 5 (May, 1984), p. 38.

19. Harold Myra, "The Glamorous Prostitutes: The myth of 'happy hookers' enjoying their trade does not match reality," *Christianity Today* (October 5, 1984), pp. 14-16 (esp. p. 15). He cites the research of Mimi Silbert.

20. "Two Women and the Passions of Abortion," *The Register* newspaper, Santa Ana, California (Sunday, September 21, 1980), pp. 18-19.

21. "Sharing the Pain of Abortion," *Time* magazine (September 26, 1983), p. 78.

22. *Ibid.*

Chapter 9

1. Tim Timmons and Stephen Arterburn, *Hooked on Life from Stuck to Starting Over* (Nashville: Oliver Nelson, A Division of Thomas Nelson Publishers, 1985), pp. 125-126.

2. Richard D. Warren, taped sermon #150, "Forgiving the Key to Living" and #84, "How to Get Rid of Guilt." A free catalogue of Rick Warren's inspirational tapes is available from Saddleback Valley Community Church, 25401 Cabot Road, Suite 215, Laguna Hills, California 92653.

3. Michael Brown and George Alan Rekers, *The Christian in an Age of Sexual Eclipse* (Wheaton, Illinois: Tyndale House Publishers, Inc., 1981), p. 31.

4. David A. Seamands, *Healing for Damaged Emotions* (Wheaton, Illinois: Victor Books, 1981), p. 22.

5. George Herbert quoted in Eleanor L. Doan, ed., *The Speaker's Sourcebook* (Grand Rapids, Michigan: Zondervan Publishing House, 1960), p. 105.

6. Richard J. Foster, *Celebration of Discipline: The Path to Spiritual Growth* (San Francisco: Harper & Row, Publishers, 1978), p. 132.

7. William L. Coleman, *Bouncing Back* (Eugene, Oregon: Harvest House Publishers, 1985), p. 92.

8. By Dr. Paul Brand and Philip Yancey, authors of *Fearfully and Wonderfully*

Made and *In His Image.* Used by permission.

9. John B. Aker, "The Ministry of Simple Touch," *Leadership, A Practical Journal for Church Leaders,* 6, no. 2 (Spring, 1985), p. 20. Used by permission.

10. Lewis B. Smedes, *Forgive and Forget: Healing the Hurts We Don't Deserve* (San Francisco: Harper & Row, Publishers, 1984), p. 73.

11. Paul Lee Tan, ed., *Encyclopedia of 7,700 Illustrations: Sign of the Times* (Rockville, Maryland: Assurance Publishers, 1979), p. 456, #1764.

12. Lewis B. Smedes, *Forgive and Forget,* pp. 76-77.

13. David Augsburger, *Caring Enough to Forgive: True Forgiveness* (Ventura, California: Regal Books, 1981), p. 56. Used by permission.

Chapter 10

1. David A. Seamands, *Healing for Damaged Emotions* (Wheaton, Illinois: Victor Books, 1981), p. 29.

2. Jerry Bridges, *The Pursuit of Holiness* (Colorado Springs: Navpress, 1978), p. 96.

3. *Ibid.*

4. From: THE MYTH OF THE GREENER GRASS by J. Allan Petersen, Copyright © 1983. Used by permission Tyndale House Publishers, Inc.

5. Edith Ogutsch, quoted in "Toward More Picturesque Speech," *Reader's Digest,* 79, no. 475 (November, 1961), p. 193.

6. Willard Gaylin, "The Emotions of Guilt Has Been Given a Bum Rap," *U.S. News and World Report* (April 30, 1984), p. 84.

7. See H.C. Hahn, "Conscience" in Colin Brown, ed., *The New International Dictionary of New Testament Theology,* 1 (Grand Rapids, Michigan: Zondervan Publishing House, 1975), p. 350.

8. Benjamin Franklin, *Poor Richard,* quoted in Frank S. Mead, ed., *The Encyclopedia of Religious Quotations* (Old Tappan, New Jersey: Fleming H. Revell Company, 1965), p. 85.

9. Alfred Martin Rehwinkle, *The Voice of Conscience* (St. Louis: Concordia Publishing House, 1956), p. 172.

10. Elisabeth Elliott, *Passion and Purity* (Old Tappan, New Jersey: Fleming H. Revell Company, 1984), p. 39. Used by permission.

11. Wilbur Rees, "$3.00 Worth of God," in Tim Hansel, *When I Relax I Feel Guilty* (Elgin, Illinois: David C. Cook Publishing Co., 1979), p. 49.

12. Name Withheld, "The War Within: An Anatomy of Lust," *Leadership, A Practical Journey for Church Leaders,* 3, no. 4 (Fall, 1982), p. 39. Used by permission.

13. Richard J. Foster, *Freedom of Simplicity* (San Francisco: Harper & Row, Publishers, 1981), p. 102.

14. William Backus and Marie Chapian, *Telling Yourself the Truth* (Minneapolis: Bethany Fellowship, 1980), pp. 81-82. Used by permission.

15. See Robert H. Schuller, *Self Esteem: The New Reformation* (Waco, Texas: Word Books, 1982), pp. 59-60.

Chapter 11

1. Mel White, *Deceived: The Jonestown Tragedy: What Every Christian Should Know* (Old Tappan, NJ: Fleming H. Revell Company, 1979).
2. Mel White, *The Other Side of Love* (Old Tappan, New Jersey: Fleming H. Revell Company, 1978), p. 150. Used by permission.
3. Name Withheld, "The Other Side of Child Molesting," *Leadership, A Practical Journal for Church Leaders,* 6, no. 3 (Summer 1985), pp. 120-125.
4. From the book BEYOND FORGIVENESS by Don Baker, copyright 1984 by Don Baker. Published by Multnomah Press, Portland, Oregon 97266. Used by permission.
5. Permission granted to reprint by Ken L. Bemis.

Chapter 12

1. From the book BEYOND FORGIVENESS by Don Baker, copyright 1984 by Don Baker. Published by Multnomah Press Portland, Oregon 97266. Used by permission.
2. *Ibid.,* pp. 55-60. Used by permission.